P9-AFC-499

Making American Foreign Policy

President—Congress Relations from the Second World War to Vietnam

Philip J. Briggs

UNIVERSITY
PRESS OF
AMERICA

Lanham • New York • London

University Press of America®, Inc.
4720 Boston Way
Lanham, Maryland 20706

3 Henrietta Street
London WC2E 8LU England

Printed in the United States of America
British Cataloging in Publication Information Available

Library of Congress Cataloging-in-Publication Data

Briggs, Philip J.
Making American foreign policy : President-Congress relations from the Second World War to Vietnam / Philip J. Briggs.
p. cm.
Includes bibliographical references and index.
1. United States—Foreign relations—1945– 2. United States—Foreign relations—1933–1945. 3. United States—Foreign Relations administration. 4. United States. Congress—History—20th century. 5. Presidents—United States—History—20th century. I. Title.
E744.B698 1990 327.73—dc20 90–23446 CIP

ISBN 0–8191–8112–9 (alk. paper)
ISBN 0–8191–8113–7 (pbk. : alk. paper)

Second Printing

The paper used in this publication meets the minimum requirements of American National Standard for Information Sciences—Permanence of Paper for Printed Library Materials, ANSI Z39.48–1984.

To Candace

CONTENTS

PREFACE

The need to understand the crucial relationship between President and Congress in the making of American foreign policy remains constant. An understanding of this relationship is vital to those who view the United States from afar, as well as its own citizenry, for it is only then that we can make intelligible the continuities and vicissitudes that characterize the formulation of foreign policy.

I have chosen to examine the three-decade period from 1943 to 1973 because each of these dates represents a major turning point in the two branch relationship. In 1943 the Congress finally adopted collective security, ending the great Wilsonian struggle over isolationism begun one generation earlier. By 1973, under the hammer blows of the Vietnam War and the Watergate scandal, the role of the Congress was changing again, this time to a more assertive position toward the President.

The intended audience for this volume includes both students and practitioners of foreign policy-making. It also includes members of the general public who would like to know more about the role of the President-Congress relationship in the making of foreign policy.

Philip J. Briggs
East Stroudsburg, PA
June 1, 1990

I

INTRODUCTION

> The accumulation of all powers, legislative, executive, and judiciary, in the same hands, whether of one, a few, or many, and whether hereditary, self-appointed, or elective, may justly be pronounced the very definition of tyranny.
>
> James Madison
> Federalist No. 47[1]

The relationship between President and Congress in the formulation of significant United States foreign policies during World War II through the Vietnam War period is the focus of this volume. The thirty year period during which these policies were developed, from 1943 to 1973, represents an era of American world power that began with the emergence of the U.S. from the Second World War as the dominant state in international relations, and ends in the quagmire of Vietnam and the legislative-executive struggle over the war power.

The case study method is utilized to illuminate the step by step procedures and politics that brought seven foreign policies in their various forms to fruition. The forms examined include congressional resolutions, an executive agreement, three treaties, and a presidential doctrine.

The case method encompasses an in-depth chronological narration and analysis of those events, options and actions which impact upon policy-makers decisions.

As such it has long been utilized by political practitioners seeking to understand how policies are actually formulated. For students of foreign policy this method has the additional advantage of imparting the feel and flavor of the political process set within the executive-congressional relationship.

Each case study leads to a number of conclusions that are clearly set-off at the end of each chapter. Taken individually, the studies explain a particular foreign policy; taken together we have a better opportunity to evaluate constitutional issues and identify common themes in the President-Congress relationship and the making of foreign policy.

Constitutional Setting

Executive-congressional relations remain the key intergovernmental relationship in the formulation of American foreign policy. The Constitution mandates its importance through the separation of powers principle which both theoretically undergirds the basic document and divides power between the President and the Congress in the making of foreign policy. Consequently, the executive-congressional relationship, as deduced from the Constitution, has been called "an invitation to struggle for the privilege of directing American foreign policy."[2]

The framers of the Constitution distrusted concentrations of power in any one branch or level of the government, believing the result of such concentrations to be oligarchy. They established instead a system of checks and balances whereby powers are actually shared by separated institutions. This sharing of powers necessitates compromise from time to time in the making of policy to avoid deadlock. In the foreign policy area the process known as bipartisanship can also avoid deadlock through cooperation between opposing political party leaders in the legislature and requiring "executive consultation with party foreign policy leaders in the Congress prior to the implementation of policy."[3] This political method was defined by Senator Arthur H. Vandenberg, its principal architect, as a common effort "to unite our official voice at the waters edge. . ."[4]

As the third branch of the national government, the judiciary or Supreme Court, plays a substantially lesser role in the formulation of foreign policy. Its main contribution is in clarifying through decisions the powers assigned to the other two branches in the Constitution. An example would be The Prize Cases (1863), in which the Court ruled in favor of President Abraham Lincoln's imposition of a naval blockade on southern ports shortly after Fort Sumter was fired upon in 1861. In sustaining the President's action the Court clarified his Commander in Chief power as follows: "If a war be made by invasion of a foreign nation, the President is not only authorized but bound to resist force by force. He does not initiate the war, but is bound to accept the challenge without waiting, for any special legislative authority. And whether the hostile party be a foreign invader, or States organized in rebellion, it is none the less a war. . . ."[5] At other times, however, the Court has declined to render decisions regarding foreign policy issues between President and Congress, instead adjudging them to be political questions not properly susceptible to legal interpretation.

The President is the key figure in the formulation of foreign policy because of specific grants of authority in the Constitution and the fact that he is elected by a national constituency. In addition to his Commander in Chief power, he also initiates treaties as stated in one of the most famous clauses in the Constitution: "He shall have Power, by and with the Advice and Consent of the Senate, to make Treaties, provided two thirds of the Senators present concur."[6] The President's Secretary of State usually negotiates a treaty which is then sent to the Senate for approval. If approved by the requisite two thirds minimum vote, it is then ratified by the President.

Some of the largest and most bitter struggles in the executive-legislative relationship have occurred over the Senate's power to "advice and consent" in treaty-making. An often cited example of conflict in this area is President Woodrow Wilson's epic and ultimately losing struggle with the Senate over approval for the Treaty of Versailles ending World War I. Consent to the treaty would have automatically ended America's isolationist foreign policy by making the United States a member of the new League of Nations as primarily designed by Wilson. The Senate finally rejected the treaty and League Covenant in 1920.

Presidents also use executive agreements instead of treaties to formulate foreign policy with other countries. These agreements do not require Senate consent although they may be voided by congressional action. The Constitution makes no explicit provision for executive agreements, but their use by Presidents has given the Chief Executive an important tool with which to bypass the Senate in reaching agreements with foreign governments. During 1940, the year before America's entry into World War II, President Franklin D. Roosevelt made an executive agreement with British Prime Minister Winston Churchill to exchange fifty old American fighting ships for British bases in the western Atlantic. This Destroyers for Bases agreement could not have achieved Senate approval as a treaty, but was vital for England's defense against the Nazi onslaught. Roosevelt was, according to one of his more noted biographers, "determined to find a way to circumvent Congress on this problem, and he found it."[7]

The President also possesses the power to appoint ambassadors and "other public Ministers and Consuls," again with the "Advice and Consent of the Senate,"[8] but with only a majority vote being required. Conversely, the President possesses the power to receive ambassadors and with it the power to recognize new states or governments. He does not share this power with the Congress and the power of recognition further solidifies his direction of foreign policy.

Although the role of the diplomat is not infrequently downgraded by Presidents who engage in direct diplomacy or summitry, their role continues to be important. This is especially true in the case of a Secretary of State who has the full confidence of the President and is largely delegated the role of directing foreign policy. An example of this kind of relationship was President Dwight D. Eisenhower and his Secretary of State John Foster Dulles. Yet, a President may turn to a personal representative to carry out important foreign negotiating missions in order to avoid the sometimes problematical question of senatorial confirmation of diplomatic officials. A classic example of this alternative was President Roosevelt's use of Harry Hopkins during World War II. Hopkins has been described by his biographer as "the second most important individual in the United States Government during the most critical period of the world's greatest war," despite the fact that he lacked any "legitimate official position nor even any desk of his own except a card table in his bedroom. However, the bedroom was in the White House."[9]

The President may also use the constitutional requirement that, "He shall from time to time give to the Congress information of the State of the Union, and recommend to their Consideration such Measures as he shall judge necessary and expedient;"[10] to declare a new foreign policy. On December 2, 1823, President James Monroe used this annual message requirement to proclaim the doctrine that bears his name: "that the American Continents, by the free and independent condition which they have assumed and maintain, are henceforth not to be considered as subjects for future colonization by any European Power. . . ."[11]

As Chief Executive of the government the President "may require the Opinion, in writing, of the principal Officer in each of the executive Departments, upon any Subject relating to the Duties of their respective Offices."[12] He therefore has the continuous support of numerous executive agencies and departments who are responsible to him in carrying out the nation's foreign policies. Closely related is the President's Chief of State or ceremonial head of government role. Taken together, these powers afford the President much of the authority necessary to lead the Republic in foreign affairs. This leadership power, as it relates to the Congress, was clarified in the supreme Court case *United States v. Curtiss-Wright Export Corporation* (1936). The Court upheld the validity of an arms embargo proclaimed by President Roosevelt under authority previously granted in a broadly stated joint resolution of the Congress. The Court reinforced the President's preeminent position by stating: "The President is the sole organ of the Federal government in the field of international relations--a power which does not require as a basis for its exercise an act of Congress, but which, of course, like every other governmental power, must be exercised in subordination to the applicable provisions of the Constitution."[13]

As both Head of State and Chief Executive, the media naturally follows the activities of the President and records his public (and sometimes private) utterances, more completely than any member of the Congress.

A President's ability to communicate effectively is therefore one of the great potential powers of the office which reinforces his leadership position in foreign affairs. John F. Kennedy effectively used this power during his relatively brief tenure in the White House (1961-63). He also remarked upon how beneficial regular preparation for press conferences were to him-- "It's like preparing for a final exam twice a month,"[14] he commented.

The power of the Congress in the formulation of foreign policy predates the ratification of the Constitution itself. Indeed, during the Revolutionary War the Continental Congress established a Committee for Foreign Affairs in 1777 to conduct the external relations of the newly independent republic. Despite the fact that this arrangement for conducting foreign policy did not work well, the Articles of Confederation following the Revolution largely replicated the same arrangement with the same results obtained under the original Committee for Foreign Affairs.

At the Constitutional Convention in 1787, the Founders reacted to this congressional ineffectiveness in the conduct of the new nation's external relations by strengthening the powers of the executive branch in foreign policy. Yet, the suspicion of executive power remained strong and it was the esteemed Benjamin Franklin of Pennsylvania who argued at the Philadelphia Convention that all money bills should originate in the House of Representatives so "that the people should know who had disposed of their money and how it had been disposed of."[15] Partly as a result of this continuing suspicion of executive power the Constitution states that, "All Bills for raising Revenue shall originate in the House of Representatives; but the Senate may propose or concur with Amendments as on other Bills."[16] The Congress also possesses the "Power to lay and collect Taxes, Duties, Imports and excises, to pay the Debts and provide for the Common Defense and general Welfare of the United States;" and, "To raise and support Armies."[17] Taken together these power over the purse requirements give the Congress approval over foreign policies requiring expenditures.

The Congress, however, may be reluctant to stop funding an ongoing foreign policy, especially if that policy involves the support of U.S. armed forces in combat. An important exception to this congressional reluctance occurred during the Vietnam War. In 1970 South Vietnamese and United States forces crossed into Cambodia from Vietnam in an effort to disrupt North Vietnamese supply lines. The Congress had not been consulted and a national frontier had been crossed touching off a new round in the widening gulf between President and Congress over the war. Congress then attempted to ban the use of funds for operations in Cambodia via passage of the Cooper-Church amendment. However, by the time the amendment went into force (July 1, 1970), the administration of President Richard M. Nixon had withdrawn U.S. ground forces from Cambodia.

The Congress also possesses the power, "To declare War, grant Letters of Marque and Reprisal, and make Rules concerning Captures on Land and Water."[18] Although the declaration of war power was assigned to the Congress by the Founders at the Constitutional Convention of 1787, in practice the President's power as Commander in Chief to independently order the armed forces into hostilities has occurred far more often than actual war declarations by the legislature. Letters of marque and reprisal, which allowed individuals to attack and seize the shipping and property of enemy nations without being considered pirates, was banned by the Pact of Paris in 1856.

The Cases Studied

For Americans, collective security represented a foreign policy choice opposite from isolationism and synonymous with internationalism. It is most clearly associated with the League of Nations and the United Nations concept in which (theoretically), an aggressor state is identified and collectively suppressed. It has also included membership in regional security organizations, bilateral treaties and unilateral declarations of support for countries in a specific geographical area.

Congressional participation in the development of American collective security policy began after the Japanese attack upon Pearl Harbor, December 7, 1941. The torpedo bombers that attacked the fleet at Pearl Harbor were able to cripple American sea power temporarily, but the tradition and credibility of isolationism was finally and permanently destroyed. Before that event, the majority legislative view had supported George Washington's admonition against permanent alliances and generally embraced hemispheric isolationism as reinforced by the Monroe Doctrine of 1823. The epic struggle between President Woodrow Wilson and the Senate over approval of the League of Nations beginning in 1919, turned largely on the same two issues: peacetime entangling alliances and the tradition of isolationism.

The Senate's rejection of the League (1920) established a new scenario in which the majority isolationists maintained their dominance over the minority internationalists, with each side basing their position upon both political and moral arguments. For the internationalists, the carnage resulting from trench warfare on the western front during World War I demonstrated that balance of power mechanisms for maintaining peace were futile. Isolationist's morality was similarly aroused by the emotional belief, based largely upon the biased Nye Committee Hearings of 1934, that the Republic had been duped into joining the Great War by "Merchants of Death."[19]

Congressional passage of four Neutrality Acts beginning in 1935, while signs of war were growing in Europe and Asia, gave further testament to the continued political power of isolationism. Yet, President Roosevelt and his Secretary of State Cordell Hull, both Wilsonian internationalists, wished to preserve executive freedom of action in foreign affairs even though the Neutrality Laws were aimed in the opposite direction--to insure that another President could not lead the nation into war.

However, after the 1939 Nazi-Soviet attack upon Poland which began World War II in Europe, Roosevelt found ways to aid the allied powers. The Lend-Lease Act of early 1941 fitted the President's "arsenal of democracy"[20] role for the Republic, but it received considerable isolationist opposition. Nevertheless, its final approving vote was 260 to 165 in the House and 60 to 31 in the Senate, demonstrating the new majority that favored the President's pro-allied stance.

Soon thereafter, Roosevelt pressed forward toward a new foreign policy based upon collective security in the postwar world. He took an historic step in that direction during August, 1941, when he and British Prime Minister Churchill referred, in a joint declaration known as the Atlantic Charter, to the future development of a collective security organization, ". . . pending the establishment of a wider and permanent system of general security."[21]

The grim memory of the League struggle could not be put to rest, however, until the Congress had also committed itself to the same collective security goal. How the Congress formally abandoned isolationism and approved collective security is the subject of the first study, "Congress and Collective security: The Resolutions of 1943."

Congressional approval for a United Nations organization was directly related to the specific content of its Charter and congressional participation in its development. Franklin Roosevelt, intent upon not repeating the errors of Woodrow Wilson, formed a bipartisan congressional delegation to attend the 1945 San Francisco Charter Conference including former isolationist leader, Senator Vandenberg of Michigan. The United States delegation insisted that the Charter include Article 51, which refers to the right of nations to self-defend either individually or collectively.[22] The inclusion of this article was critical, as it became the legal basis upon which the North Atlantic Treaty Organization (NATO) was founded in 1949.

As Cold War politics stalemated the United Nations Security Council, a new search for security through regional alliances began. American participation in the evolving North Atlantic Alliance became the main preoccupation of British, French and American political-military planners during the late 1940's. The role of the Congress and especially the Senate with its treaty-approval power became critical in this development; just as it had in the final acceptance of the United Nations collective security concept in 1943.

President - Congress relations were therefore also critical to the formation of NATO, especially since U.S. participation meant disregarding George Washington's farewell address admonition "to steer clear of permanent alliances with any portion of the foreign world."[23] The political methodology that allowed for a cooperative posture between the two branches as they struggled with this basic change in the nation's foreign policy was bipartisanship. How the Congress finally accepted the North Atlantic Alliance and the role of bipartisanship is the subject of the second study, "Congress and Bipartisanship: The Formation of NATO, 1949."

The development of NATO took place without the inclusion of an important potential member state--Spain. General Francisco Franco and his regime were fully ensconced in power at Madrid while the North Atlantic Alliance was being formed, but his former links with the Axis Powers during World War II had made him anathema to the West European democracies.

Franco was not without resources, however, in his quest to become an alliance partner. Congressional ties with Spain during the administration of Harry S. Truman and the beginning of the Eisenhower Administration in 1953, present us with a case study in the important role of foreign lobbying activity on Capitol Hill and its success in influencing the direction of United States foreign policy. The role of the U.S. military is also brought into focus as it influenced Washington's new Spanish policy.

Unlike the congressional resolutions and treaty which are the subject of the first two chapters respectively, the Pact of Madrid was an executive agreement not requiring congressional approval. Yet, the role of Senate members was especially important in bringing the agreement into existence. How the Spanish Lobby, members of the Congress and the military establishment, influenced the United States to form a quasi-alliance with Spain is the subject of the third study, "Congress and Franco Spain: The Pact of Madrid, 1953."

On the other side of the world, the defeat of the Nationalist Chinese forces in 1949 brought on the so-called loss of China issue in American politics which greatly heightened its partisan tone. Also, during February 1950, Senator Joseph R. McCarthy, a Republican Senator from Wisconsin, claimed in a speech that he had a list of 205 names in the State Department "who have been named as members of the Communist Party and members of a spy ring."[24] Although "McCarthy had no list,"[25] the kind of witch-hunting that would bear his name had begun, further exacerbating the executive-congressional relationship during the closing years of President Truman's term in office.

The outbreak of the Korean War in June of 1950 brought the Cold War to a new height with U.S. armed forces engaged in combat under the United Nations flag. As that war dragged on, a Republican Administration was elected in 1952 for the first time in twenty years. Against this backdrop of heightened Cold War tensions and the rise of McCarthyism in the early 1950's, U.S.-China policy took a new turn as fighting between Nationalist and Communist forces developed in the Formosa Strait separating the mainland of China from Taiwan. Taiwan (or Formosa) is a large island to which the Nationalist forces had retreated in 1949.

This Formosa Strait confrontation of 1954-55 was evaluated differently by members of the legislative and executive branches of the government, and especially by Secretary of State Dulles and members of the Senate. Nevertheless, the Eisenhower Administration negotiated a formal alliance with the defeated Nationalist Chinese on Taiwan and also requested a supporting joint resolution from the Congress. Congressional reaction to and final approval of the resolution and treaty with the Nationalist Government is the focus of the third study, "Congress and the Cold War: U.S.-China Policy, 1955."

A second area resolution followed in 1957 when the Eisenhower Administration requested from the Congress a Middle East Resolution also known as the Eisenhower Doctrine. Because political occurrences or diplomatic events are usually related to preceding events, we find the U.S. role in the Middle East to be largely motivated by a combination of long-term economic (oil) and strategic concerns shaped by Cold War perceptions.

Secretary of State Dulles once again played a prominent role in devising this policy, including the Middle East Resolution itself, which in his view became necessary following the rapid British-French loss of power in the wake of the disastrous Suez War of 1956. That Middle East war was precipitated by the Egyptian seizure of the Suez Canal--which was in turn precipitated by the U.S. decision not to fund Egypt's Aswan High Dam.

The result of this curious chain of events was

perceived by Dulles and Eisenhower as producing "a serious power vacuum"[26] which they believed must be filled by the United States, least the Soviet Union be tempted to do so. Congressional resistance to the Eisenhower Doctrine was, however, considerable. How that resistance was met and overcome is the subject of the fourth study, "Congress and the Middle East: The Eisenhower Doctrine, 1957."

President John F. Kennedy's commitment to arms control was demonstrated during the first year of his administration when he established the U.S. Arms Control and Disarmament Agency. But intermittent nuclear testing in the atmosphere had continued in both the Soviet Union and the United States with hazardous results. Speaking to his science adviser Jerome Wiesner in his White House office on a rainy afternoon following a U.S. nuclear test, he asked how fallout was returned to the earth. Wiesner said, "It comes down in rain." The President turned and looked at the rain falling on the Rose Garden and asked, "you mean there might be radioactive contamination in that rain out there right now?" Wiesner answered: "Possibly." The President continued looking at the rain for several minutes and according to two of his closest confidantes they "never saw him more depressed."[27]

The Cuban Missile Crisis of 1962 demonstrated to the world that a nuclear holocaust was a distinct possibility and its occurrence provided an impetus for a ban on nuclear testing. Yet many obstacles remained. Difficult questions of verification for a test ban treaty plus potential military opposition had to be overcome. Most of all, opposition by conservative Senators might prove insurmountable in the President's quest for consent to ratification of the treaty itself.

How John F. Kennedy achieved this historic nuclear arms treaty through the bipartisan method is the subject of the fifth study, "Kennedy and the Congress: The Nuclear Test Ban Treaty, 1963."

Richard M. Nixon was elected President of the United States in 1968 during a particularly stormy period in executive-congressional relations due mainly to the highly unpopular Vietnam War. His own political party, the Republicans, remained in a minority status in the Congress during his entire tenure as President.

Despite this divided government characteristic of American Government during his administration, he failed to consult congressional leaders prior to the aforementioned U.S.-South Vietnamese Cambodian incursion in 1970. That event and others contributed to a period of congressional reassertion in foreign policymaking which roughly coincided with Nixon's years in the White House.

Congressional assertiveness in foreign policymaking was centered mainly on the war power--specifically the commitment of U.S. armed forces into combat without explicit congressional consent. It was, and remains, a difficult question to ponder since Presidents have frequently committed the armed forces to hostilities without a congressional declaration of war. But the public mood aroused by Vietnam, coupled with a congressional determination to have no more such wars, led directly to passage of the War Powers Resolution; an attempt to reinvigorate the legislative role in this key foreign policy area.

In 1972 Richard Nixon was overwhelmingly re-elected, but a seemingly unrelated event known as the Watergate scandal also began that same year and it would eventually lead to his resignation from the Presidency in 1974. That same scandal would also play a critical role in aiding the War Powers Resolution to become law.

The origins of Watergate and its specific causes are still being debated, but undoubtedly part of the reason for its occurrence and Nixon's inability to work more successfully with the Congress had to do with his personality. Tip O'Neill, who was House Majority Leader during this time period, has described the former President as follows: "Although Nixon was a brilliant guy, he had a quirk in his personality that made him suspicious of everybody. . . ."[28]

This tumultuous time period in executive-congressional relations is examined in the last study, "Nixon versus the Congress: The War Powers Resolution, 1973."

Taken together, the seven case studies afford us an opportunity to evaluate the constitutional issues raised and identify the common themes revealed by the studies in a final chapter. The concluding chapter ends with a look at the executive-congressional relationship in the post-Vietnam War era. Each study may also be examined with reference to the key document(s) related to the policy produced by referring to the appropriate reference in the appendices. One such document is, for instance, President Kennedy's letter to Senate Republican Minority Leader Everett McKinley Dirksen and Senate Majority Leader Mike Mansfield, which played an important role in making it possible for Dirksen to support the Nuclear Test Ban Treaty.

We have avoided the tyranny described by James Madison in an excerpt from his Federalist No. 47 at the beginning of this chapter. But the separation of powers between President and Congress has also produced numerous conflicts in the making of foreign policy. How those conflicts have been met and overcome, with varying results, bears close examination. Let us begin.

Notes

[1]*The Federalist Papers: Alexander Hamilton, James Madison, John Jay*, Introduction by Clinton Rossiter (New York: The New American Library, 1964), 301.

[2]Edward S. Corwin, *The President: Office and Powers, 1787-1957* (New York: New York University Press, 1957), 171.

[3]See author's, "Senator Vandenberg, Bipartisanship, and the Origin of United Nations Article 51," *Mid-America: An Historical Review* 60 (October 1978): 164.

[4]Vandenberg to a constituent, 5 January 1950, in Arthur H. Vandenberg, Jr., ed., *The Private Papers of Senator Vandenberg* (Boston: Houghton Mifflin Company, 1952), 552.

[5]*The Prize Cases*, 2 Bl. (67 U.S.) 635 (1863).

[6]Johny H. Killian, ed., *The Constitution of the United States of America: Analysis and Interpretation* (Washington, D.C.: U.S. Government Printing Office, 1987), 14.

[7]Robert E. Sherwood, *Roosevelt and Hopkins: An Intimate History* (New York: Harper & Brothers, 1950), 175.

[8]Killian, *The Constitution of the United States*, 14.

[9]Sherwood, *Roosevelt and Hopkins*, 212.

[10]Killian, *The Constitution of the United States*, 14-15.

[11]Samuel Flagg Bemis, *A Diplomatic History Of The United States* (New York: Henry Holt & Company, 1947), 210.

[12]Killian, *The Constitution of the United States*, 14.

[13]*United States v. Curtiss - Wright Export Corp.*, 299 U.S. 304 (1936).

[14]Quoted in, Theodore C. Sorensen, Kennedy (New York: Harper & Row, 1965), 325.

[15]Quoted in author's, "Franklin and the Bicentennial" (Annual Newsletter, Pennsylvania Political Science Association, 1987), 2.

[16]Killian, The Constitution of the United States, 7.

[17]Ibid., 8-9.

[18]Ibid., 9.

[19]Quote from book title by, Helmuth C. Englebrecht and F. C. Hanighen, eds., Merchants of Death (New York: Dodd, Mead & Company, 1934). A powerful indictment of arms merchants.

[20]Roosevelt used this phrase during a fireside chat on 29 December 1940. Samuel I. Rosenman, comp., The Public Papers And Addresses Of Franklin D. Roosevelt, 13 vols. (New York: Russell & Russell, 1969) 9: 643.

[21]Ibid., Vol. 10, 315. For a complete text of the Atlantic Charter see Appendix A.

[22]For a case study on this development see author's, "Senator Vandenberg, Bipartisanship, and the Origin of United Nation's Article 51," Mid-America 60 (October 1978): 163-69.

[23]Henry Steele Commager, ed., Documents of American History (New York: Appleton-Century-Crofts, 1968), 174.

[24]David M. Oshinsky, A Conspiracy So Immense: The World of Joe McCarthy (New York: The Free Press, 1983), 109.

[25]Ibid.

[26]Townsend Hoopes, The Devil And John Foster Dulles: The Diplomacy of the Eisenhower Era (Boston: Little, Brown & Company, 1972), 285.

[27]Kenneth P. O'Donnell and David F. Powers with Joe McCarthy, "Johnny, We Hardly Knew Ye" (Boston: Little, Brown & Company, 1972), 285.

[28]Tip O'Neill with William Novak, Man Of The House: The Life and Political Memoirs of Speaker Tip O'Neill (New York: St. Martin's Press, 1987), 288.

II

CONGRESS AND COLLECTIVE SECURITY: THE RESOLUTIONS OF 1943*

The experience of World War I convinced Americans that they should avoid international commitments and refuse to participate in future foreign wars. The war to save the world for democracy set in motion a nationalist reaction to the idea of collective security which was to last through the 1930's. Only the hard realities of Hitler's success in conquering Europe turned the nation toward a policy of international commitment.[1]

Pearl Harbor struck a crippling blow to isolationism. Many of the hard-core noninterventionists, including Senator Arthur H. Vandenberg, who had been the darling of the American isolationists and their favorite candidate for the Republican nomination in 1940, turned away from isolationism after the Japanese attack on December 7, 1941.[2]

After the war began the nation appeared to reject isolationism, though no official legislative action was initiated to adopt a policy of internationalism. Congress waited until 1943 before it gave official approval to the principle of collective security. En-

---

*Author's article, original version first published in World Affairs 132 (March 1970): 332-44, and in author's edited volume, Politics in America: Readings and Documents (New York: MSS Information Corp., 1972), 208-20, distributed by Irvington Publishing, Inc., New York City.

dorsement came in the form of two resolutions, one passed by the House, called the Fulbright Resolution, and another by the Senate, entitled the Connally Resolution.

Congress gave strong bipartisan support to the resolutions amidst a spirit of cooperation vastly different from the legislative-executive struggle which characterized the peace-making efforts following World War I. What factors gave rise to bipartisanship and why was conflict between the branches of government kept at a relatively low level? Finally, who was principally responsible for the cooperative endeavor which officially sanctioned and legitimized the precepts of collective security?

The President Sets the Stage

After the outbreak of World War II in Europe, the Roosevelt Administration began to take steps, independent of the isolationist-dominated Congress, to involve the United States in both the war and in an international organization for peace-keeping. Aboard the American cruiser Augusta off the coast of Newfoundland on August 9, 1941, President Franklin D. Roosevelt and Britain's Prime Minister Winston Churchill met in secret to discuss a wide range of topics associated with the war. A joint declaration was issued which became known as the Atlantic Charter; the last principle mentioned in this declaration included a statement concerning the establishment of a permanent system of general security.

On New Year's Day 1942 the representatives of twenty-six nations gathered in the White House and signed the Declaration of the United Nations. At this time the term United Nations referred to the grand coalition and not the future international organization. The Declaration specifically upheld the principles and purposes embodied in the Atlantic Charter. It also pledged all signatory governments not to make a separate peace with the Axis Powers. Thus, Roosevelt had successfully broken the tradition of nonentangling alliances via an executive agreement, for this Declaration was never submitted to the Senate for its consent.

President Roosevelt had long been sympathetic to the internationalist cause. The President knew well, however, from the tragic experience of Woodrow Wilson, that the disposition of the executive branch toward the establishment of an international organization with American participation was one thing, and the attitude of Congress, and especially the Senate with its treaty approval powers, was quite another. Thus, during the war Roosevelt was haunted with the knowledge that partisan politics had once destroyed his country's chance for involvement in an international peace-keeping organization.

Even though the President had demanded an end to domestic politics of a partisan nature and had even suggested that the two national party organizations be converted to civilian defense, the regular off-year congressional contests were held in 1942. Roosevelt avoided Wilson's mistake of asking for a Democratic Congress, yet his party still came close to losing control of Congress.[3]

In the elections the Republicans gained enough seats in the House to nearly equal the total held by the Democrats, with 216 Democrats to 212 Republicans and 4 third party representatives by the middle of 1943. The majority party was now compelled to consult Republican leadership in the House before taking legislative action. Eight seats were also lost by the Democrats in the senatorial elections of that year.

In general the year 1943 saw a turning against Roosevelt's domestic policies; the conservative coalition of Southern Democrats and Republicans had become a more potent force than previously. In June 1943 Congress enacted over a presidential veto the War Labor Disputes Act, and throughout the year it rebuffed repeated attempts by the administration to sequester further legislative powers through a third War Powers Act.[4] Clearly, a need now existed for bipartisan, or nonpartisan, as Secretary of State Cordell Hull preferred to call it, support for American foreign policy, especially after the congressional elections of 1942.

Republicans to be Consulted

Republican interest in a role in foreign policymaking was expressed through Senator Vandenberg, a convert to the cause of internationalism, who in 1943 was a powerful member of the Senate Foreign Relations

Committee.[5]

A sense of frustration over lack of information bothered Vandenberg and on December 15, 1941, he wrote President Roosevelt a letter suggesting the creation of a joint congressional committee on war cooperation. He felt that the executive branch would be more willing to share information with Congress if it could be done through a dependable partnership of the two major parties. Although Roosevelt answered this request with a very conciliatory letter, nothing came of the suggestion at that time. Possibly the less than cordial relations between the two men in the past prevented the President from using Vandenberg's request to begin foreign policy collaboration between the two major parties and the executive branch of government.

Nevertheless, Vandenberg and several other Republican members of the Senate Foreign Relations Committee continued to press for more information from the State Department. They carried their complaint to Senator Tom Connally (Democrat of Texas), chairman of their committee. One month after Pearl Harbor, Senator Connally, in response to the Vandenberg request, asked Hull to send State Department representatives to Capitol Hill on a regular basis to discuss their special fields of knowledge with the Foreign Relations Committee. The first meeting took place on January 6, 1942, with Assistant Secretary of State Breckenridge Long representing his department.[6]

Early in 1942 Secretary of State Hull took a cautious but important step in the evolution of a bipartisan foreign policy when he launched his Advisory Committee on Postwar Foreign Policy. Its membership gradually expanded to a total of forty-five participants, including leading members of both parties in the Senate and House of Representatives; the State, War, Navy, and other departments; the Library of Congress; the White House staff; and the other government agencies.[7]

In the Spring of 1943 the fortunes of war were finally beginning to turn against the Axis Powers. Devastated areas of the war zones were being recovered and the need for relief in these areas had become apparent. Discussions on a United Nations Relief and Rehabilitation Administration (UNRRA) agreement, begun during the recent visit of Anthony Eden to Washington, were continued with Great Britain, the Soviet Union, and China. While these negotiations were in progress, the State Department continued to hold discussions with the Senate Foreign Relations Committee and the House Committee on Foreign Affairs. In early June Roosevelt called the majority and minority leaders of the Senate, Alben W. Barkley (Democrat of Kentucky) and Charles L. McNary (Republican of Oregon) respectively, as well as their counterparts in the House, John W. McCormack (Democrat of Massachusetts) and Joseph W. Martin, Jr. (Republican of Massachusetts), to a conference at the White House. There the congressional leaders agreed not to raise objection to an executive agreement whereby the United States would participate in the establishment of UNRRA via an executive agreement; legislative approval then would follow the negotiations with other concerned countries.[8]

The administration's decision to use an executive agreement and thus bypass Congress touched off an immediate reaction from Senator Vandenberg that was to result eventually in a greater degree of cooperation between the two branches and the two parties than had previously existed. Vandenberg quickly introduced a resolution in the Senate to ascertain whether or not the draft agreement was, in fact, a treaty that must therefore be submitted to the Senate for approval. He then sent letters to the minority leaders in both houses of Congress asking if they had approved the use of an executive agreement; they replied by telegram stating they had not agreed that Congress should be bypassed.[9]

This turn of events inflamed Senator Connally, the Democratic Chairman of the Foreign Relations Committee, even more than Vandenberg. Connally called a meeting of his committee and invited Hull and Assistant Secretary of State Dean Acheson, who was primarily responsible for designing UNRRA. The meeting was stormy, with Hull finally admitting that he was personally opposed to bypassing the Senate. At this juncture Connally offered a compromise and suggested that UNRRA be presented as a joint resolution which would require only simple majorities in both houses for passage, instead of a treaty which would require a two-thirds majority of the Senate. Connally added that the House should be involved in the matter because large sums of money would need to be appropriated under UNRRA; Hull agreed and even asked Connally to help write UNRRA in bill form for congressional approval. Senator Connally later noted in reference to UNRRA that it was one instance in which the Senate gave its prior "advice" during the construction of the bill as well as its later "consent."[10]

Senator Vandenberg also agreed with this compromise and dropped his original demand that the agreement be submitted as a treaty. In the late summer of 1943 Vandenberg enthusiastically referred to the procedures being used to make UNRRA acceptable to both branches of government as "a new and direct system of consultation between the State Department and the Senate Foreign Relations Committee which should be able to avoid many of the stalemates of which we are historically aware."[11] The stage was now set for Congress to acquiesce in favor of American collaboration in maintaining the peace that was yet to be won.

The House Acts First

The House of Representatives was becoming increasingly involved with the problems of planning for the postwar world, due partly to the decision to submit UNRRA in the form of a joint resolution, but also to growing sentiment in the House to place that body on record as favoring American cooperation in the establishment of a security organization.

Representative J. William Fulbright (Democrat of Arkansas) had been elected to the Seventy-Eighth Congress on November 3, 1942, a relatively short time prior to the introduction of the important resolution that would bear his name. Fulbright had been both a Rhodes Scholar and President of the University of Arkansas before his election. He brought with him to the House a different comprehension of what a Representative's role should be in the making of foreign policy: it included an increasing involvement by the House in foreign policy-making.

The Foreign Affairs Committee at that time consisted of twenty-five members, fourteen Democrats and eleven Republicans. The Fulbright Resolution received the affirmative vote of every member of the committee except two absentees, but it was understood that some members would seek to add amendments on the floor.

Actually Fulbright's original draft of the resolution included support for an international police force but this part had been deleted.[12] The House resolution was concurrent (H. Con. Res. 25) so that the Senate could follow its lead and simply concur if it so desired; it did not. The resolution, reported out on June 16, 1943, read as follows:

> Resolved by the House of Representatives that the Congress hereby expresses itself as favoring the creation of appropriate international machinery with power adequate to establish and to maintain a just and lasting peace among the nations of the world, and as favoring participation of the United States therein.[13]

Debate on the resolution was delayed at least partly because of Secretary of State Hull's insistence "on thorough organization in the Senate and House so as to secure an overwhelming vote."[14] The President had written to Hull less than two weeks after the Fulbright Resolution had been introduced into the House, suggesting that he thought it a resolution worth backing. Hull replied that he had already spoken to the Speaker of the House, Representative Sam Rayburn (Democrat of Texas), and was informed that there would be over fifty Republican votes against it at that time. In order to whittle down the numbers in opposition, Rayburn met with Representatives Fulbright, James W. Wadsworth (Republican of New York), and Majority Leader McCormack. It was then agreed that the resolution would not be taken up until the House reconvened in September.[15]

Although sentiment had clearly been building during the summer, both in and out of Congress, for some kind of resolution supporting the establishment of a security organization, considerable opposition still remained when debate finally began in September. The Fulbright Resolution was brought up under a suspension of the rules which precluded amendment. Opposition formed around those who felt the resolution might be interpreted by the executive branch as an invitation to disregard the constitutional process concerned with ratification of treaties.

An attempt to amend the resolution was agreed upon

by the Republican members of the House Foreign Affairs Committee. This amended version was given the backing of the House minority leadership. The amendment to the resolution would simply add the words "through its constitutional processes."[16] Representative Hamilton Fish (Republican of New York), speaking for the minority position, explained the meaning of this amendment: he noted his own support for its inclusion and then referred to the basic mistrust of the Chief Executive he shared with some of his colleagues, by stating that there was fear some "secret commitments will be entered into and that Congress will be bypassed."[17] On September 21, 1943, the House voted on the amended Fulbright Resolution. The House, in what Representative Sol Bloom, Chairman of the House Committee on Foreign Affairs, referred to as "a vote uninfluenced by party differences,"[18] passed the resolution 360 to 29.

Hull Facilitates Congressional Action

Cordell Hull, President Roosevelt's Secretary of State for over a decade, was widely respected in Congress. This was the result of having received the bulk of his political socialization through long and successful tenure in the House, followed by election to the Senate in 1930 from his home state of Tennessee. It was generally believed in Congress that due to this experience Hull completely respected the prerogatives and procedures of that body, and could therefore be trusted never to ignore them.

Because of Hull's considerable influence in Democratic councils (he was Chairman of the Democratic National Committee from 1921-24), he was able to help Roosevelt gain the Democratic nomination in 1932. The Roosevelt-Hull relationship was further solidified by their similar stands on the leading foreign policy question of their generation. Both men were determined to establish an internationalist foreign policy after the war by insuring American participation in an international collective security organization. Both men were also firm Wilsonian internationalists, yet the relationship between Roosevelt and Hull was never close. Because they differed in temperament as well as their approach to foreign policy problems, while not differing substantially with one another regarding overall objectives, Roosevelt frequently worked around his Secretary of State. This was especially apparent when the President sent special envoys to important summit meetings and was receptive to advice from other members of the executive establishment.

Nevertheless, an open rift between Roosevelt and Hull never occurred, and when Hull finally retired in 1944 because of advancing age and ill health, he had held the position of Secretary of State longer than any of his predecessors. Roosevelt's reliance upon Hull was in the important area of congressional relations and this "concept of his dependence on Hull was justified by the enormous success of the Moscow Conference in October, and its consequent profound effect on Congressional opinion."[19]

During the spring and summer of 1943 Hull had worked hard to create the kind of atmosphere that would be conducive to the passing of House-and-Senate-supported resolutions putting the legislative branch squarely behind American participation in a security organization. He seldom lost an opportunity to impress upon senators and representatives of both parties two main points: first, that "a world organization to maintain the peace, by force if necessary, was absolutely imperative, and the United States had to be one of its principal members. The other was that our policy in this respect should be entirely nonpartisan."[20] In this case, Hull frequently invited senators and representatives to visit his office when the details of these proposed policies and strategies were examined closely.

Hull knew that congressional assent to a postwar collective security organization would strengthen his hand when he approached other nations seeking their cooperation, especially Great Britain and the Soviet Union. A Foreign Ministers' Conference in Moscow had been agreed on during the Quebec Conference of August 1943. Both Roosevelt and Hull hoped agreement would be reached at the Moscow Conference on a number of major political decisions affecting the postwar world. It was also agreed that a four nation declaration (the United States, Great Britain, the Soviet Union and China) should be sought that outlined, via a broad set of principles, a collective security organization.

Both Roosevelt and Hull were concerned that the wartime unity evoked in the democratic nations (especially the United States) would be lost after the war.

They recalled Wilson's failure to rally support for his League of Nations and wished to cement commitments to postwar cooperation while the guns were still booming.

In the spring of 1943 a brief resolution pertaining to postwar international cooperation was drawn up at the State Department in response to a request from Senator Scott W. Lucas (Democrat of Illinois), acting President Pro Tempore of the Senate. In accordance with Hull's strategy that any such resolution should receive overwhelming bipartisan support, he discussed the State Department's resolution with leading Democratic and Republican senators. Senator Charles Q. McNary (Republican of Oregon), Minority Leader, promised Hull his complete cooperation.[21] When the Connally Resolution on postwar collaboration was finally reported out of the Senate Foreign Relations Committee, it was to a large extent a product of collaboration between the Committee and the State Department.

On October 30th Hull and the foreign ministers of Great Britain and the Soviet Union, as well as the Chinese ambassador, signed the Four Nation Declaration in Moscow. In it they declared their recognition of the necessity of establishing "at the earliest practicable date a general international organization, based on the principle of the sovereign equality of all peace-loving states, and open to membership by all such states, large and small, for the maintenance of international peace and security."[22] Hull now declared that with the signing of the Four Nation Declaration, it was "probable that the United States would be a member of a new security organization."[23]

Although the administration continued to fear that debate in the Senate concerning American participation in an international organization would become a bitter partisan quarrel, the aging Secretary of State's flight to Moscow in the cause of postwar collaboration undoubtedly played a large role in placating the opposition to the Connally Resolution when debate finally began.

Thus Hull's strategy to gain American acceptance of the collective security concept by careful development of a favorable consensus was successful. That strategy may best be summarized in his own words spoken in the spring of 1943: "There were still some elements in our population who might run away from this proposition like a horse at the rustle of a leaf; and if we were not careful they would get away as fast as a wild stallion."[24]

The Senate Follows Suit

Just three days after the House passed the Fulbright Resolution, Senator Connally made it plain he did not intend to take any similar proposed resolution to the Senate floor before the forthcoming major foreign power conferences, and possibly not very soon thereafter. He was determined not to begin an "ill-considered debate in the Senate with regards to subjects of vital interest to our allies and which might produce irritations or vexations at a critical period in the prosecution of the war."[25]

Of particular concern to Connally was the introduction of the so-called B_2H_2 Resolution, reported to the Senate on March 16, 1943, which outlined solutions to postwar problems in specific terms. B_2H_2 stood for the last initials of a bipartisan group of senators who were its authors; they were Senator Joseph Ball (Republican of Minnesota), Senator Harold Burton (Republican of Ohio), Senator Carl Hatch (Democrat of New Mexico), and Senator Lester Hill (Democrat of Alabama).

Connally, noting that none of the authors of B_2H_2 were serving on the Foreign Relations Committee (whose members had the added benefit of working closely with the State Department on postwar problems) stated that their resolution "went too far in spelling out details."[26] He felt that debate on this resolution would trigger a highly partisan controversy which he wanted to avoid. The President, Connally claimed, shared his opinion and had commented to him, that "those senators are hurting our efforts for a workable international organization."[27]

Connally's reaction to the Fulbright Resolution was also critical. He remarked that it was "mild and cryptic,"[28] thus eliminating the possibility of simple Senate concurrence with the House resolution.

When Congress convened again in the fall, Connally introduced his own resolution (S. Res. 192) on October 21, 1943. With Secretary of State Hull in Moscow seeking firmer allied commitments to a security organization, and the B_2H_2 Resolution already introduced in the Senate amid a growing clamor for action, Connally felt compelled to introduce his own resolution. Unlike the B_2H_2 Resolution, which included controversial stipulations,[29] the Connally Resolution was a brief, general statement which read as follows when introduced:

> Resolved, that war against all enemies be waged until complete victory is achieved;
>
> That the United States cooperate with its comrades-in-arms in securing a just and honorable peace;
>
> That the United States, acting through its constitutional processes, join with free and sovereign nations in the establishment and maintenance of international authority with power to prevent aggression and to preserve the peace of the world.[30]

Connally believed his resolution went as far as any resolution could go and remain acceptable to a majority of his colleagues in the Senate.[31] It had already received substantial support from the Senate Foreign Relations Committee where it was reported out by a vote of twenty to two. The main opposition from within the Committee came from Senator Claude Pepper (Democrat of Florida), whom Connally characterized as "spokesman for the B_2H_2 group."[32]

The ensuing debate revealed the three main arguments of the opposition. First, there were those senators, namely the B_2H_2 group, who did not feel the Connally Resolution was specific enough; second, there were those senators concerned that the resolution did not clearly safeguard the Senate's prerogatives in the treaty-making process; and, finally, there remained some isolationist sentiment opposed to any postwar international involvement.

In answer to those senators who remained isolationist in their sentiments, Senator Connally himself produced what was probably the strongest argument when he stated: "Isolation has failed. Let us try collective security."[33] This charge the isolationist argument could not counter effectively, and thus the main challenge to the Connally Resolution came from the B_2H_2 adherents and those concerned with safeguarding the treaty-approving prerogatives of the Senate.

Giving the Connally Resolution important Republican support during the debate was Senator Vandenberg. The former leader of isolationists in the Senate, Vandenberg now swung his full weight behind the Connally Resolution and opposed the B_2H_2 Resolution, because "we withhold our blueprints until we are at grips with the realities of tomorrow and the disclosure of the intentions of others."[34]

Senator John Danaher (Republican of Connecticut) strongly presented the case of those concerned that the Senate might be ignored in the final establishment of an international organization. The thrust of his argument was that the executive branch might choose to look upon the impending resolution as ratification in advance. In answering this challenge, both Connally and Vandenberg argued that the advice and consent powers of the Senate in the treaty-making process imply two different functions, and that passage of Senate Resolution 192 would only be an exercise of the former.[35]

While the debate in the Senate wore on, the Moscow Foreign Ministers' Conference proceeded on schedule. On October 30 the three foreign ministers and the Chinese ambassador signed the Four Nation Declaration. Secretary Hull proudly noted that "now there was no longer any doubt that an international organization to keep the peace, by force if necessary, would be set up after the war."[36]

The signing of the Declaration in Moscow did not, however, precipitate a vote on the Connally Resolution. Debate in the Senate continued to drag on before a three-quarters empty chamber after the first two days of discussions on the resolution.[37] However, the executive branch was snow becoming increasingly uneasy over the inability or unwillingness of the Senate to bring the resolution to a vote. Assistant Secretary of State Breckenridge Long has recorded in his diary (entry of November 3, 1943) the Department of State's growing alarm over the Senate's lack of action after the Four Power Declaration had been signed in Moscow. Long recounts how the Department feared "the action of the

Senate might serve to divide the executive from the legislative branch and would be of assistance to Germany."[38] After consultation with the Acting Secretary of State and the White House, it was decided that Long should go to the Senate and talk to Connally. Noting that "up to this point, we had considered it a Senate matter,"[39] Long proceeded to the Senate where he impressed upon Connally, in a private conversation, "that the Senate was in a position where it should take some stand on the Moscow Resolution. Otherwise, its position would be misunderstood."[40] Connally expressed agreement with these sentiments and Long has credited his action with having played a "considerable part in the maneuver"[41] that resulted in final passage of the Connally Resolution.

A compromise was now in order, and on November 3rd Senator Connally introduced two amendments in an effort to appease the forces opposing his resolution, even though he personally felt their inclusion was "unnecessary."[42] The first amendment was an attempt to placate the B_2H_2 group by specifically mentioning the creation of an international organization at the "earliest practicable date."[43] This amendment was in fact the fourth section of the Four Power agreement. By this maneuver, the Senate resolution was brought into agreement with the commitments Secretary of State Hull had already made in Moscow. Undoubtedly the inclusion of this amendment was made more palatable to the less internationalist minded senators because the esteemed and trusted "Cordell Hull, Secretary of State, stood behind it."[44]

The second amendment was an attempt to placate the fears of those who felt the President might not consult the Senate again when he chose to implement the purposes of the resolution through a treaty. These two amendments, which were then added to the original Connally Resolution, read as follows:

> That the Senate recognizes the necessity of there being established at the earliest practicable date a general international organization based on the principle of the sovereign equality of all peace-loving states, and open to membership by all such states, large and small, for the

> maintenance of international peace and security.
>
> That, pursuant to the Constitution of the United States, any treaty made to effect the purposes of this resolution, on behalf of the Government of the United States with any other nation or any association of nations, shall be made only by and with the advice and consent of the Senate of the United States, provided two-thirds of the Senators present concur.[45]

The next day, November 4th, a rumor spread throughout the Senate that under international law the Four Power Declaration could be carried out solely by presidential action, as Roosevelt had done in the "destroyers for bases" arrangement of 1940. The word then passed that if the Senate approved any of the Declaration of Moscow, it would be giving blanket advance endorsement to treaties negotiated with other nations by the executive. Once again, the trust most Senators had for Cordell Hull, whose strong defense of constitutional processes was well known, played a strategic part in snuffing out this rumor; the moment a close State Department aide of the Secretary's repudiated the story, the flurry ended.[46]

The following day, November 5th, the amended Connally Resolution was brought to a vote and passed by an overwhelmingly bipartisan vote of 85 yeas to 5 nays.[47] The five dissenting votes were cast by three Republicans, Senators Hiram W. Johnson of California, Henrik Shipstead of Minnesota, and William Langer of North Dakota, plus two Democrats, Senators Robert R. Reynolds of North Carolina and Burton K. Wheeler of Montana. Geographical area rather than party affiliation is more relevant in evaluating those "no" votes, with three of the five nays being cast by senators from the Midwest (two Republicans and on Democrat) where isolationist sentiment remained strongest.

A Bipartisan Accomplishment

The passage of the Fulbright and Connally resolutions expressing congressional support for the creation of international machinery with power to prevent aggression and preserve world peace was a triumph for bipartisanship. Congress' action indicated that broad agreement had been reached by the executive and legislative branches as well as by Republicans and Democrats on the approach the nation would take to international relations after the war had been won.

President Roosevelt--aware of the tragic experience of Woodrow Wilson--set the stage for this achievement. He sought the cooperation of Congress at critical junctures in his effort to lead the nation along the path to collective security.

Senator Arthur H. Vandenberg won for the Republicans the right to be consulted, and thus made bipartisanship possible. Vandenberg accomplished this goal by securing access to relevant State Department information and by insuring that a direct system of consultation between the State Department and the Senate Foreign Relations Committee was established.

Secretary of State Cordell Hull played a crucial role in developing a consensus in favor of American participation in an international peace-keeping organization, in both houses of Congress, and among the general public as well. The President recognized the special trust and esteem congressional members placed in their former colleague and relied heavily upon him to gain their support; Roosevelt's trust in Hull proved to be well-founded.

The Congress itself provided the final test and both houses performed admirably. Both parties in Congress joined together to produce heavy majorities for the Fulbright Resolution in the House and the Connally Resolution in the Senate. Passage of these measures was a milestone victory for a bipartisan foreign policy and for collective security. Congress' action marked a major departure from the isolationist policy which pervaded the country after World War I and gave strong indication that the United States would place its hope for peace on a policy of international involvement and cooperation.

Epilogue

During the height of the Vietnam War in 1970, J.

William Fulbright, who was elected to the U.S. Senate in 1944 and was currently serving as Chairman of its Foreign Relations Committee, read and commented on the above study. Fulbright had become a strong critic of the Southeast Asian war and the particular role of the President in America's involvement. His comment read as follows: "The desire of the executive to bypass the Congress is not a new phenomenon so the struggle continues."[48]

Notes

[1]Selig Adler, The Isolationist Impulse: Its Twentieth Century Reactions (New York: Free Press, 1966), 251.

[2]Arthur H. Vandenberg, Jr., ed., The Private Papers of Senator Vandenberg (Boston: Houghton Mifflin Company, 1952), 1.

[3]James MacGregor Burns, Roosevelt: The Lion and the Fox (New York: Harcourt, Brace & World, Inc., 1956), 465.

[4]Edward S. Corwin, The President: Office and Powers 1787-1957: History and Analysis of Practice and Opinion (New York: New York University Press, 1957), 276.

[5]Vandenberg, Private Papers, 22.

[6]Tom Connally, My Name is Tom Connally (New York: Thomas Y. Crowell Company, 1954), 261.

[7]Cordell Hull, The Memoirs of Cordell Hull (New York: The Macmillan Company, 1948), 1635.

[8]Daniel S. Cheever and H. Field Haviland, Jr., American Foreign Policy and the Separation of Powers (Cambridge, Mass.: Harvard University Press, 1952), 98.

[9]Vandenberg, Private Papers, 68.

[10]Connally, My Name is Tom Connally, 262-63.

[11]Vandenberg, Private Papers, 73.

[12]Bradford H. Westerfield, Foreign Policy and Party Politics: Pearl Harbor to Korea (New Haven: Yale University Press, 1955), 149.

[13]Sol Bloom, The Autobiography of Sol Bloom (New York: G. P. Putnam's Sons, 1948), 265.

[14]Hull, Memoirs, 1263.

[15]Ibid., 1262-63.

[16]*Congressional Record*, 78th Cong., 1st sess., 1943, 89, pt 6:7647.

[17]Ibid.

[18]Bloom, *Autobiography*, 265.

[19]Robert E. Sherwood, *Roosevelt and Hopkins: An Intimate History* (New York: Grossett & Dunlap, 1950), 717.

[20]Hull, *Memoirs*, 1259.

[21]Ibid., 1261-62.

[22]Harold C. Syrett, ed., *American Historical Documents* (New York: Barnes & Noble, Inc., 1960), 394.

[23]Hull, *Memoirs*, 1307.

[24]Ibid., 1261.

[25]*New York Times*, 25 September 1943.

[26]Connally, *My Name is Tom Connally*, 263.

[27]Ibid.

[28]Ibid.

[29]*Cong. Rec.*, 89, pt 7:8844.

[30]Senate Committee on Foreign Relations, *Declaration of War and Peace Aims of the United States*, 78th Cong., 1st sess., 1943, S. Rept. 478, 1.

[31]Connally, *My Name is Tom Connally*, 264.

[32]Ibid.

[33]*Cong. Rec.*, 89, pt 7:8665.

[34]Ibid.

[35]Ibid., 9001.

[36]Hull, *Memoirs*, 1307.

[37]T.R.B., "Washington Notes," The New Republic: A Journal of Opinion 109 (November 1943): 652.

[38]Fred L. Israel, ed., The War Diary of Breckenridge Long: Selections from the Years 1939-1944 (Lincoln: University of Nebraska Press, 1966), 331-32.

[39]Ibid., 331.

[40]Ibid., 332.

[41]Ibid., 333.

[42]Connally, My Name is Tom Connally, 264.

[43]Cong. Rec., 89, pt 7:9222.

[44]New York Times, 5 November 1943.

[45]Cong. Rec., 89 pt 7:9222.

[46]New York Times, 5 November 1943.

[47]For full text of Fulbright and Connally Resolutions see Appendix A. Text quoted from, A Decade of American Foreign Policy: Basic Documents, 1941-1949, Revised Edition (Washington, D.C.: Department of State, 1985), 11, 15.

[48]J. William Fulbright, letter to the author, 26 May 1970.

III

CONGRESS AND BIPARTISANSHIP:

THE FORMATION OF NATO, 1949

The bipartisan origins of United States foreign policy formulation are found during the World War II period with approval by the Congress of the Fulbright and Connally Resolutions during 1943. With the passage of those resolutions the U.S. commitment to a peace-keeping international organization was secured and the former isolationist Republican leader, Senator Arthur H. Vandenberg of Michigan, emerged as a bipartisan proponent committed to internationalism. Vandenberg's own definition of bipartisanship was a common effort to "unite our official voice at the water's edge. . . ."[1]

As World War II drew to a close and the Cold War developed, Vandenberg participated at presidential request in the United Nations Charter Conference held in San Francisco during the spring of 1945. The result of the conference was a U.N. Charter the Senate approved containing Article 51 and other stipulations (Chapter VIII), supporting regional defense pacts. Vandenberg once again played an important role in this development upon which subsequent regional alliances such as the Organization of American States (OAS), was established in 1948 and the North Atlantic Treaty Organization (NATO), was formed in 1949. Although the key author of U.N. Article 51 was perennial presidential candidate Harold Stassen, Vandenberg supplied sufficient political pressure to insure its inclusion in the Charter.[2] The conditions under which a bipartisan foreign policy may succeed are examined below.

Bipartisan Conditions

Several conditions may be identified as being either ideal or necessary for the existence of a bipartisan foreign policy. The first Chief of Staff of the Senate Foreign Relations Committee and former Assistant Secretary of State in the Eisenhower Administration, Francis O. Wilcox, has identified one essential and three ideal conditions as follows:

> First, when the White House and the administration are controlled by one party, and the Congress is controlled by the other party - as in the case of the 80th Congress - when cooperation becomes absolutely essential; the government can't function in that kind of a situation unless you have a bipartisan approach. Secondly, when there is a fairly good consensus in the country about the basic principles or goals of our foreign policy and the way it should be conducted. . . . Thirdly, the kind of leadership on Capitol Hill that can command the confidence of the Congress and the executive and be willing to deemphasize politics while working for the national interest. And fourthly the kind of strong leadership in the White House that is willing to accord Congress its rightful place in the constitutional scheme of things and is willing to consult frequently with Congress on important foreign policy questions.[3]

The last noted of the ideal conditions is also essential, however, for the existence of a bipartisan foreign policy and it may be stated more specifically as follows: "Executive consultation with party foreign policy leaders in the Congress prior to the implementation of policy."[4] This condition was established in 1943 by Vandenberg in his wartime dealings with the Roosevelt Administration over the struggle to establish a United Nations Relief and Rehabilitation Administration (UNRRA) Agreement.[5] Of additional importance was the emerging role of Vandenberg as a congressional leader who could command respect among his colleagues and rise above partisan politics in the national interest--thus conforming to the third condition identified above.

Consensus, the first ideal condition identified by Wilcox, was achieved in the postwar period via adoption of the containment thesis as put forward in the writings of a moody, intellectual Foreign Service officer, George Kennan. Kennan's basic views were enunciated in his "Long Telegram," 1946, which warned of the Kremlin's expansionist ambitions and then in a 1947 Foreign Affairs journal article titled "The Sources of Soviet Conduct," which formulated the theory of containing the Soviet Union.[6] Despite his own later misgivings as to the manner in which his theory was adopted, former Secretary of State Henry Kissinger stated that "Kennan came as close to authoring the diplomatic doctrine of his era as any diplomat in our history."[7] The actual adoption of the containment thesis as U.S. foreign policy occurred through congressional passage of the 1947 Greek-Turkish Aid Act or Truman Doctrine. That act received large bipartisan congressional voting majorities as follows: House 287 to 107, Senate 67 to 23.

The necessity for a bipartisan foreign policy during the 80th Congress, 1947-48, as referred to by Wilcox above, was determined by the results of the 1946 congressional elections in which the Republican Party regained majority party status for the first time since 1930. A divided government scenario resulted with the White House and administration still under Democratic Party control in the personage of President Harry S. Truman. Thus, all four conditions were in existence for a bipartisan foreign policy during the critical formative years of NATO including the two essential conditions--the first and last, and the two ideal conditions--the second and third.

The Truman Administration moved quickly to encourage bipartisan action on foreign policy by nominating General George C. Marshall for Secretary of State in early 1947. Marshall was highly respected by the Congress as one of the principal architects of victory in World War II. With no previous record in politics to defend he was acceptable to both Republicans and Democrats. As Chairman of the Foreign Relations Committee Vandenberg aided in obtaining his unanimous approval by the Senate. Marshall picked a former Assistant Secretary of War, Robert A. Lovett, as his Under Secretary of State replacing the more acerbic Dean Acheson. Lovett's key role was to act as the State Department liaison person with the Senate and when Acheson took Lovett to meet Vandenberg he stated, "I've known Bob since college and I hope you will be agreeable to accept his services." Vandenberg replied, "I welcome you to the job of Under Secretary of State and may God have mercy on your soul."[8]

Forming NATO

The year 1947 saw a continuing deterioration in Soviet-American relations into the mold of mutual hostility known as the Cold War. The development of the Truman Doctrine, the Marshall Plan, the consolidation of the German blocs and the breakdown of diplomacy between East and West led to an agreement in principle between British Secretary of State Ernest Bevin and Marshall that some kind of western alliance was necessary.[9] A major triggering mechanism for western rearmament occurred shortly thereafter when, during February, 1948, the Communists seized power in Czechoslovakia following the protest resignation of the non-Communist ministers of the Prague cabinet.

A crisis atmosphere soon permeated both the administration and the Republican foreign policy leadership in the Congress. President Truman felt that much more would have to be done to bolster Western Europe's "Will to resist."[10] Senator Vandenberg, in a major speech endorsing Marshall Plan aid, referred to the recent Czech fate as an example of democracy having been "gutted."[11] Vandenberg's reaction was predictable considering his long-standing view of the Soviet Union: he opposed American recognition of the Soviet Government during the 1920's and he denounced the Roosevelt-Litvinov Agreement of 1933, extending diplomatic recognition to the Soviet State. Given the large number of his constituents who were of Polish ancestry, he was especially sensitive to, and critical of, Poland's fate following the Yalta Agreements of 1945.[12]

A full-blown but artificial war scare followed when on March 5th, General Lucius D. Clay, the U.S. Military Governor in Germany, sent a top secret telegram expressing the feeling that war with Russia "may come with dramatic suddenness." Clay's telegram was sent to Lieutenant General Stephen J. Chamberlain, Director of Intelligence, but was meant to influence congressional action on pending military appropriations bills. It was not related, according to Clay, to ". . . any official report in the absence of supporting data but my feeling is real."[13] Five days after formation of the Brussels Pact, on March 22nd, and via Bevin's initiative, secret negotiations began in Washington on the formation of an Atlantic alliance. Congressional delegates were not included, partly because the administration feared provoking congressional isolationists. Ironically, because the British delegation included the Soviet spy Donald MacLean, the Russians were presumably well-informed.[14] State Department officials were soon busy developing plans for obtaining senatorial "advice" regarding eventual union with the Brussels Pact nations. To seek "consent" for an alliance treaty from the Senate Republican majority during a presidential election year was not considered feasible. The possible use of an executive agreement, or joint resolution, was also rejected since it was assumed the Senate would insist upon its treaty-approval prerogative in the formation of any such alliance. All efforts were therefore aimed at obtaining a favorable Senate resolution.

On April 11, 1948, Marshall and Lovett called on Vandenberg with a proposal that the United States aid the Brussels Pact nations of Western Europe. The Senator responded by suggesting that the administration's desire for a military treaty be supplemented with resolutions which seek to revise the United Nations Charter. He also suggested that the administration should leave it to the Senate to initiate a course of action which the administration could then follow.[15]

Vandenberg's motivation for Senate initiation of this historic foreign policy is worth pondering. According to one member of the British Foreign Office at the time, "The Presidential election was now in the offing, and Senator Vandenberg shied at something which would give so prominent a role to Truman, the prospective Democratic candidate for the Presidency."[16] Because Truman would have a prominent role in the administration proposal--announcing an Atlantic conference and declaring American support for the Brussels Pact--this observation seems plausible, but is probably incorrect. Instead, Vandenberg's view of how the resolution should be constructed was based upon the concerns of congressional colleagues who were "anxious about the United Nations,"[17] plus his interpretation of U.N. Article 51 which would allow an alliance to develop "within the Charter but outside the veto."[18]

Pressure to form the alliance continued to mount from Western Europe. During a top secret meeting on April 15, 1948, between French Embassy Minister Armand Berard and Theodore Achilles of the State Department's Office of European Affairs, Berard referred "to the dangers inherent in the present European situation and the need for speed" on the American part. Achilles responded by recognizing "the urgency, but great importance to having whatever policy we adopted a fully bipartisan American policy."[19]

Clearly the administration was committed to bipartisanship. Yet, the degree to which the evolving U.S. alliance policy would be formed on a fully bipartisan basis, despite the existence of both ideal and necessary conditions, remained to be seen.

Fully Bipartisan?

When the National Security Council met on April 22nd, the plan suggested by Vandenberg was explained by Lovett. Accordingly, it was noted that the Senate should first produce an advisory expression of support for a regional agreement, and that the President would then immediately concur by stating his interest.[20] On April 30th, Senator Tom Connally (Democrat of Texas), ranking minority member of the Senate Foreign Relations Committee, expressed his concern to the President over the lack of American involvement in a West European defense system. Truman responded enthusiastically by saying he would instruct the Secretary of State, and his Undersecretary, to consult with the Foreign Relations Committee regarding possible American participation in the Brussels Alliance.[21] Obviously the administration was not keeping Connally fully informed. Its efforts, at this stage, were aimed solely at Republican leader Vandenberg.

Lovett soon began meeting with the Senate Foreign Relations Committee where it was agreed that the Senate should pass a resolution indicating its desire to back a West European regional defense alliance. As various senators introduced resolutions to that effect, Vandenberg referred them to Lovett to condense into two or three drafts for the committee's final consideration. Connally claimed that from this point on Lovett began to ignore the Democratic members of the committee and concentrated only on the Republicans.[22]

In fact, a private collaboration on a resolution was occurring between Vandenberg and Lovett. For three or four weeks during this period Lovett would stop by Vandenberg's apartment, number 500G, in the old Park-Wardman Hotel. Their objective was to develop a draft resolution that would reflect the goals outlined in the April 11th meeting with Marshall. During this collaboration, Marshall kept in touch daily with what all three men referred to as the "500G meetings."[23]

Vandenberg's view of how the resolution should be constructed was also based upon his familiarity with U.N. Article 51 which acknowledges the "inherent right of individual or collective self-defense."[24] In other words, the West would formulate a regional defense alliance without violating the Charter of the United Nations--a point he knew was a significant concern to many of his Senate colleagues. At the same time, he believed any such U.S. effort toward the potential or actual use of regional agreements should be coupled with an additional effort to strengthen the peace-keeping machinery of the U.N. itself.

Eventually, at a 500G meeting, Lovett produced a State Department draft resolution three pages long. Vandenberg said it was "too long" and that he would take a turn at drafting the proposal. Twenty minutes later he produced a condensed version of the State Department draft that became known as the Vandenberg Resolution.[25] The sense-of-the Senate resolution advised the President, "that this Government, by constitutional process," should pursue the resolution's objectives within the United Nations Charter. Six evenly divided objectives followed with the intention of either strengthening the U.N. by, for instance, eliminating the veto from all questions involving the pacific settlement of disputes, or promoting regional self-defense arrangements in which the U.S. would eventually be associated.[26]

The administration did consult with additional

Republican leaders. At an April 27th conference held at Blair House, John Foster Dulles, the foreign policy confidante of Republican Governor Thomas E. Dewey of New York (the leading contender for the 1948 Republican presidential nomination), was invited along with Vandenberg, Marshall and Lovett. The Undersecretary noted the growing fear in European capitals regarding possible Soviet intentions.[27] He then suggested that these concerns could best be mollified by a regional pact such as the Rio Treaty. Vandenberg then produced the resolution he and Lovett had been drafting jointly. Dulles, although impressed with the clarity of the resolution, expressed doubt about treating the situation so formally. Instead he proposed that a European commitment would be better begun via an executive declaration such as President Monroe had announced in 1823, the Monroe Doctrine.[28] On May 11th the draft resolution was nevertheless made public and as Lovett himself would later recount, it was "largely" in Vandenberg's phraseology.[29]

Two days later French Ambassador Henri Bonnet inquired from Lovett as to whether the now publicized resolution, if passed by the Senate, could be interpreted as, "one-half of a guarantee?" But Lovett, fully aware of congressional concerns, quickly disabused Bonnet of any such notion by stating: "We had never thought of any guarantees and that if the Ambassador, or his government, were thinking of guarantees from us they would be well advised to get the idea out of their heads."[30]

Congressional Opposition

Three closed Foreign Relations Committee sessions on the resolution occurred during mid-May at which Undersecretary Lovett gave extensive testimony. There was considerable concern among committee members that automatic commitments in the event of an attack should not be made. Several senators also wanted it clearly understood that actual implementation of the resolution should be submitted to the Congress for a final determination, so that the advice function of the Senate would not be confused with the consent function. After reassurances on these matters by both Lovett and Vandenberg, the committee unanimously approved the Vandenberg Resolution on May 19, 1948, and submitted it to the Senate for consideration.[31]

West European impatience with the intricacies of U.S. legislative-executive relations and the formation of the alliance continued. On June 1st British Foreign Secretary Bevin stated in a top secret telegram that "I cannot agree that the situation in Europe will not further deteriorate if conversations on security are postponed until Congress rises."[32] Despite Bevin's prodding, the administration's gaze was now fixed upon the Congress and the fate of the Vandenberg Resolution.

Senator Vandenberg was at the height of his influence in the Senate when the resolution was introduced on June 11, 1948. As a senior senator with considerable prestige on both sides of the aisle, he could hold his own in debate and was widely respected for his ability in this area. He was a clear contender for his party's presidential nomination--if he wanted to pursue it--and the acknowledged spokesman for a bipartisan foreign policy. His appearance was not, however, commanding: balding, bespectacled and slightly plump, but his political technique was polished.

His journalist friend New York Times columnist James Reston, explained this technique by observing that Vandenberg's skill in maneuvering proposals through Congress was accomplished by anticipating and then removing any arguments that might threaten to block congressional acceptance. In addition, his dual role in the 80th Congress as President pro-tem of the Senate and Chairman of the Foreign Relations Committee put him in an advantageous position from which to influence foreign policy legislation.[33] As a former journalist himself, Vandenberg also remained in close touch with members of the press via frequent off the record sessions,[34] thus cementing his relationship with the Fifth Estate.

Vandenberg also possessed a "passionate Constitutionalism" according to political thinker Walter Lippmann. Commenting on the "violence of the struggle" between President and Congress during early 1952 after Vandenberg had passed from the scene, leaving Robert A. Taft as the leading Republican in the Senate, Lippmann added that "neither Truman nor Taft has shown a proper respect and loyalty where the Constitution was meant to be supreme." They had "flagrantly failed" to act "to preserve the spirit and meaning of the separation of powers." All of this had occurred, according to Lippmann, because they are no longer "kept in order by the moderating effect of Vandenberg."[35]

Liberal Democratic Senator Claude D. Pepper was left to mount the only real challenge to the resolution. He was at least Vandenberg's equal in oratorical skills, but lacked the bipartisan coalition support behind the foreign policy leader. Pepper argued that collective security was being abandoned for regionalism coupled with military and economic commitments, thus bringing back the balance of power principle as the only means of keeping world peace. In addition, he wished to have stricken from the resolution all references to military aid. Pepper's efforts were supported by Senators Kenneth McKellar (Democrat of Tennessee), and Glen H. Taylor (Democrat of Idaho), who was Henry Wallace's Vice Presidential running mate for the November election.[36]

The critical difference between Pepper's position and that of Vandenberg was his defense of the existing structure of the United Nations rather than the creation of a new regional organization which Vandenberg proposed. Claude Pepper noted in retrospect:

> I would like to have seen a maximum effort to make the United Nations work as an organization to preserve the security of all nations without a NATO like the Locarno Pact negotiated outside the League of Nations--I think contributing to its weakness.[37]

Vandenberg's counter-assertion that the resolution "encourages individual and collective self-defense against armed aggression within the charter and outside the veto,"[38] was a more immediately persuasive argument. The Pepper amendment on military aid was defeated 61 to 6, and after just one long day of debate (the Senate was rushing to adjourn), the Vandenberg Resolution as originally introduced was passed 64 to 4 with a total of 28 mostly isolationist senators, including Taft of Ohio, abstaining.

Thus, a more than sufficient vote for passage of the resolution was quickly mustered, which also equaled the minimum two-thirds majority vote that would be necessary for passage of the subsequent treaty. Senator

Taft's non-opposition at this critical juncture was an important factor. Although opposed to the bipartisan position, he was probably unwilling to trigger Vandenberg's opposition to his own possible presidential nomination at the upcoming Republican convention in Philadelphia. Taft's biographer, James T. Patterson, has noted that the Ohio Republican "may have hoped to mollify Republican internationalists, Arthur Vandenberg in particular, on the eve of the convention" by announcing that the Senate would stay in session until the European Recovery Program was funded.[39]

Ironically, Vandenberg's polished technique and political influence may have been too successful for his bipartisan effort to be fully achieved--acting instead as an inhibition on the Senate's consideration of both the Vandenberg Resolution and the North Atlantic Treaty. Claude Pepper believed that it was, recalling in addition that, "At that time, Senator Vandenberg dominated the policy and the position of the Senate and our government in the field of foreign affairs."[40]

A legislative effort similar to the Vandenberg Resolution was also occurring in the House of Representatives. During May, 1948, the House Committee on Foreign Affairs under the chairmanship of Representative Charles Eaton, a New Jersey Republican, held hearings to consider "the relationship of the United States to the United Nations." The committee then drew up its own bill and reported it to the House on June 9th. Among other points, it sought to encourage "regional self-defense arrangements under the UN charter." However, no further action was taken on the House bill,[41] leaving the Senate's Vandenberg Resolution as the sole advisory expression of the Congress on the developing alliance.

At the Republican convention beginning on June 21st, Governor Dewey easily won his party's presidential nomination and fully accepted the bipartisan foreign policy planks written by Vandenberg. These events occurred against a backdrop of heightened Cold War tensions as the Soviet Union completed their land blockade of West Berlin during the same month. The election campaign that followed was characterized by Truman's hard-hitting attacks upon the Republican controlled legislature which he repeatedly charged with being a do-nothing Congress. His tactics necessarily put a strain upon the President-Congress relationship and the bipartisan formation of NATO, but they did not cause a schism between Truman and Vandenberg. The main reason a break between them did not occur was due to the President's private assurance to Vandenberg during the heated campaign that, "Nothing will be done without consultation with you."[42]

Both Dewey and third party candidate Henry Wallace, a controversial liberal who attacked the bipartisan foreign policy as being too hard-line toward the Soviet Union, were defeated by Truman. Both the Senate and House also returned to their former Democratic majorities in 1949. Because the Truman Administration had maintained Democratic control of the White House, the results of the 1948 election are referred to as a maintaining election.[43] In addition, the bipartisan foreign policy would no longer be "absolutely essential,"[44] in that the executive and legislative branches were now controlled by the same party.

The Treaty Approved

During a private White House meeting the night before the signing of the North Atlantic Treaty, President Truman spoke to the Foreign Ministers of the signatory states. His remarks bespeak of an active, power balancing role for the new alliance while at the same time eschewing military action.

> I mean rather the building up of a power balance sufficient to destroy the debilitating fear of Soviet aggression and then, from this secure power base, taking active measures, on the one hand to remove in the non-Soviet world the social and economic pressures on which Communism thrives, and on the other hand to create active counterpressure to undermine the base of Soviet power itself.[45]

The treaty was signed the next day (April 4, 1949), by the twelve signatory nations. Its key provisions were contained in Article 5 where the parties agreed that "an armed attack against one or more of them in Europe or North America shall be considered an attack against them all." It further stated that, "if such an armed attack occurs, each of them, in exercise of the right of individual or collective self-defense recognized by Article 51 of the Charter of the United Nations" will assist via "such action as it deems necessary, including the use of armed force, to restore and maintain the security of the North Atlantic area."[46]

The only specific U.N. Charter reference in the treaty was Article 51. Vandenberg wanted the treaty more broadly based on the Charter by references in the treaty text to Chapter VIII, the regional chapter. However, Pepper argued successfully before his colleagues on the Foreign Relations Committee that the treaty was not truly regional because: "I do not agree that when you cross 3,000 miles of ocean and put two states into that kind of group that you have a regional arrangement within the contemplation of the charter." Therefore, according to Pepper, further inclusions would be, "setting up something which may be potentially a world organization certainly inconsistent with the concept of the United Nations."[47]

Thus, the North Atlantic Treaty was legally based upon Article 51 alone. No conflict or inconsistency resulted according to Vandenberg because he claimed "51 was written to be applied on a regional basis if anybody wanted to apply it on a regional basis."[48] On June 6th, the committee unanimously reported the treaty favorably to the Senate. Clearly then, the inclusion of Article 51 in the Charter had "paved the way for the NATO Treaty" as later remarked by Francis O. Wilcox, Vandenberg's Chief of Staff on the Foreign Relations Committee.[49]

Because Article 5 of the treaty did not technically violate the congressional power to declare war, a major potential isolationist argument was undercut, even though isolationist sentiment against the treaty continued on the floor of the Senate led by Taft. A content analysis of the twelve day floor debate reveals the issue had taken an economic turn with members expressing concern that the Congress would be obligated to approve military assistance programs submitted later.[50] The great debate on balance of power versus collective security was essentially over.

On July 21, 1949, the treaty was approved by a vote of 82-13, followed by presidential ratification four days later. Under the Democratic controlled 81st Congress, the number of approving votes increased by 18. All of the additional votes for the Treaty came from Democratic members. However, Republican support remained constant at 32 vote for the Resolution and the Treaty despite Taft's outspoken opposition to the Treaty and the party's loss of 8 Senate seats in the November, 1948, elections.

Summing Up

The development of NATO as the Grand Alliance of the West saw the President-Congress relationship confronting fundamental issues raised by the Cold War. The internationalist struggle to lead the United States into the United Nations had been won previously in 1943 with approval by the Congress of the Fulbright and Connally Resolutions. However, Soviet-American confrontational events following World War II, plus much West European prodding, demanded a new U.S. peacetime military presence in a regional alliance.

It fell upon the Republican controlled 80th Congress and the Democratic Presidency of Harry Truman to bring about U.S. acceptance of the NATO concept. The political method used to accomplish this historic task was bipartisanship. The degree to which this method was successful may be measured against the ideal and essential conditions necessary for its existence as enumerated and defined in the first several pages of this study. We must also measure the success of the alliance itself by its four plus decade record without a war in Europe. With respect to bipartisanship, all four of the essential and ideal conditions necessary for it to succeed were present at the creation of NATO.

The period during which the Senate passed the Vandenberg Resolution, the 80th Congress, 1947-48, saw the legislative and executive branches controlled by opposing political parties making the bipartisan approach between them essential. Secondly, a broad government consensus had developed over what U.S. foreign policy should be in the postwar era with the adoption of containment in 1947. NATO's development in 1949 conformed to the general containment thesis already enunciated. Public opinion was also supportive. When a

George Gallop poll in March, 1948, asked "What policy do you think we should follow toward Russia?" a plurality responded that the U.S. should "prepare to fight, build up armed forces."[51]

Capital Hill leadership capable of rallying the legislative branch was also abundantly available in the personage of Senator Vandenberg. The Michigan Republican and former isolationist must be considered one of the most important congressional foreign policy leaders in the entire postwar era. Finally, the necessary executive consultation with party foreign policy leaders in the Congress, prior to the implementation of policy, was closely adhered to by the Truman Administration in the formation of NATO--despite the strains of the 1948 presidential election campaign.

Ironically, Vandenberg's congressional leadership in the formation of the alliance also became a factor in denying this important foreign policy from being classified as fully bipartisan. The administration did not keep Tom Connally, the ranking member of the Senate Foreign Relations Committee, informed during the early stages of the alliance's formation--preferring instead to key on Vandenberg. Also, Senator Claude Pepper, who mounted the only concerted effort to defeat the Vandenberg Resolution, believed that the Republican Senator dominated the congressional foreign policy view at that time to the detriment of full legislative deliberation.

Nevertheless, Vandenberg's tactic for gaining congressional acceptance of a peacetime alliance was soundly based upon the United Nations Charter. His within the Charter but outside the veto approach, via the use of Article 51, and the Vandenberg Resolution provisions calling for the strengthening of the U.N., strongly appealed to his Senate colleagues. In addition, because the treaty text did not technically violate the congressional power to declare war, a major constitutional argument against Senate approval was not available to the isolationist opposition.

The results of the 1948 elections, which gave the Democrats a voting majority in the 81st Congress and maintained the Truman Administration in the White House, made bipartisanship no longer essential for the Senate's consent to ratification. Yet, the crucial Vandenberg Resolution had been passed earlier via the bipartisan method and Republican support in the Senate remained firm at 32 votes for both the resolution and the treaty.

The main arguments against the bipartisan method are essentially three in number. They are first, that real consultation between the two branches rarely occurs; secondly, that it stifles congressional debate and finally, that it increases presidential power at the expense of Congress. Vandenberg was keenly aware of all these criticisms and strongly argued against them publicly and in correspondence. In a Lincoln Day speech at Detroit during early 1949, he referred to the substantial consultation that had occurred by stating that his party "helped to formulate foreign policy before it ever reached the legislative stage. Otherwise it would not have worked." Regarding inhibitions on debate, Vandenberg had written that it actually ". . . encourages factual attack if such be warranted through a clarification of the real issues involved." With reference to presidential power being enhanced by making the Congress a rubber stamp, Vandenberg simply stated that bipartisanship was not "a carbon copy process," but rather a "meeting of minds."[52]

In conclusion, the bipartisan method will remain difficult to fully achieve even when all essential and ideal conditions are present for its success. At the same time, a pragmatic commitment to unity, in particular foreign policy areas, remains as vital to a constitutional system built upon a separation of powers principle as are critics' concerns that such unity may result in excessive concentrations of power. Because the American political system invites and requires both conflict and consensus, bipartisanship will continue to aid the President-Congress relationship in the formation of foreign policy. It did so with obvious success in the development of NATO.

Notes

[1]Vandenberg to a constituent, 5 January 1950, Arthur H. Vandenberg, Jr., ed., The Private Papers of Senator Vandenberg (Boston: Houghton Mifflin Company, 1952), 552.

[2]See author's, "Senator Vandenberg, Bipartisanship and the Origin of United Nations Article 51," Mid-America: An Historical Review 60 (October 1978): 163-69.

[3]Francis O. Wilcox, Chief of Staff, Senate Foreign Relations Committee, 1947-1955, Oral History Interviews, February 1 to June 13, 1984 (Washington, D.C.: Senate Historical Office, 1985), 205-6.

[4]This condition is originally noted in "Senator Vandenberg, Bipartisanship and the Origin of United Nations Article 51," Mid America, 164.

[5]Refer to development of UNRRA in Chapter II, 22-24.

[6]Full text of Long Telegram in Foreign Relations of the United States 1946 (Washington, D.C.: U.S. Government Printing Office, 1969), 696-709.

[7]As quoted in Walter Isaacson and Evan Thomas, The Wise Men: Six Friends And The World They Made (New York: Simon & Schuster, Inc., 1986), 24.

[8]Ibid., 417.

[9]Daniel Yergin, Shattered Peace: The Origins of the Cold War and the National Security State (Boston: Houghton Mifflin Company, 1977), 334.

[10]Harry S. Truman, Memoirs: Years of Trial and Hope, 1946-1952, vol. 2 (New York: Doubleday & Company, Inc., 1956), 243.

[11]Arthur H. Vandenberg, "The Economic Cooperation Administration: A Plan For Peace, Stability and Freedom," Vital Speeches of the Day 14 (15 March 1948): 322.

[12]For a critical examination of Vandenberg's anti-Soviet views and bipartisanship see, Thomas Michael Hill, "Senator Arthur H. Vandenberg, the Politics of Bipartisanship, and the Origins of Anti-Soviet Consensus, 1941-1946," World Affairs 138 (1975-76): 219-41. On the Polish question see his letter of 27 July 1946, to Frank Januszewski, owner of the Polish Daily News of Detroit attacking the Yalta Agreements, Private Papers, 314.

[13]Jean Edward Smith, ed., The Papers of General Lucius D. Clay: Germany 1945-54, vol. 2 (Bloomington: Indiana University Press, 1974), 568-69.

[14]Lord Gladwyn, The Memoirs of Lord Gladwyn (New York: Weybright & Talley, 1972), 214-16. MacLean defected to the Soviet Union in 1951.

[15]James A. Robinson, Congress and Foreign Policy-Making: A Study in Legislative Influence and Initiative (Homewood, Illinois: The Dorsey Press, 1967), 45.

[16]Sir Nicholas Henderson, The Birth of NATO (Boulder, Colorado: Westview Press, 1983), 27.

[17]Vandenberg in conversation with State Department Assistant Secretary Dean Rusk, 13 April 1948. Foreign Relations of the United States, Memoranda of Conversation of the Secretary of State, 1947-1952, Microfiche Publication 486 (Washington, D.C.: Department of State, 1988).

[18]Vandenberg to a constituent, 9 December 1948, Private Papers, 418-19.

[19]Memoranda of Conversation, 15 April 1948, no. 492.

[20]Walter Millis, ed. The Forrestal Diaries (New York: The Viking Press, 1951), 423-24.

[21]Tom Connally, My Name is Tom Connally (New York: Thomas Y. Crowell Company, 1954), 328.

[22]Ibid.

[23]Vandenberg, Private Papers, 404.

[24]See, "Senator Vandenberg, Bipartisanship and the Origin of United Nations Article 51," Mid America, 168.

[25]Isaacson and Thomas, The Wise Men, 450.

[26]See full text of resolution in Appendix B. Text quoted from, U.S. Congress, Committee on Foreign Relations, The Vandenberg Resolution and the North Atlantic Treaty, 80th Cong., 2nd Sess. and 81st Cong., 1st Sess. (Washington, D.C.: U.S. Government Printing Office, 1973), 327-28.

[27]Four days earlier Lovett delivered a top secret telegram to Truman from Britain's Foreign Secretary Bevin urging the United States to organize a West European defense. See vol. 2, Truman's Memoirs, 244-45.

[28]John Foster Dulles, War or Peace (New York: Macmillan Company, 1950), 96.

[29]Vandenberg, Private Papers, 406.

[30]Memoranda of Conversation, 13 May 1948, no. 552.

[31]Hearings, The Vandenberg Resolution and the North Atlantic Treaty, 1-66, passim.

[32]Full text of telegram with Memoranda of Conversation, 14 June 1948, no. 592.

[33]James Reston, "Events Spotlight Vandenberg's Dual Role," New York Times Magazine, 28 March 1948, 51.

[34]See Vandenberg, Private Papers, 329-30.

[35]Clinton Rossiter and James Lare, eds., The Essential Lippmann: A Political Philosophy for Liberal Democracy (New York: Vintage Books, 1965), 287-89.

[36]Remarks in, Congressional Record, 80th Cong., 2nd sess., 1948, 94, pt 6: 7837.

[37]Letter to the author from Representative Claude Pepper, 23 June 1980. Following the last multilateral effort to strengthen the League of Nations through the Geneva Protocol, which failed, a series of bilateral treaties were concluded in 1925 known as the Locarno

Pact. Taken together these treaties formed a regional agreement.

[38] Cong. Rec., 94 pt 6: 7792.

[39] See Patterson, Mr. Republican: A Biography of Robert A. Taft (Boston: Houghton Mifflin Company, 1972), 329.

[40] Letter, Rep. Claude Pepper, 23 June 1980.

[41] Congressional Digest 27, 8 & 9 (August-September, 1948): 199.

[42] See Vandenberg diary entry of 23 October 1948 in, Private Papers, 459-60.

[43] Richard S. Kirkendall, "Election of 1948," in Arthur M. Schlesinger, Jr., ed., History of American Presidential Elections, 1789-1968, vol. 4 (New York: McGraw-Hill Book Co., 1971), 3144.

[44] Wilcox, Chief of Staff, Senate Foreign Relations Committee, 205.

[45] Memoranda of Conversation, 3 April 1949, no. 897.

[46] See treaty text in Hearings, The Vandenberg Resolution and the North Atlantic Treaty, 360-63.

[47] Ibid., 315, 318.

[48] Ibid., 316.

[49] Letter to the author from Francis O. Wilcox, 23 February 1979.

[50] See Table Four, "Selected Congressional Controversies, 1945-1970," in James Clotfeter, The Military in American Politics (New York: Harper & Row, 1973), 167.

[51] Ralph B. Levering with a foreword by George Gallop, The Public and American Foreign Policy, 1918-1978 (New York: William Morrow & Company, 1978), 98.

[52]On consultation and presidential power see Vandenberg's Lincoln Day speech at Detroit, 14 February 1949. Regarding debate see letter to Robert E. Hannegan, Chairman of the Democratic National Committee, 28 October 1946, all in Private Papers, 550.

IV

CONGRESS AND FRANCO SPAIN:

THE PACT OF MADRID, 1953

In 1946 the United States, Britain and France jointly requested that the Spanish people peacefully end, by political means, the dictatorial government of General Francisco Franco. Seven years later, with the full development of the Cold War, the United States established bases in Spain through the Pact of Madrid, thus beginning a de facto military alliance between the two countries. The following case study will examine this reversal in U.S. foreign policy with particular emphasis upon the role of the Congress and its relations with the administration of President Harry S. Truman.

Franco Spain and U.S. Foreign Policy

The Franco regime came to power as the winning side in the Spanish Civil War from 1936-39 that overthrew the Republican Government of Spain during an era of Fascist and Nazi dictatorships in Italy and Germany. Although Franco subsequently signed the Anti-Comintern Pact of 1939 with Hitler, Mussolini and the Imperial Japanese Government, Spain did not become a belligerent during World War II, the major reason being "Hitler's unwillingness to satisfy Franco's imperial aspirations."[1] As the tide of battle turned against the axis powers, Franco reluctantly retreated into a more strict neutrality. In October, 1943, he declared Spain neutral instead of simply a non-belligerent, and strengthened his ties with Portugal, a nation allied to Great Britain since 1384.

As the war drew to a conclusion and an allied victory appeared imminent, President Roosevelt wrote to Mr. Norman Armour, the new American Ambassador to Spain on March 10, 1945. Although the United States had maintained full diplomatic relations with the Franco regime since shortly after it assumed power, he stated: "I can see no place in the community of nations for governments founded on Fascist principles."[2]

On July 17, 1945, at the Potsdam Conference, Joseph Stalin argued that diplomatic relations should be broken off with the Franco regime, but Winston Churchill demurred and President Truman, "who disliked the Franco Government, agreed that the question should be studied."[3] Nevertheless, the Big Three did agree that Spain should not be admitted to the United Nations. Thus, after the war the Franco Government "underwent an ostracism that was almost complete for two years."[4] The intended purpose of this policy by the principal powers was to encourage liberal Spanish elements to change the leadership and disposition of their government.

In response to a Polish delegation resolution proposed during April, 1946, that U.N. members "who maintain diplomatic relations with the Franco Government . . . sever such relations immediately,"[5] and a less severe version proposed by the United States, a compromise resolution was adopted by the General Assembly on December 12, 1946. It recommended that the "Franco Government of Spain be debarred from membership. . . ." Another recommendation called for all members to "immediately recall from Madrid their ambassadors and ministers plenipotentiary accredited there."[6] The United States withdrew Ambassador Armour from Madrid in compliance with the resolution and left a charge d'affaires to head the United States Embassy.

On March 4, 1946, the United States, the United Kingdom and France released a Tripartite Declaration regarding their disposition toward the Spanish Government. While carefully noting there was no intention of interfering with Spanish internal affairs they expressed hope that liberal elements would find a means of bringing into existence "a peaceful withdrawal of Franco, the abolition of the Falange, and the establishment of an interim or caretaker government. . . ."[7] A promise was then included that if the Spanish nation moved in this direction, full diplomatic relations would be restored and badly needed economic aid would be made available.[8]

General Franco attempted to break his regime out of its enforced isolation by seeking friends in the Middle East and Pakistan on the basis of his nation's historical but slender link with Islam. He also sought friendship with Argentina during this period,[9] and his regime remained staunchly anti-Communist. Internally, the economy was his most pressing problem, but an uprising against the government could not be totally discounted with one well-known Spanish writer describing Franco's Spain as "a military state at war with its people."[10]

Former Prime Minister Churchill delivered his famous "Iron Curtain" speech at Fulton, Missouri on March 5, 1946: "From Stettin in the Baltic to Trieste in the Adriatic, an iron curtain has descended across the continent."[11] Three months later on June 6, 1946, U.S. Secretary of the Navy James V. Forrestal proposed to Secretary of State James Byrnes that cruisers should be sent into the Mediterranean "so that we may establish the custom of the American flag being flown in those waters."[12] Soon thereafter naval planners became interested in obtaining bases for the new Mediterranean squadron.

As the governments of England and France moved toward a military alliance, which would eventually culminate in the development of the North Atlantic Treaty Organization and the rearming of West Germany, the United States began to shift its policy toward Spain. Since a basic tenet of the evolving NATO strategy was "that the basis of the alliance be expanded as far as possible,"[13] the future development of military bases in Spain also fell under the scrutiny of U.S. military planners.

Thus, during 1947 the United States led the movement to defeat a U.N. resolution reaffirming the 1946 resolution on the recall of ambassadors from Madrid. Although the Truman Administration contended that the original resolution was still binding, and continued to deny the Spanish Government all forms of economic aid, its stand at the U.N. was interpreted by Madrid as lifting the diplomatic sanctions against the Spanish Government.[14] At the same time, George F. Kennan, head of the State Department's policy planning group and principal author of the newly embraced policy of containment, was arguing for a reappraisal of our policy toward Spain. Importantly, it was Kennan's assertion that securing the Mediterranean and the Straits of Gibraltar could not be considered without Spain.[15]

New Secretary of State George C. Marshall was also in favor of reevaluating U.S. policy toward Spain. He urged the rescinding of the U.N. ban on exchanging ambassadors with Spain. Yet, his awareness of England and France's aversion to Franco, and "their fear of a policy of defense behind the Pyrenees,"[16] dissuaded him from pressing for Spain's inclusion in his own foreign aid proposal known as the Marshall Plan.

As U.S. foreign policy planners became increasingly desirous of including Spain within the emerging Atlantic Alliance, they reevaluated the policy of ostracism. That policy, it was now believed, had failed in its primary purpose of encouraging liberal elements to peacefully topple the Franco regime. Instead the Spanish dictator seemed as secure as ever with his opposition at home divided and ineffectual. Franco's acceptability at home and abroad was also increased during 1947 by a plebiscitic vote on a Law of Succession which embodied the monarchial principle. With 15,200,000 votes cast out of an electorate of nearly 17,200,000, 14,145,163 voted yes "under conditions which observers testified to be fair."[17] Therefore, by 1948 support was growing in the Congress, the State Department and the Pentagon for a change in U.S. policy toward Spain.

Secretary of State Marshall retired at the end of 1948 and was succeeded by Dean Acheson the following year. According to Acheson: "Mr. Truman held deep-seated convictions on many subjects, among them, for instance, a dislike of Franco and Catholic obscurantism in Spain."[18] However, 1948 was a presidential election year and most political experts were predicting a defeat for Truman. Under the circumstances the President made a small reconciliation gesture toward Spain. During March he sent Myron C. Taylor, his Vatican envoy, to Madrid with instructions for Franco as to how he could gain U.S. support. Some observers asserted that the President was simply attempting to gain favor with American Catholic voters during an election year.[19]

Nevertheless, as massive Marshall Plan aid began to pour into many areas of Western Europe, it became painfully evident to Franco that Spain was not to be a recipient. President Truman was still considered an implacable foe of better relations with the Franco regime as it then existed. General Franco therefore hoped the predictions that Truman would be defeated in the 1948 elections were true. In the meantime, the Spanish Embassy in Washington, D.C. began a program to influence both the legislative and executive branches of the U.S. Government toward improved relations with Spain.

The Spanish Lobby

Efforts by Foreign Ministers accredited to the United States attempting to influence its external affairs began during the administration of the first American President, George Washington. The activities of the new French Minister in 1793, Citizen Edmond Genet, aimed at using American soil for the outfitting of French privateers against English ships and other plans, were opposed by the President. When Genet threatened to go over the President's head and appeal directly to the American people for support, "Washington indignantly requested his recall."[20] Despite Genet's maladroit tactics and their ultimate failure, foreign efforts to influence U.S. policy have long continued. Indeed, by the early 1970's some 400 "foreign agents" were registered with the State Department. These so-called agents were in fact American professional lobbyists hired by foreign governments.[21]

General Franco was not without friends on Capitol Hill. He was aware of both representatives and senators who supported his quest for U.S. aid. He also knew that American military planners desired an arrangement by which bases in Spain could be established. Events, too, were working to make his position more acceptable. In 1948, Berlin was blockaded and the nations of Western Europe increased their search for security. Also, Franco Spain appeared more staunchly anti-Communist than either France or Italy, where large Communist parties were active. In order to exploit this beachhead of acceptability in the American governmental establishment, a Spanish lobby was established in Washington during 1948.

Senor Don Jose Felix de Lequerica, an experienced diplomat, was charged with the responsibility of heading the Spanish Government's attempt to gain economic support and increased political acceptability from the United States. As Ambassador-without-Portfolio he became, in effect, chief of the Spanish delegation to Washington. On the advice of friendly congressman, he retained the services of Charles Patrick Clark, an honors graduate from Georgetown University who had served on the staffs of several congressional committees. It would be Clark's responsibility to mobilize and coordinate support among the various governmental groups sympathetic to a policy of closer relations with Spain. The Spanish cause became brighter soon after Clark was retained.[22]

The groups that Clark enlisted in the Spanish cause were varied and motivated by different reasons. Within the Congress some members supported the Spanish Lobby partly because of their religious sympathy for Catholic Spain. Significantly, this group acted as a legislative counterforce to Truman's known antipathy for Franco and Spanish Catholicism. Its most important member was Senator Patrick A. McCarren, a Nevada Democrat, who received the Grand Cross of the Order of Isabella la Catholica from the Spanish Dictator in 1953, just prior to the signing of the Pact of Madrid "for his efforts to improve Spanish-American relations."[23] Other members of this group were Republican Senators Owen Brewster of Maine, Styles Bridges of New Hampshire and Joseph McCarthy of Wisconsin. The Senate condemned McCarthy in 1955 for his unfounded charges that public officials were Communists. Representatives in this category included A. E. O'Konski, a Republican of Wisconsin, Eugene Keogh, a Democrat of New York, and the future Speaker of the House, John W. McCormack of Massachusetts.

A second area of important support came from within the military establishment which was concerned with maintaining the fleet's Mediterranean lifeline and a related desire to include Spain in the developing North Atlantic alliance. This desire was to remain partially muffled among flag rank officers so long as it was clear that the President was not in favor of closer relations with Spain. A final group from which the Spanish Lobby was able to gain significant support was the growing number of anti-administration representatives and senators, including such influential figures as Republican Senator Robert Taft of Ohio.

Although President Truman was re-elected in 1948, events were occurring that would indirectly aid the cause of the Spanish Lobby. Truman had consistently attacked the Republican controlled 80th Congress in his successful bid for re-election. By previous agreement, a bipartisan foreign policy was to be maintained; however, this agreement did not cover the administration's China policy because, according to Republican Senator Arthur H. Vandenberg of Michigan, the kind of advance consultation between Republicans and the administration regarding European questions had not been conducted on the same scale regarding Far Eastern policy.[24]

As the Nationalist Chinese cause became more bleak, criticism of the administration's Far East policy became more common. However, while the highly respected Secretary of State Marshall remained in office until the end of 1948, these attacks remained muffled. His successor, Secretary of State Dean Acheson, was not similarly spared. When the Nationalists were finally routed from the mainland in 1949, the Republican attacks upon the administration became vitriolic.

The bipartisan foreign policy was breaking down under a hail of bitter accusations primarily related to the administration's so-called loss of China. It was to collapse completely when in February, 1950, Senator McCarthy injected the whole China question deeper into the antagonisms of partisan politics by announcing, without presenting any evidence, that the State Department was completely infested with Communists.[25] In June of that same year the Korean War began. The two political parties briefly closed ranks with this event, but soon reverted back into a bitter partisan debate. A scapegoat was in order and the most accessible target for the Republicans was Secretary of State Dean Acheson.

During December, 1950, the Republicans caucused in the House and adopted a resolution that declared the Secretary of State had lost the confidence of both the Congress and the American people; Senate Republicans followed by demanding he be replaced. Senator McCarran, a consistent critic of the Secretary and congressional leader of Spanish Lobby forces added, "Whether what had been said about him is either proper or correct doesn't matter now."[26] The Truman-MacArthur controversy, which began with the General's dismissal in April, 1951, touched off new and even more virulent criticisms of the administration. Again, Acheson bore the brunt of the Republicans' partisan attack: the bipartisan foreign policy was temporarily dead.

The combination of defeat for the Chiang Kai-shek forces in 1949, Senator McCarthy's "witch hunting," the Korean War and incessant right wing attacks, had thrown the administration on the defensive. In the context of these events the government's policy toward Spain was relatively unimportant. However, the Spanish Lobby was aided considerably by the administration's increasingly vulnerable position. Luck of sorts was running with the Franco forces.

The main groups that coalesced to change the administration's foreign policy--Catholic representatives and senators, the military establishment, and anti-administration forces, gave the Spanish Lobby a bipartisan coloration. Yet, this bipartisan support was not a product of close executive-congressional collaboration as exemplified by passage of the Vandenberg Resolution in 1948, which supported future U.S. involvement in the Western Alliance. President Truman was never sympathetic to the Spanish cause and executive-congressional relations were strained in general by 1949.

In the spring of 1948, the pro-Spanish forces delivered a blow to the administration's Spanish policy. While the Economic Cooperation Act, which was to implement the Marshall Plan, was being debated on the floor of the House, Representative Alvin O'Konski offered an amendment whereby Spain would become a participating member. In Representative O'Konski's hard-hitting speech on behalf of his amendment, he pointed to the large Communist blocs within Italy and France who were slated to receive Marshall Plan aid. He then claimed that if war broke out within a week, "you would find that the fighting front would be Spain, the only country which would offer effective resistance."[27]

The Truman Administration was now caught within the crisis atmosphere engendered by the Cold War. At this time it was attempting to gain senatorial acceptance for American involvement in a European alliance and had therefore been describing the Soviet Union's threat vividly. The atmosphere created made the acquisition of all possible allies seem justifiable. Under these conditions, Representative O'Konski's logic seemed almost compelling; however, in a later House-Senate conference, his amendment was dropped. The show of strength by the pro-Spanish forces was significant. Although they had not achieved their objectives in the 80th Congress, they were greatly heartened by the widespread support they were gaining.

This near victory was soon to be tempered by a series of events the Spanish Lobby considered a defeat: the unexpected re-election of President Truman in November of 1948, and the subsequent retirement of George Marshall as Secretary of State at the end of the year. Truman's position was sympathetic to that of the United Nations declaration on relations with Spain, and his re-election was neither expected nor desired by the Spanish Lobby. Secretary Marshall had shared the view of most military officers who considered closer relations with Spain desirable. His retirement meant the loss of one influential voice close to the President who desired closer relations with Spain.

Dean Acheson, Marshall's replacement beginning in January, 1949, rejected the Wilsonian assumption that faith could achieve peace under law, and he saw little room in his analysis of world events for sentiment. He also emphasized the difference between ideal and real conditions in decision-making.[28]

Acheson concluded that the key to blocking the Soviet threat was to use the combined forces of the North Atlantic Community. This Europe-first orientation brought him to the viewpoint that nothing should be done to antagonize America's European allies, and bringing Spain into closer relations with the West could only serve that purpose. Any attempt to include Spain would therefore be detrimental to the alliance since it would jeopardize its very existence. In addition, Acheson also evidently shared some of President Truman's emotional aversion to Franco. In a letter to this author, he recalled having had "little enthusiasm for an agreement" with Spain.[29]

Acheson's opposition to the Franco regime soon became the target of the Spanish Lobby forces in Congress. Hearings before a Senate Subcommittee on Appropriations during May, 1949, on State Department requests, were used to attack the administration's Spanish policy. Senator McCarran, Chairman of the subcommittee, insisted that the United States did not even recognize the Spanish nation. This was not in fact the case: by the time this committee hearing took place, the United States had for eleven years given recognition to the Franco regime. In compliance with the U.N. recommendation of 1946, only an ambassador was missing. Nevertheless, the Franco regime sought full diplomatic recognition from Washington. By so doing, the United States would be successfully harnessed to Franco's quest for enhanced prestige. Also, economic aid could more easily be obtained from Washington, even though it need not necessarily be used for the American objective of strengthening the Western Alliance.

Senator McCarran also questioned Acheson as to what was being done to bring about smoother relations between the United States and Spain. Acheson answered in a way that reflected his concern over the reactions of the European allies: he noted that the Spanish Government could make "considerable progress in doing away with some of the more oppressive practices which they have," and also that "they can go quite a distance toward coming closer to the views of some of their neighbors."[30] McCarran, leading Senate spokesman for the Spanish Lobby and right wing critic of State Department officials, responded sharply that he was not in favor of the Secretary's policy with reference to Spain, and until it was changed he was going to "examine your appropriations with a fine-tooth comb."[31]

The announcement of the Soviet Union's atomic explosion in August, 1949, also affected the congressional view toward the role of Spain. Senator Taft reportedly declared that "we must adjust our relations with Spain because of that discovery."[32] In addition during 1949, it was also reported in secret by the U.S. Chargé in Spain to Secretary of State Acheson that U.S. policy encouraging Spain to liberalize and change is, "completely neutralized by the attitude and statements of such people as Senator Taft and Senator McCarran."[33]

Acheson did not believe that the United Nations ban on ambassadors had been effective in trying to bring about a moderate regime in Spain. He was also aware of the strategic advantages Spain could bring to the defense of Western Europe against the potential threat of the Soviet Union he believed existed, if it could be acceptably integrated into a European alliance system. Accordingly, when the question of rescinding the recommendation on ambassadors was brought to a vote in the General Assembly in 1949, the United States abstained from voting. The "ban on ambassadors" recommendation was retained by a margin of only a few votes.

U.S. military officers lent increasing support to congressional attacks upon the Truman Administration's Spanish policy during 1949. When it was decided to organize the NATO fleets under a single command during the year, the competition between British and American naval officers intensified. American naval strategists believed they needed bases strategically located with respect to both the Atlantic and the Mediterranean, and independent of the need to use British facilities. By so doing the American naval presence in the Mediterranean could be further secured against the Soviet Union. Thus, naval officers began to make more overt efforts to bring Spain into the developing Western Alliance. Admiral Richard L. Connally, Commander of the United States Naval Forces in the Eastern Atlantic and Mediterranean, finally received permission from the State Department in September, 1949, to visit Spanish ports with elements of the fleet. Connally's visit was followed by another courtesy call with elements of the 6th Fleet soon after. The Franco regime was gaining a new aura of respectability through these naval visits.[34]

Junketeering became an additional technique employed by those members of Congress attempting to change the administration's foreign policy toward Spain. In the fall of 1949, Senators McCarran and Owen Brewster (Republican of Maine), plus Representatives James J. Murphy (Democrat of New York), and James P. Richards (Democrat of South Carolina) among others, visited Spain and returned with glowing reports of friendship with the Franco Government.[35] In the late fall of 1949, a subcommittee of the Senate Appropriations Committee returned from Spain, whose members included Senators Dennis Chavez (Democrat of New Mexico), John C. Stennis (Democrat of Mississippi) and John L. McClellan (Democrat of Arkansas). The committee unanimously agreed that both economic aid and full diplomatic recognition should be given to the Spanish Government.[36]

The Administration Weakens

The year 1950 was one of crisis and complexity for American foreign policy planners. Congressional pressures continued on the administration to strengthen the newly formed North Atlantic Treaty Organization by including Spain. A significant break developed in the administration's position in January, 1950: Senator Tom Connally (Democrat of Texas), who had regained his Chairmanship of the Senate Foreign Relations Committee from Senator Vandenberg in the Democratic sweep of 1948, requested clarification of the administration's Spanish policy from Dean Acheson.

Acheson, now embattled by right wing congressional criticism over the administration's China policy (the following month Spanish Lobby supporter Senator McCarthy would claim the State Department was infested with Communists), used his reply to justify a turnabout on this issue. While noting that the whole question of Spanish policy had been magnified by controversy "to a position among our present day foreign policy problems which is disproportionate to its intrinsic importance," he added that it had still been possible to treat the Spanish question on a broad bipartisan basis through the American delegation at the U.N.[37] Acheson went on to explain how he felt the withdrawal of ambassadors from Spain in compliance with the 1946 U.N. resolution had been a mistake, since instead of weakening the Franco Government, it had only strengthened it. Thus, Acheson announced, the United States was ready to vote for a resolution in the General Assembly leaving it up to each nation as to whether or not it wished to send an ambassador or minister to Spain. However, this change in policy was not to be interpreted as approval of the present Spanish regime, but merely as an effort to return to more normal practices in the exchange of diplomatic representatives, and to remove the issue from available use "by hostile propaganda to create unnecessary divisions within the United Nations and among our own people."[38]

Regarding the question of Spanish affiliation with European recovery programs, Acheson noted that the Spanish regime was still quite unacceptable to many of its close neighbors. In this matter he noted, "the Western European nations must have a leading voice." Finally, the highly sought after funds the Spanish Government desired must be obtained via the Export-Import Bank, he maintained. However, Spain's application would be evaluated according to the Bank's regular policies, which included an evaluation of the applicant's ability to pay. Acheson further contended that the plight of the Spanish economy could be avoided considerably through steps that could be taken by the Spanish Government itself. These would include lifting the restrictions on foreign investors, such as the 25 percent ceiling on participation of foreign investors in Spanish business ventures.[39]

Acheson's turnabout toward Spain was probably an attempt to placate his critics who considered the lack of an American ambassador in Madrid as an important missing link in their drive to make the Spanish regime more acceptable to Washington, and thus more eligible for aid. To be sure, Acheson regarded the absence of an American ambassador in Madrid as having failed in its intended purpose of encouraging liberalization of the regime. Instead, he felt it had needlessly injected a note of moral condescension into American policy toward Spain's own internal affairs. However, mass funding would still be withheld and it was highly doubtful, considering the poor state of Spain's economy, that the Export-Import Bank would extend credit.

Acheson had not completely closed the door on Franco, however, and if Franco were willing to make certain internal changes, the possibility for better relations with Washington existed. Spanish nationalism was also a factor in this problem. Spain's refusal to grant greater privileges to foreign investors was in part a nationalistic response, and the importance of Spanish nationalism was to become more apparent when actual negotiations over the Pact of Madrid took place.

Added fuel for the fire of increasingly partisan politics was supplied by Mao Tse-tung's visit to Moscow during February to sign a thirty year treaty of friendship, mutual assistance and alliance with the Soviet Union. With this event, the constant flaying of the State Department by the China Lobby in Congress began to reach new heights.

With the State Department preoccupied in defending its Far Eastern policy against heavy partisan criticism, the pro-Spanish forces now concentrated their fire on the argument that the Spanish people lacked basic freedoms. This emotion-laden issue, especially the question of religious freedom, evidently concerned the President more than his Secretary of State. Truman had once remarked that "the situation in Spain is intolerable. Do you know that a Baptist who dies in Spain must even be buried in the middle of the night?"[40] In essence, the Spanish Lobby's attack was now being shifted against the Truman position since the Secretary of State was developing a more tolerant stance toward Spain.

In March, Senator Brewster led the first attack of the session against the administration's Spanish policy from the floor of the Senate. In his lengthy address, Brewster referred repeatedly to the question of freedom of religious worship in Spain. In an effort to answer the charge that the Protestant religion was discriminated against, Brewster quoted extensively from a letter he had received on this question from one Max H. Klein, President of the American Chamber of Commerce in Barcelona, who was also a Catholic. Klein, according to Brewster, had personally "never heard of any such thing as a Protestant problem in Spain" until he had read a recent article in the New York Herald Tribune.[41]

In another speech related to this issue, Representative Richards, Chairman of the House Foreign Affairs Committee, generally endorsed the administration's foreign policies, but differed sharply with its Spanish policy. His speech, delivered less than two weeks prior to the onset of the Korean War, reinforced Senator Brewster's contention that Protestants were free to worship in Spain. He then broadened the whole argument regarding religious toleration to include the treatment of Jews and Moslems, with the conclusion that they also enjoyed religious freedom. Like Senator Brewster before him, he referred to a number of different sources in his attempt to prove that religious tolerance did in fact exist in Spain.[42]

During 1950, Spain was finally included in Marshall Plan appropriations. A possible factor in this victory for Franco was the large sums of money ($108,250 during 1950 alone) the Spanish Embassy made available to their lobby organizer Clark. Clark hoped to insure that aid proposed for Spain would not be obliterated during House and Senate debates. During March and April of 1950 Clark began paying Congressman Keogh "checks averaging about $1,000 a month, allegedly for advice on a Federal tax case (though it is against the law for a Congressman to accept fees in a Federal tax case)." This money was returned later when the matter was brought to the attention of the Justice Department. On April 25, 1950, Clark made out "check No. 3393 for $1,000 in cash and asked his secretary to cash it at the Mayflower Hotel in $100 bills." Clark then told his secretary that he had "a date to pay gin rummy with Senator Owen Brewster that evening. He also remarked, 'Hurry up and get the cash or Brewster will be hopping mad.'" Two days later Senator Brewster introduced an amendment to include Marshall Plan appropriations for Spain. However, in this case the Senate defeated the amendment.[43]

Monetary payments probably also affected Spain's relations with the West earlier in 1941 and 1942, when Spanish neutrality was bolstered by a secret British conspiracy in which a number of Spanish Generals received gifts of money so that they "would insist on Spain maintaining her neutrality." The money was deposited in New York with the knowledge of the U.S. Office of Strategic Services (OSS).[44] Nor would such dealings have shocked Franco. Don Juan, Pretender to the throne of Spain, who spoke with the Caudillo aboard a yacht during 1948, remarked that "Franco is a complete cynic about men. I recall that in our conference on the yacht, he remarked that anybody could be bought."[45]

With the invasion of South Korea in June, 1950, pressure upon the administration to change its Spanish policy became intense. Shortly after that war began, Senator Harry P. Cain (Republican of Washington) spoke out on behalf of friendlier relations with Spain. His remarks are of interest because his reference to the military position on this matter, in support of his own contention, illustrates the growing alliance between Spanish Lobby supports in Congress and the military establishment. Senator Cain made a special effort to keep his conversation with General Omar Bradley, Chairman of the Joint Chiefs of Staff, in such a perspective that it would not endanger his relationship with the Commander in Chief. Thus, Cain noted Bradley's remark that it is the job of the military establishment to plan on the basis of "what you in the Congress and those in the White House and those in authority in other high political offices in the United States and around the world give us to work with." However, Cain then added quickly that in his opinion General Bradley "would by no means deny a solitary thing I have said in support of Spain so far."[46]

As the Korean War continued, the last remaining vestiges of bipartisan support for American foreign policy were destroyed. The Truman Administration could no longer count on congressional support for its Spanish policy. At the same time, the question of a loan for Spain remained crucial to the pro-Spanish forces. Under these conditions, the continued efforts of "Brewster, Keogh, McCarran and an assist by another paid lobbyist, Max Truett, son-in-law of Vice President Barkley . . ." began to achieve results.[47] McCarran decided it was a propitious moment to push through a Spanish loan in the Senate. In this effort, he marshalled the aid of members of the military establishment in persuading key members of the Senate to support a loan.

McCarran organized a secret meeting at which he brought together key members of the Senate and military during July, 1950, while he claimed "headlines were telling us to get ready for a Dunkirk in Korea." McCarran explained he was about to introduce a bill to loan $100,000,000 to Spain. "While they were digesting this loathsome request," he then added that he would also begin a drive to bring Spain into NATO, which left the senators in the room "beyond shock." McCarran did not disclose the names of the army officers who were used as added persuasion on the senators present. However, he did add that army men of cabinet rank had kept out of the argument, but that the "shirt-sleeve boys in the Pentagon wanted it."[48]

McCarran's campaign for aid to the Franco regime was now carried to the floor of the Senate. On August 1, 1950, the first successful Spanish loan (the McCarran Amendment) was passed by a vote of 65 to 15. During the course of the debate over the amendment, Senator Wayne Morse (who was at that time a Republican of Oregon) spoke on the moral dilemma that closer relations with Spain presented. In his speech called "A Wrestle

With One's Conscience," Morse noted that he hated "with all my soul and being, everything that is Communistic. But likewise, I hate with an equal hatred, and with all my soul and being, everything that is Fascist." Morse also referred to the key role of the United Nations in helping solve this moral dilemma by adding that the "first test to our making a loan to Spain is whether or not Franco Spain can meet the tests of the United Nations for membership." [49] Morse favored such a change in the U.N.'s position.

Two days later, an attempt was made in the Senate to have the Spanish loan reconsidered. Senate liberals, such as Hubert Humphrey (Democrat of Minnesota) and Herbert Lehman (Democrat of New York), made eloquent speeches in an effort to beat back the onslaught of support the Spanish loan appeared to have. This support included such Senate leaders as Tom Connally, Chairman of the Foreign Relations Committee. Senator Humphrey echoed the argument of Secretary of State Acheson that the concerns of Spain's neighbors must be considered, especially those of England and France, in contemplating any change in American relations with Madrid. Humphrey referred to the loan as an action that had apparently been taken on the advice of the military, instead of the advice of those concerned with formulating policies for political organization. He also referred to the reaction of France to such developments when he noted that this was an action "which runs counter to the definite purposes and proposals of the French Government." Senator Lehman then raised an important point closely related to the moral dilemma which closer relations with the Franco regime would pose for the United States. He asked: "Is it not a fact that this gives the Soviet government a propaganda weapon which it will use to the fullest extent in advancing the thesis that we are not sincerely democratic, but that we are ready to support a Fascist government." [50]

Despite these strong protests, the motion to set aside the Spanish loan of $62,500,000 was beaten decisively by the same vote by which it was supported initially, 65 to 15. It was a significant defeat for the administration's Spanish policy. Only a few hours before the final vote, President Truman had denounced the Spanish loan. [51] However, when Truman signed the General Appropriations Bill (H.R. 7786) on September 5, 1950, of which the Spanish loan was a part, he let it be known that he did not consider the Spanish loan mandatory and that funds would continue to be withheld from Spain until certain pre-conditions were met. These included mutually advantageous arrangements regarding both the purposes for which the money would eventually be spent and the terms of repayment. Money would be loaned to Spain, Truman concluded, when it was in the best interests of American foreign policy to do so.[52]

The following month, on October 31, 1950, a Special Political Committee of the General Assembly of the United Nations passed a resolution repealing that portion of the 1946 U.N. resolution pertaining to the exchange of ambassadors with Spain. The committee suggested that nations wishing to resume full diplomatic relations with Spain could now do so with U.N. sanction. The General Assembly approved the committee's resolution the following month. In both instances, the United States delegation voted with the majority. Despite the fact that President Truman stated there was "no hurry"[53] to appoint an ambassador to Madrid, he nominated Stanton Griffis as American Ambassador to Spain in December, 1950, less than two months later.

During the spring of 1951, congressional pressure to include Spain in Western military preparations continued. In a joint Foreign Relations and Armed Services Committee Report issued in March on the assignment of ground forces to Europe, it was recommended that "all available assistance to the North Atlantic Treaty Organization should be sought. To this end Spain, Yugoslavia, Greece, and Turkey are important."[54] The following month, an amendment suggested by Senator Joseph McCarthy and modified by Senator Brewster, expressing the sense of the Senate as favoring revision of European defense plans to include "the utilization on a voluntary basis of the military and other resources of Western Germany and Spain" was successfully tacked onto Senate Resolution 99 authorizing the dispatch of ground forces to duty in Europe.[55] In June, Senator McCarran announced that he intended to ask Congress for a new loan of $100,000.000 to Spain. He said he would propose the new loan in the form of an amendment to an appropriations bill.[56]

The activities of the Spanish Lobby were becoming increasingly newsworthy however, and the following June an incident attested to the fact that those in the

Lobby did not like their activities publicized. Shortly after Senator Brewster was defeated in the Maine Republican primary, the columnist Drew Pearson was punched in the jaw by Patrick Clark who remarked, according to Pearson: "Take this for what you did to Brewster." Clark later stated that he was sick and tired of Pearson's calling him a lobbyist. Pearson, in a column prior to this, had referred to Clark as a lobbyist for Generalissimmo Francisco Franco of Spain and had also discussed Brewster's alleged part in obtaining American aid for Spain.[57]

The State Department proceeded to reconsider its Spanish policy throughout 1950. George Kennan was Director of the Department's Policy Planning Staff and Counselor to the Secretary of State. Yet, his influence within the Department was waning and by mid-September, 1949, he was informed that Policy Planning memos would no longer go directly to Acheson "who preferred to be advised by people, not institutions."[58] Nevertheless, during January, 1950, Kennan developed a wide-ranging memorandum analyzing the current status of U.S. foreign policy. His cautionary advice to Acheson read as follows:

> As for Spain-importance of problem is exaggerated. It has been discussed far more in press than in Government. It is true: U.N. resolution has not proved useful in weakening Franco and establishing more democratic regime. We would be glad to see it removed from books, and diplomatic relations normalized. Perhaps this will soon be possible. This will depend largely on our European allies, whose hand we don't wish to force. But this does not mean we would then rush to other extreme and shower Franco with loans or welcome him as ally. We must insist on retaining dignity and reserve of our position toward those who repudiate ideals of government we happen to believe in.[59]

By early 1951 Acheson had finally removed himself from the ranks of the opposition and Admiral Forrest P. Sherman, Chief of Naval Operations, began to forcefully argue for closer relations with Spain in National Security Council meetings during the spring of 1951. Sherman had grained an excellent reputation as healer of the fierce inter-service rivalries that had characterized the recent battle to unify the armed forces. It was also known that he was the officer who would probably soon replace General Omar Bradley as Chairman of the Joint Chiefs of Staff. On July 16, 1951, Sherman left for Europe with the President's authorization to talk to the Spanish Government.[60] Sherman's approach to Spanish policy had evidently influenced Truman.

On July 18, just two days after Sherman's departure for Spain, Acheson announced that the United States was in fact seeking to negotiate an agreement that would bring Spain into Western defense arrangements, presumably to strengthen NATO against the possibility of a Soviet attack. At the same time, he sought to placate the concerns and fears of Paris and London by noting that they would continue to receive "clear priority" for American aid, and Western Europe would not be abandoned for a defensive position behind the Pyrenees.[61] Importantly, President Truman commented the following day that American policy toward Spain had been shifted "on the advice of the Department of Defense."[62]

Negotiations and Agreement

It was to be two long years after the Sherman visit before a final agreement was signed with the Franco regime. After the United States changed its official position toward Spain in July, 1951, Franco lost some of his eagerness and took on a more reserved posture toward the ensuing negotiations.

To some extent, Franco's slight reticence was based upon domestic opposition he received from extreme traditionalists, nationalists and Catholics. The traditionalists felt the proposed treaty would destroy Spain's long tradition of isolation and neutrality. The nationalists were most annoyed with the establishment of foreign bases on Spanish soil, and the conservative Catholic group did not like the idea of forming a relationship with Protestant America. The strongest dissenting group was the conservative Catholics led by Cardinal Segura of Seville. In response to this pressure, Franco first concluded a concordat with the Vatican in August, 1953, giving his regime the official sanction of the Church before the agreements with the United States were concluded the following month.[63]

The Truman Administration did not pursue the negotiations avidly because the President continued to show little enthusiasm for the proposed alliance. Truman noted during a press conference on February 7, 1952, just two months before formal negotiations started, that "he was not very fond" of Franco Spain.[64]

The Spanish Lobby remained active during these long deliberations. Their sympathizers now had little difficulty in marshalling enough support in the Senate and with some effort, in the House as well, to include a $100,000,000 item for Spain in a foreign aid bill passed in October, 1951.[65] Senator McCarran had announced his quest for this additional Spanish appropriation to the press the previous June; he had now achieved this objective. In the meantime, Dr. Sidney Sufrin of Syracuse University had been heading up an economic survey mission to Spain for the administration. He returned with a report suggesting that Spain would need economic aid totaling about $150,000,000 per year for raw materials and the improvement of power production and transport facilities. The amount of aid finally appropriated, Sufrin concluded, would have to depend ultimately "on how badly the armed services wanted military bases on the Iberian peninsula."[66]

Negotiations continued to drag along both before and after the November, 1952 presidential election. Informed Spanish sources claimed the main reason the agreements had not been signed was the desire of President Truman to wait and let President-elect Eisenhower take the final responsibility for consummation of the agreements upon his inauguration in January.[67] Eisenhower and his Secretary of State, John Foster Dulles, did not share Truman's reticence about a pact with Madrid, and a good deal of animation was quickly infused into the negotiations under the new administration in Washington.

On September 26, 1953, three bilateral agreements were signed between the two countries: a Defense Agreement, an Economic Aid Agreement, and a Mutual Defense Assistance Agreement.[68] Upon signature, they took effect immediately and were known collectively as the

Pact of Madrid. Because they were executive agreements, they did not require approval by the Senate. Although mutual obligations in case of war had not been included in the agreements, a quasi-alliance had in fact been established between the United States and Spain.

Conclusions

Congressional initiative, aided in some cases by what were probably paid Spanish Lobby supporters, played an important role in bringing about a change in the Truman-Acheson position toward Spain. Spanish Lobby supporters in Congress also skillfully coalesced with supporters within the military establishment. This alliance of congressional and military supporters of a more sympathetic policy toward Franco Spain was able to mount a formidable challenge to the administration's policy. Thus, while it is clear that President Truman was able to delay the final consummation of the Pact of Madrid while he was in office, he had become increasingly isolated in his opposition to the Franco regime and had in fact relented to the establishment of formal negotiations with Madrid.

The bipartisan foreign policy had collapsed under the blows of bitter partisan attacks during the Truman Administration, probably beginning with the President's own slashing attack on the Republican controlled 80th Congress in 1948. This was followed by partisan attacks upon his own administration over the so-called loss of China, the McCarthy accusations about Communists in the administration, and the Korean War. Nevertheless, support for Spain in Congress retained a bipartisan image. This was so because only a small minority of Senate liberals such as Morse, Humphrey and Lehman remained opposed to closer relations with Franco Spain. Many conservatives, Catholics, and the growing number of anti-Trumanites in both political parties were successfully integrated, with the help of the Spanish Lobby, into pro-Spanish forces.

The kinds of pressures used by these pro-Spanish forces in Congress to gain executive support for their policy were varied. In general, their campaign was characterized by a lack of subtlety, especially when led by the major pro-Spanish exponent in Congress, Senator McCarran. Appropriations bills were authorized for Spain without being requested by the administration, and State Department witnesses were badgered at committee hearings. Yet, while this kind of confrontation undoubtedly influenced the administration's change of policy, it was the military's opinion during a time of crisis (the Korean War) that the administration found most irresistible. However, here again certain senators played a key role in leading the views of the military to the press and the public. In this way, additional pressure was undoubtedly mounted upon the administration to change its policy toward Spain.

To the pro-Spanish groups in Congress, the ideological problem of more closely relating to a nation ruled by a Fascist dictatorship was overshadowed by the threat of possible Soviet expansionism in Western Europe. Ideological concerns had little bearing on the military's desire to incorporate Spain into Western defense plans. Their primary concern was simply to strengthen NATO. Importantly, President Truman was to credit these Department of Defense concerns with the change in U.S. foreign policy toward Spain.

The Spanish Lobby was clearly an effective force in its attempts to change U.S.-Spanish relations. It was probably one of the most effective foreign lobbies ever to operate on American soil. Although support for the Spanish cause existed in Congress and the military establishment before the Spanish Lobby really came into existence, its role in influencing Congress to seek a change in the administration's policy, and in that sense manipulate the executive-congressional relationship was very significant.

For Franco, the Pact of Madrid meant huge sums of money to help keep his regime afloat. Also, the existence of a quasi-alliance between Madrid and Washington symbolized at least tacit approval of the Spanish Government by the United States. At the same time the military establishment finally gained access to the bases it needed at a critical point in the Cold War.

Epilogue

Following the death of Franco in 1975, the monarchy was restored under Juan Carlos and Spain became a parliamentary democracy. In 1976 the United States and Spain concluded a Treaty of Friendship and Cooperation giving the United States continued access to military bases in Spain. The estimated annual cost incurred by the United States for the use of these bases between 1953 and 1974 was $90 million.[69]

Notes

[1]Arthur P. Whitaker, Spain and Defense of the West: Ally and Liability (New York: Harper & Brothers, 1961), 9.

[2]A Decade of American Foreign Policy: Basic Documents, 1941-1949, Revised Edition (Washington, D.C.: Department of State, 1985), 604.

[3]Robert J. Donovan, Conflict And Crisis: The Presidency of Harry S. Truman, 1945-1948 (New York: W. W. Norton & Company, 1977), 74.

[4]Whitaker, Spain and Defense of the West, 22.

[5]Yearbook of the United Nations, 1946-47 (Lake Success, New York: 1947), 345.

[6]A Decade of American Foreign Policy: Basic Documents, 1941-1949, Revised Edition, 606.

[7]Ibid.

[8]Ibid., 607.

[9]D.K.M.K., "Franco's Foreign Policy: From U.N. Outcast to U.S. Partner," The World Today 9 (December 1953): 513.

[10]Salvador de Madariaga, Spain: A Modern History (New York: Frederick A. Praeger, 1958), 603.

[11]Winston Churchill, "Alliance of English-Speaking People," Vital Speeches Of The Day 12 (15 March 1946): 331.

[12]Walter Millis, ed., The Forrestal Diaries (New York: The Viking Press, 1951), 171.

[13]Walter Lafeber, America, Russia, and the Cold War, 1945-1984 (New York: Alfred A. Knopf, 1985), 127.

[14]Whitaker, Spain and Defense of the West, 30-31.

[15]Millis, Forrestal Diaries, 328.

[16]Theodore J. Lowi, Bases in Spain (Indianapolis and New York: The Bobbs-Merrill Company, Inc., 1963), 7.

[17]Paul Johnson, Modern Times: The World from the Twenties to the Eighties (New York: Harper & Row, Publishers, Inc., 1983), 608.

[18]Dean Acheson, Present At The Creation: My Years in the State Department (New York: W.W. Norton & Company, 1969), 169.

[19]Lowi, Bases In Spain, 7.

[20]Samuel Flagg Bemis, A Diplomatic History Of The United States (New York: Henry Holt & Company, 1951), 98.

[21]William Ebenstein, C. Herman Pritchett, Henry A. Turner and Dean Mann, eds., American Democracy In World Perspective (New York: Harper & Row, 1973), 289.

[22]Lowi, Bases in Spain, 7-8.

[23]As quoted in Lowi, Bases, 29.

[24]Arthur H. Vandenberg, Jr., ed., The Private Papers Of Senator Vandenberg (Boston: Houghton Mifflin Company, 1952), 526.

[25]Norman A. Graebner, "Dean G. Acheson," in Norman A. Graebner, ed., An Uncertain Tradition: American Secretaries of State in the Twentieth Century (New York: McGraw-Hill Book Company, Inc., 1961), 282.

[26]Ibid., 284.

[27]Congressional Record, 80th Cong., 2nd sess., 1948, 94, pt 3: 3656.

[28]Graebner, "Acheson," An Uncertain Tradition, 269-70.

[29]Letter to the author from Dean Acheson, 4 December 1967.

[30]Hearings, State, Commerce, Justice, Judiciary Appropriations, 1950 Senate, Subcommittee on Appropriations, 81st Congress, 1st Session, 5 May 1949, 92-4.

[31]Ibid.

[32]Communication dated 3 October 1949, from the Chargé in Spain, Paul T. Culbertson, to the Secretary of State, Foreign Relations of the United States 1949, vol. 4 (Washington, D.C.: United States Government Printing Office, 1975), 761.

[33]Ibid.

[34]Lowi, Bases In Spain, 9-10.

[35]New York Times, 1 October 1949, 16 and 27 October 1949, 15.

[36]Ibid., 2 November 1949, 9; New York Herald Tribune, 28 November 1949, as cited in Lowi, Bases In Spain, 11-12.

[37]Dean Acheson, "Return to Normal Exchange of Diplomatic Representation With Spain Urged," Department of State Bulletin 22 (January, 1950), 156.

[38]Ibid., 157.

[39]Ibid., 158.

[40]Stanton Griffis, Lying in State (Garden City: Doubleday & Company, Inc., 1952), 269.

[41]Cong. Rec., 96, pt 3: 3178.

[42]Ibid., 8559-62.

[43]Spanish Lobby monetary figures in, Drew Pearson and Jack Anderson, The Case Against Congress: A Compelling Indictment of Corruption on Capitol Hill (New York: Simon and Schuster, 1968), 355-56.

[44]Anthony Cave Brown, The Last Hero: Wild Bill Donovan (New York: Vintage Books, 1984), 224-26.

[45]Memorandum of Conversation dated 27 July 1949, Foreign Relations of the United States 1949, vol. 4, 755.

[46]Cong. Rec., 96, pt 7: 9531.

[47]Pearson & Anderson, The Case Against Congress, 356.

[48]Pat McCarran, "Why Shouldn't the Spanish Fight for Us?," The Saturday Evening Post 223 (April, 1951), 25.

[49]Cong. Rec., 96 pt 9: 11464-65.

[50]Ibid., 11685.

[51]New York Herald Tribune, 4 August 1950, 1.

[52]New York Times, 7 September 1950, 1.

[53]Ibid., 8 February 1952, 1.

[54]U.S., Congress, Senate, Committees on Foreign Relations and Armed Services, Assignment Of Ground Forces Of The United States To Duty In The European Area, S. Rept. 175, 82nd Cong., 1st sess., 1951, 19.

[55]Cong. Rec., 97 pt 3: 3269.

[56]New York Times, 3 June 1951, 34.

[57]Ibid., 9 June 1952, 13.

[58]Walter Isaacson and Evan Thomas, The Wise Men: Six Friends And The World They Made, Acheson, Bohlen, Harriman, Kennan, Lovett, McCloy (New York: Simon & Schuster, Inc., 1986), 474.

[59]Memorandum by the Counselor (Kennan) to the Secretary of State, 6 January 1950, Foreign Relations of the United States 1950, vol. 1 (Washington, D.C.: U.S. Government Printing Office, 1977), 135-36.

[60]Lowi, Bases In Spain, 22-24.

[61]New York Times, 19 July 1951, 1, 6.

[62]Ibid., 20 July 1951, 4.

[63]Whitaker, Spain, 41.

[64]New York Times, 8 February 1952, 1.

[65]Ibid., 21 October 1951, 1.

[66]Ibid., 4 January 1952, 1.

[67]Ibid., 31 December 1952, 4.

[68]See full text of Defense Agreement in Appendix C. Text quoted from, The Department of State Bulletin 29 (October, 1953), 436.

[69]Charles W. Kegley, Jr. and Eugene R. Wittkopf, American Foreign Policy: Pattern And Process (New York: St. Martin's Press, 1982), 122.

V

CONGRESS AND THE COLD WAR: U.S.-CHINA POLICY, 1966*

Perhaps no other foreign policy area brought forth the emotional anti-Communism characteristic of the 1950's as did American relations with the Peoples Republic of China. The so-called loss of China issue beginning in 1949, severely strained the bipartisan approach to foreign policy formulation. In addition, Senator Joseph McCarthy's Communists in government charges during the Korean War, while American forces were engaged in combat with the Peoples Liberation Army, further exacerbated relations between the two parties and the legislative and executive branches. Ominously, the possibility of a preventive strike on the Peoples Republic also became the focus of serious consideration and possible implementation during the Formosa Strait confrontation of 1954-55.

Bipartisan foreign policy formulation was already a ten year old political process when the administration of Dwight D. Eisenhower took office in 1953. The new Republican Chief Executive's reliance upon bipartisanship increased after 1954 when the Congress once again returned to Democratic control. Liberal critics of the bipartisan coalition were to clearly emerge during the 1950's, in effect replacing the isolationist challengers of the 1940's.[1]

Eisenhower's relations with the Congress and his policy making role in general, are the subject of consid-

---

*Author's article originally published in <u>The China Quarterly</u> 85 (March 1981): 80-95. Reprinted with permission of the publisher.

erable revisionism at the present time. In general, these studies have upgraded the assessment of his leadership from the more passive image he acquired during his administration and immediately afterwards. However, before such reassessments can approach a definitive level, new studies of his administration's role in the formulation of key foreign policies must be completed as new documentation becomes available.[2]

The middle 1950's is a particularly germane period for an examination of Cold War Sino-American relations because it was during the first Formosa Strait confrontation that the United States formally allied itself with the defeated regime of Generalissimo Chiang Kai-shek on Taiwan. The instruments chosen by the administration for formal involvement-the Formosa Resolution and the Mutual Security Pact with Taipei-deeply involved the Congress. Illumination of the Cold War congressional role in this development must begin earlier, however, with the final route of the Nationalist forces from the mainland during 1949.

Truman and Chiang

By 1949 the United States had largely cast its lot with the defeated forces of Chiang Kai-shek on Taiwan. It refused even de facto recognition of the new mainland government and successfully rallied enough votes to exclude the Peoples Republic from the United Nations.

However, the Truman Administration did not totally embrace the Nationalist Government. Military aid was not immediately forthcoming despite strong congressional criticism. In addition, two days after the North Koreans attacked South Korea, Truman attempted to neutralize Taiwan by assigning the Seventh Fleet to the Formosa Straits and calling upon Chiang to cease all war operations against the mainland. He also refused to accept a Nationalist offer to send troops for use in Korea, largely because of his highly negative view of those forces and their leadership.[3]

Even after the Peoples Liberation Army crossed the Yalu in great force during October and November of 1950, bringing Chinese and American forces into direct combat, Truman stated that the final status of Taiwan, "must await the restoration of security in the Pacific, a peace settlement with Japan or consideration by the United

Nations."[4]

Dulles and Eisenhower

The son of a northern New York Presbyterian Minister, John Foster Dulles was a fervent anti-Communist who saw international politics as a universalist confrontation between christianity and communism. His uncompromising moralism was coupled with a determination to implement his *idee fixe* through tactical maneuvers rather than long range planning.[5]

As President Eisenhower's Secretary of State in the first Republican administration since 1932, Dulles quickly assumed command over who should be involved in foreign policy formulation. He was domineering, impulsive and sometimes arrogant according to Sherman Adams, but also intelligent and knowledgeable. His powers of persuasion were considerable and when he decided upon a course of action he argued his point strongly and Eisenhower usually concurred.[6]

According to Adams, the President could also be forceful and was not "pushed around by anybody," including the vocal criticisms of Senate Republican Majority Leader William F. Knowland of California, a spokesman for China Lobby (Republic of China), positions. His decision-making process, influenced by a long military career, was more methodical than his predecessor. The Eisenhower approach was to bring up policy questions for discussion with members of the National Security Council. In the final analysis, however, it was usually Dulles' advice that guided the President. This was particularly true during periods of foreign policy crisis when, according to Adams, the specific policy innovations chosen were "due to Dulles and not to Eisenhower."[7]

Of additional importance were the political beliefs shared by the President and his Secretary of State. Eisenhower possessed an internationalist outlook and was identified with the progressive wing of his party. At the same time Dulles' own Republicanism was "more in the mold of Dwight Eisenhower."[8] Both men also wished to maintain strong bipartisan support in Congress and actively sought Democratic support. Eisenhower, aided by his wide popularity, had "friends on both sides of the aisle," and his administration possessed greater underlying congressional support then appeared to be the case.[9]

Of special significance was the area of shared beliefs both men held with respect to foreign policy formulation. Two basic rules guided Eisenhower's decision-making according to Adams: "Don't make mistakes in a hurry and secondly, if you do, share them."[10] The President's second rule dovetailed well with Dulles' penchant for tactical approaches to problems. Most notably, the Dulles formulated Formosa Resolution was tactical in its conception and had the result of sharing responsibility between President and Congress for subsequent presidential action in the Formosa Strait.

The New Look

During the presidential campaign of 1952, the Republican Party attempted to carve out a radically different foreign policy from that of the Truman Administration, whose Far Eastern policies were under heavy partisan attack. The architect of this policy and leading Republican foreign policy spokesman was Dulles. Labeling the Truman Administration's policy of containment "negative, futile and immoral" in the party platform, he proposed instead a new policy of "liberation."

Reflecting his Secretary of State's new policy, Eisenhower declared during his first State of the Union message that the Seventh Fleet would "no longer be employed to shield Communist China."[11] The administration's decision to end Taiwan's neutralization had the fateful additional effect, as noted by former China Hand O. Edmund Clubb, of the U.S. becoming "automatically involved in the civil war of its protege, Generalissimo Chiang Kai-shek."[12]

Eisenhower then requested his new Joint Chiefs of Staff, chaired by Admiral Arthur W. Radford, to develop a forward projection of military needs based on the assumption that defense expenditures had to continue for an indefinite period in the future. The resulting J.C.S. paper emphasized the military concept of deterrence. However, as Radford later noted: "The power to retaliate --our atomic offensive--was the basis of our deterrent . . . ."[13] This "New Look" was subsequently adopted by the National Security Council and afterwards referred to as Massive Retaliation by Dulles.

Legislative-Executive Relations

The spell of the whole McCarthy witch hunting episode hung fresh over the 84th Congress. It was not until December 2, 1954, that the extremist Republican Senator from Wisconsin had finally been censured by his colleagues. While Eisenhower was critical of McCarthy type actions, he never publicly repudiated the Senator's activities.[14] Dulles was equally determined not to fall prey to the same soft on communism charges that bedeviled his predecessor Dean Acheson. He placated any possible right wing criticism toward the administration's China policy during 1954 by, for instance, dismissing one of the last Department of State China Hands and ostentatiously refusing to shake hands with Premier Cho En-lai at a conference in neutral territory.[15]

Dulles had also criticized the way in which bipartisanship occurred between the parties in the recent past, claiming that the Democratic Platforms of 1948 and 1952 had taken "100% credit for all good results, giving no recognition whatever to Republican cooperation." Yet, he continued to call for a sharing of responsibility between the parties, based upon a new code of ethics in which credits and debits should also be shared.[16] Significantly, as Secretary of State he worked diligently and successfully to cultivate cooperative congressional relations, especially with leading southern Democrats like Senators Walter George of Georgia, Lyndon Johnson of Texas and John Sparkman of Alabama.[17]

The congressional elections of 1954 saw the Republicans revert to their former minority party status in the 84th Congress. There were now forty-eight Democrats, forty-seven Republicans, and one Independent (Wayne Morse), who was committed to vote with the Democratic reorganization of the Senate. To meet this potential challenge to administration policy-making, a promise was made to senior Democratic and Republican members of foreign affairs committees (Foreign Relations and Armed Forces), to "participate in evolving national policy." The administration's use of bipartisanship was also an important method of isolating right wing Republicans and received important southern Democratic support.[18]

Of particular concern to Dulles was continued support from the Senate Foreign Relations Committee. Undoubtedly because of Senator Walter George's cooperative attitude toward the administration, Dulles preferred that he become chairman of the Foreign Relations Committee over Theodore Francis Green of Rhode Island. Thus, because Dulles "chose him," Eisenhower prevailed upon George to accept the Chairmanship at a White House meeting in January.[19]

A small group of thirteen bipartisan liberals (mostly Democrats), occasionally formed a counter bloc against the bipartisan coalition of Republicans and Southern Democrats in the Senate. Members included Hubert Humphrey and Wayne Morse, however, the driving force behind this group was Herbert H. Lehman of New York. As a former Governor of his state and Director General of the United Nations Relief and Rehabilitation Administration, Lehman was a well established political figure before election to the Senate. In addition, he was looked upon by younger liberals like Humphrey as a "real stalwart," for the liberal cause.[20]

Lehman and Dulles had already clashed in a bitter, 1949, New York State campaign for senator in which Lehman defeated the future Secretary of State. They were to clash again over the administration's China Policy with the Democratic Senator playing a lead role in opposition.

Into the Abyss

Two months after the United States signed a collective security agreement with South Korea, Chiang proposed a security treaty with the United States. Although Dulles did not immediately respond to this proposal, Senator Alexander Wiley, Republican Chairman of the Senate Foreign Relations Committee was enthusiastic.

Following Dulles' Massive Retaliation speech on January 12, 1954, and a false report from Taipei that agreement was near on a bilateral defense pact with the United States, Peking began a campaign to bloc any American treaty with the Nationalists.[21]

During August Prime Minister Cho En-lai claimed the Peoples Republic would "liberate" Taiwan from the Nationalists. Eisenhower responded on August 17th by stating that any such invasion "would have to run over the Seventh Fleet."[22] On September 8th, Peoples Liberation Army forces (P.L.A.) commenced a heavy shelling of the Nationalist's held Quemoy Islands from nearby Amoy harbor.

Although held by the Nationalists, the offshore islands (Quemoys, Matsu, Tachens), had always been considered part of China and were, as British Foreign Secretary Anthony Eden noted, "in a different category from Taiwan."[23] Taiwan and the Pescadores had been a colony of China until 1895 when they were ceded to Japan by the Treaty of Shimonoseki. At the Cairo Conference of 1943, the allies stated in the Cairo Declaration their intention to return Taiwan, the Pescadores and Manchuria to the Republic of China and following the Japanese defeat the Nationalists brought Taiwan under de facto control.

As the P.L.A. continued to bombard Quemoy, Eisenhower met with his Security Council on September 12th. Admiral Arthur Radford, Chairman of the Joint Chiefs of Staff, proposed that the Nationalists bomb the mainland, with American aid if needed, to prevent the fall of Quemoy. Eisenhower rejected Radford's preventive strike proposal, siding with the minority dissenting views of General Matthew B. Ridgway, former Under Secretary of State, W. Bedell Smith and Vice President Richard M. Nixon.[24]

The level of rhetoric, however, continued to heighten with Chiang stating on October 10th that preparations for liberation of the mainland were nearly complete,[25] and Senator Knowland declaring that he wished to go beyond Dulles' Massive Retaliation Doctrine by justifying its use against Communist gains via subversion as well as overt action.[26]

Negotiations already in progress between Washington and Taipei were speeded up and a Mutual Defense treaty was signed in Washington on December 2, 1954. Eisenhower submitted the treaty for Senate approval on January 6, 1955, declaring its purpose to be "defensive and mutual in character, designed to deter any attempt by the Chinese Communist regime to bring its aggressive military ambitions to bear against the treaty area."[27] The treaty area included Taiwan, the Pescadores and the island territories in the west Pacific under American jurisdiction, including the Ryukyus, former Japanese mandated islands and Guam. However, Article VI referred only obliquely to the offshore islands by making the provisions of mutual defense applicable to "such other territories as may be determined by mutual agreement."[28]

Immediate congressional criticism followed as concern rose over Chiang's intentions and ability to involve the nation in war. In an effort to mute these concerns, Dulles negotiated but did not divulge publicly, an exchange of supplementary treaty notes with Taipei on December 10th, agreeing that the use of force would be a matter decided upon jointly. Chiang was thus once again restrained by obtaining his promise not to attack the mainland without first receiving approval from Washington.

Military action continued unabated against the offshore islands. Chinese air units launched strikes against the Tachens and the island of Ichiang to their north. On January 18th the P.L.A. invaded and captured Ichiang. Dulles immediately proclaimed that the loss of Ichiang was of "no particular importance." He added that the Tachens, now also under bombardment, were not "in any sense essential to the defense of Formosa and the Pescadores."[29] However, the New York Times reported that because the pending Mutual Defense Treaty did not mention the Quemoys, Tachens or Matsu it was being "interpreted rather widely," that the Seventh Fleet would not defend them.[30]

Dulles quickly suggested a new course of action to Eisenhower improbably linking the defense of Taiwan, across the wide (120 miles) Formosa Strait with that of certain offshore islands. The plan included American assistance in evacuating the Tachens while at the same time declaring that the United States would assist in holding the Quemoys and Matsu. Agreeing with Dulles' logic, Eisenhower noted the "serious psychological consequences" to the Nationalists which would result from any evacuation of the Quemoys and Matsu.[31]

Hitting First

Dulles also suggested a warning be issued to the Peoples Republic in the form of a joint congressional resolution. The Dulles composed message asked for approval to protect Formosa, the Pescadores and the so-called related positions if it became necessary to defend the principal islands. Thus, the resolution did not specifically guarantee a defense of Matsu and the Quemoys. Instead it was left up to the President to determine if and when American forces need be committed for their defense.

Confusion and acrimonious controversy resulted from the resolution's wording because the degree of congressional authorization requested for the use of force was unclear. Yet, Eisenhower claimed in his accompanying message to Congress that he already possessed constitutional authority to act, but that passage of the resolution would "make clear the unified and serious intentions of our government, our Congress and our people."[32]

According to Dulles, Eisenhower did not wish to give the impression that the resolution was a war message "or anything which is going to lead to war," so he chose not to personally deliver it before a Joint Session of the Congress.[33] Nevertheless, Prime Minister Chou En-lai of the Peoples Republic did equate the resolution with a war message and he restated his government's intentions regarding Taiwan.[34]

Executive Hearings on the Formosa Resolution began on January 24, 1955, before the combined Senate Foreign Relations and Armed Forces Committees with Senator George presiding. The combined committees possessed a "profound distrust of Chiang and his intentions," coupled with the mistaken belief that vis-a-vis the Soviet Union, the deterrent value of American nuclear forces had "evaporated."[35] Dulles attempted to quell Senate fears regarding Chiang by divulging to the committee the contents of the supplementary treaty notes of December 10th with Taipei.

Dulles also stated that the basic administration rationale for the resolution as being "not just a problem of geography but a problem very largely of psychology." More ominously, he noted the resolution would allow the President to feel authorized, if need be, to "hit first." He also called for a willingness to act "boldly and alone," if necessary, because "if everybody waits and says 'after you, Gaston,' I know what is going to happen. We will be fighting here in the streets of Washington."[36]

Ridgway Not Consulted

The divergence of testimony between Admiral Radford, who supported the resolution and also believed that Chiang, with full American support could return to the mainland,[37] and General Ridgway's dissenting view provided a dramatic highlight. Wayne Morse requested and Senator George reluctantly agreed, that Ridgway be allowed to testify as an unscheduled witness.

In answering a question submitted by Morse, Ridgway stated that his "opinion was not asked," thus indicating that the resolution lacked the unanimous endorsement of the Joint Chiefs of Staff.[38] Ridgway also revealed he did not believe sufficient American ground forces were available to successfully intervene on the Chinese mainland as envisioned by Radford. The President had not, as noted later by Morse, consulted with the general who headed the American Army.[39]

Critical reaction to the resolution was strong, including Morse's comment that the authority sought by the President "could very well mean war." Yet, the House quickly and overwhelmingly approved on January 25th the President's request with Democratic Speaker Sam Rayburn of Texas stating: "If the President wants it done this way, it will be done this way-and promptly."[40]

Two efforts were made in the Joint Senate Committee to either amend or substitute for the administration's resolution. Democratic Senator Estes Kefauver wanted to limit the area of American responsibility to Taiwan and Hubert Humphrey offered a substitute resolution requesting the President to call upon the "United Nations to take prompt action to bring about a cease-fire. . . ."[41] Both of these efforts were defeated and the joint committee recommended passage of the Formosa Resolution by a 26 to 2 vote with one absent. Morse and isolationist Republican Senator William Langer of North Dakota dissented. However, from four to six senators reserved the right to change their vote on the Senate floor.[42]

Lehman, Langer and Morse

Although Dulles had already "canvassed the Congress and knew the resolution could be gotten,"[43] a bitter debate broke out on the Senate floor the same day the joint committee recommended the resolution. It took place within the highly charged atmosphere of the recently completed McCarthy censure action. Morse, commenting later, referred to that atmosphere as follows:

> In fact, as Lehman and I spoke against the Eisenhower Formosa Resolution, we

> didn't know about it at the time, but one of our colleagues pointed out that there were those in the Senate sitting by, listening to every word we said, for the purpose of seeing if we didn't say something that would permit the filing of a resolution of censure against each one of us, on the ground that we were violating some secrecy of committee confidence.[44]

Referring to his opposition role at that time Morse also recalled that he and Lehman "knew it was a preventive war resolution and we knew the Eisenhower Administration wasn't being honest with the American people."[45] Morse delivered a two hour speech attacking the resolution with a concluding statement that its passage "would legalize the position of the proponents of a preventive war."[46]

He was immediately denounced by Knowland as having endangered the security of the United States by allowing the Communists to understand or pretend that the nation was ready to provoke a war in Asia. Morse answered in a shaking voice that he was "aware what a man lets himself in for" if he argued that even the Communist dictatorship of China had the right of sovereignty.[47]

The following day, January 27th, the administration attempted to dispel fears of a preventive war via a statement from the White House. Eisenhower declared that any decision to use American forces except for self-defense or in defense of Formosa and the Pescadores "would be a decision which he would take and the responsibility for which he has not delegated."[48] Senators seeking to restrict the resolution to a defense of Formosa and the Pescadores interpreted the President's message as assurance that neither Chiang nor Radford would be delegated authority to make war or peace decisions in the Formosa Strait.[49]

Following the President's announcement, Senator George spoke on behalf of the resolution. He claimed that if a line were drawn in the Formosa Strait beyond which the United States was not obligated to defend, the result would be an enemy "sanctuary."[50] Although any such sanctuary would of course be the territory of China, George's remarks, in tandem with the President's message, all but eliminated Hubert Humphrey's opposition to the resolution.

On the third and final day of debate several substitute amendments were offered. Senator Langer's substitute forbade American armed forces from entering upon the Chinese mainland or closer than twelve miles from the coast; only Lehman and Morse joined Langer in supporting this amendment. An amendment produced by Kefauver excluding any American obligation to defend the Quemoy and Matsu Islands was defeated 75 to 11. In addition, Republican Senator George Malone's effort to put the Senate on record against continued diplomatic relations with the Soviet Union was shouted down. An amendment offered by Joseph McCarthy directing that aid be cut off to any nation trading with the Peoples Republic of China was withdrawn to speed action on the Formosa Resolution.[51]

Democratic-Liberal Senator Lehman offered the key amendment. It would have deleted from the resolution any authorization to protect "related positions . . . now in friendly hands" and the taking of "other measures" to secure Formosa.[52] His speech questioned the hast to pass the resolution and its lack of any reference to the United Nations. Most of all he questioned the Formosa Resolution's grant of authority: "Why should we write and sign this blank check?" Lehman simply did not see the necessity, nor would he vote for, a non-specific congressional resolution of support for the offshore islands. He would gladly support a "congressional sanction for the defense of Formosa and the Pescadores."[53]

The Lehman sponsored amendment was defeated 74 to 13. Of the 13 supporting votes almost all were cast by liberal Democrats. Senator John F. Kennedy, who was hospitalized at the same time as fellow future President Lyndon Johnson, paired his vote with the Senate Majority Leader. Johnson sided with the administration's resolution, Kennedy with the Lehman sponsored amendment.[54]

The final vote passing the Formosa Resolution was 85 to 3. Only Lehman, Langer and Morse dissented. Within hours Eisenhower gave his final instructions regarding the conduct of American assistance in helping to evacuate the Tachens. His orders to Admiral Radford indicated that he interpreted the resolution as affording him, for all practical purposes, the same power as a congressional declaration of war. He ordered Radford "to attack Red Chinese airfields, if self-defense so required."[55]

U.N. Agenda Items

On the same day the Formosa Resolution received Senate approval, a cease-fire resolution was proposed in the United Nations Security Council by New Zealand's Representative, Sir Leslie K. Munro. Referring simply to the "occurrence of armed hostilities between the Peoples Republic of China and the Republic of China in the area of certain islands off the coast of the mainland of China,"[56] the resolution sought to sidestep the sovereignty issue.

Two days later, however, Representative A. Sobolev countered with a draft resolution which condemned "acts of aggression by the United States of America against the Peoples Republic of China," and recommended the immediate withdrawal of all U.S. forces "from the island of Taiwan and other territories belonging to China."[57] Sobolev then followed with another draft resolution inviting a representative of the Peoples Republic to participate in Security Council deliberations concerning the Soviet resolution.[58]

A brief struggle ensued over the adoption of the Security Council agenda, or more specifically, which item should be considered first-New Zealand's or the Soviet Union's. Representative Munro, probably responding to the Soviet's proposed invitation to the Peoples Republic, added that he would also request an invitation to their representative once the agenda had been adopted.

The Soviet Union and the Republic of China opposed the inclusion of the New Zealand item. The Soviet Union called it an intervention in the domestic affairs of China and the Republic of China termed it superficial because it did not consider the problem of Communist aggression. The United States supported the New Zealand item, but not the Soviet item. The United Kingdom supported the inclusion of both items, but the New Zealand item first. The inclusion of both items was approved by the Council with the New Zealand item first along with their proposed invitation.

On February 4th, U.N. Secretary General Dag Hammarskjold cabled an invitation to the Peoples Republic to participate in the Security Council debate. Chou En-lai replied with a stinging rejection of the U.N. offer on the grounds that the New Zealand agenda item intervened in China's internal affairs and was therefore "in direct violation of the fundamental principles of the United Nations Charter." Chou also noted his government's lack of U.N. representation, thus making Security Council decisions on questions concerning China, "illegal and null and void."[59]

The Security Council subsequently (February 14th) voted to adjourn its consideration of the New Zealand item, but not proceed to the Soviet item. The result was stalemate at Turtle Bay.

Treaty Ties Approved

The administration's strategy for Senate approval remained essentially the same as it had been for the resolution--a reliance upon the bipartisan majority of conservative Democrats and internationalist Republicans for passage. For right wing critics emphasis was placed upon the combination of resolution plus treaty to insure the defense of Chinese Nationalist territories. Liberal critics were to be pacified by reference to the supplementary letters exchanged between Dulles and Foreign Minister Yeh (finally released on February 7th), restraining Chiang, plus Eisenhower's assurance that he alone would decide if American forces should strike the mainland.

The administration's call for quick passage of the treaty was strongly reinforced by Senate approval of the Formosa Resolution and the stalemate at the United Nations. Dulles continued to repeat the administration's psychological rationale for immediate action by declaring that the Communists were "probing our resolution." He also suggested that no action be taken on a Humphrey proposed resolution putting the Senate formally behind U.N. cease-fire talks which they had rejected, except on terms unacceptable to the United States. Humphrey agreed and dropped his proposal.[60]

Dulles also explained that there would be no expansion of the American commitment to "other territories," as mentioned in the treaty without consent of the Senate. His verbal assurances were not enough on this point. Although the Foreign Relations Committee recommended the treaty by an 11 to 2 vote on February 8th with Langer and Morse objecting, three understandings were included. They were first, that no military action should be taken in "other territories" without advance Senate consent; that the treaty did not give Chiang's regime any claim to sovereignty over Formosa; and finally, that the treaty was defensive and applied only through joint agreement in the event of an armed attack.[61]

According to Senator George the inclusion of the understandings in the committee report was "entirely agreeable" to Secretary Dulles. Morse, however, denounced the understandings as having no "substantial status." He characterized the pact as "a treaty with Knowland" and Lehman labeled it a "treaty with Chiang Kai-Shek."[62]

On February 9th Eisenhower announced that the evacuation of the Tachens was proceeding according to plan, giving the impression that the evacuation and pending treaty formed a coordinated effort in which timing played a key role. On the Senate floor Morse with Lehman and Langer co-sponsored two reservations designed to accomplish via the legally binding reservation route what the committee had attempted to achieve through its understandings.

Their first reservation invalidated the treaty section pertaining to possible American defense of "other territories" currently held by the Nationalists. The second reservation stipulated that the treaty shall not "be construed as affecting or modifying the legal status or sovereignty of the territories to which it applies."[63]

George claimed the reservations would require re-negotiation of the treaty and that the understandings had "in every practical way the force of reservations." Both reservations were defeated by large majorities and the treaty was approved 64 to 6.[64]

At the Bandung Afro-Asian Conference in April Chou En-lai suggested that direct talks be initiated with the United States to ease tensions in the Far East. The administration agreed and talks began at Geneva. Although nothing was settled, the first Formosa Strait confrontation faded, but America's treaty commitment to Taipei would remain in place for a quarter of a century.[65]

Summing Up

Congressional passage of the Formosa Resolution and the Mutual Defense Treaty with the Republic of China was due largely to the stability of the bipartisan coalition Eisenhower and Dulles were able to maintain and rely upon during the period of confrontation in the Formosa Strait. A significant additional factor which made opposition to those measures most difficult was the McCarthyite atmosphere still existent during the 84th Congress. The extreme pressure generated by that atmosphere and described vividly by Morse on the congressional debate, clearly inhibited a full discussion of what was a preventive war resolution.

The administration's insistence that a crisis existed in which the will of the United States was being tested also meant that critics of the resolution could more easily be accused of endangering national security as Senator Knowland claimed Morse was doing during the debate. Yet, Prime Minister Winston Churchill's observation to Eisenhower (February 15, 1955) that the offshore islands were not necessary for the defense of Formosa because the United States could easily "drown any Chinese would-be-invaders of Formosa,"[66] was a graphic reference to the actual lack of crisis surrounding Formosa's security.

The New Look concept, originating with Admiral Radford and the Joint Chiefs of Staff and later referred to as Massive Retaliation by Dulles; plus the EisenhowerDulles acceptance of a "hit first" scenario if need be against China, more than justified Senate critics misgivings over the administration's intentions. Despite the President's statement that he had not delegated any decision to use American forces and Adams' later assertion that Radford was not "trigger-happy," Ridgway's non-consultation remains at best a puzzlement and at worst a clear effort to ignore the voice of the army's commander.

The abortive agenda dance at the United Nations played itself out in predictable fashion. Given administration opposition to Hubert Humphrey's proposed resolutions placing the Senate behind U.N. cease-fire efforts and the Peoples Republic absolute rejection of an invitation from a body within which it was not represented, little more could be expected than the stalemate that resulted.

Eisenhower's direction of events during the period of confrontation was dependent upon and essentially determined by John Foster Dulles. On the tactical level, the Formosa Resolution was a Dulles contrivance and his psychological interpretation of its necessity was fully supported by the President. The important mission of successfully maintaining bipartisan support was also a task fulfilled by the Secretary of State, as the Congress reverted back to Democratic majorities in 1955. While Eisenhower's wide personal popularity undoubtedly aided Dulles' efforts at implementation, Sherman Adams' observation that the policy innovations chosen were "due to Dulles and not to Eisenhower," was clearly the case and re-assessments of Eisenhower's leadership must remain cognizant of this fact.

Final bipartisan opposition to the executive initiated resolution and treaty was unable to substitute, stall or mitigate by reservation the administration's China policy. Indeed, Lehman, Langer and Morse could only offer a stubborn rear-guard action against overwhelming odds in an effort to prevent policies that would largely divide the Peoples Republic of China and the United States for a generation.

Notes

[1]For a critical analysis of bipartisanship during the first Eisenhower term see, Gary W. Reichard, "Divisions and Dissent: Democrats and Foreign Policy, 1952-1956," Political Science Quarterly 93 (Spring 1978): 51-72.

[2]For a review article reassessing Eisenhower's leadership see Victor De Santis, "Eisenhower Revisionism," Review of Politics 38 (April, 1976), 190-207. An example of documentation becoming available is U.S. Congress, Senate, Executive Sessions Of The Senate Foreign Relations Committee (Historical Series), Vol. 3, 84th Cong., 1st sess., 1955, published April, 1978. Hereafter referred to as Executive Sessions.

[3]For Truman's views see, Merle Miller's Plain Speaking: an oral biography of Harry S. Truman (New York: Berkley Publishing Corporation, 1974), especially 304.

[4]U.S. Congress, Senate, Committee on Foreign Relations, Authorizing the President to Employ the Armed Forces of the United States for Protecting the Security of Formosa, the Pescadores, and Related Positions and Territories of that Area, S. Rept. 13, 84th Cong., 1st sess., 1955, 3. Hereafter referred to as Authorizing the President.

[5]For incisive views of the Dulles personality and political style see, Townsend Hoopes, "God and John Foster Dulles," Foreign Policy 13 (Winter 1973-74), 154-77, and his The Devil and John Foster Dulles: The Diplomacy of the Eisenhower Era (Boston: Little, Brown & Company, 1973).

[6]Author interview with Presidential Assistant Sherman Adams in Hanover, New Hampshire, 14 November 1967.

[7]Ibid.

[8]Representative Charles H. Halleck, recorded interview, the John Foster Dulles Papers, Princeton, New Jersey.

[9]Author interview with Adams.

[10]Ibid.

[11]Eisenhower, State of the Union Message, 2 February 1953, Vital Speeches Of The Day 19 (15 February 1953): 258-64.

[12]See Clubb's Twentieth Century China (New York: Columbia University Press, 1964), 341. For an excellent early analysis of the Formosa problem see his "Formosa and the Offshore Islands in American Policy, 1950-1955," Political Science Quarterly 74 (December 1959): 517-31.

[13]Admiral Arthur W. Radford, recorded interview, Dulles Papers.

[14]For a pertinent study on Senator McCarthy see Robert Griffith, The Politics of Fear: Joseph McCarthy and the Senate (Lexington: University Press of Kentucky, 1970).

[15]Dulles fired John Patton Davies on 5 November 1954. See Chapter 10 in The China Hands: America's Foreign Service Officers and What Befell Them, E. J. Kahn, Jr. (New York: The Viking Press, 1975).

[16]Remarks from address before American Bar Association, San Francisco, Calif., 16 September 1952, Dulles Papers.

[17]Senator Sparkman has recalled that Dulles ". . . coordinated and cooperated quite well with Congress," recorded interview, Dulles Papers.

[18]Lyndon Johnson was for instance, supportive of the administration's bipartisan approach. See New York Times, 15 December 1954, 1.

[19]Author interview with Adams. George was entitled by seniority to the chairmanship of either the Finance or Foreign Relations Committee.

[20]Senator Hubert Humphrey, recorded interview, The Herbert H. Lehman Papers, Columbia University, School of International Affairs, New York City, N.Y.

[21]Hoopes, The Devil and John Foster Dulles, 263-64.

[22] See Robert J. Donovan, Eisenhower: The Inside Story (New York: Harper & Brothers, 1956), 300.

[23] Anthony Eden, The Memoirs of Anthony Eden: Full Circle (Boston: Houghton Mifflin Company, 1960), 342.

[24] See Wayne Morse's speech in Congressional Record, 84th Cong., 1st sess., 1955, 101, pt 1: 747, Eisenhower's Mandate For Change, 1953-1956 (New York: Doubleday & Company, Inc., 1963), 554-55, and Hoopes, The Devil and John Foster Dulles, 265-66.

[25] Clubb, Twentieth Century China, 342.

[26] New York Times, 16 November 1954, 1.

[27] U.S. Congress, Senate, Message From The President Of The United States Transmitting A Mutual Defense Treaty Between The United States of America And The Republic Of China, S. Doc. Executive A, 84th Cong., 1st sess., 1954.

[28] For complete text of the treaty and supplementary notes see U.S. Congress, House, Collective Defense Treaties, H. Doc., 90th Cong., 1st sess., 1967, 101-4.

[29] New York Times, 19 January 1955, 3.

[30] Ibid.

[31] Eisenhower, Mandate For Change, 558.

[32] Authorizing the President, 5-6.

[33] Transcript of background news conference, 24 January 1955, Dulles Papers.

[34] Eisenhower, Mandate For Change, 550.

[35] See remarks by Senator John Sparkman in Preface to Executive Sessions, 4-5.

[36] Hearings on S.J.R. 28, Ibid., 24 January 1955, 68, 84 and 92.

[37] Ibid., 25 January 1955, 216.

[38] Ibid., 182.

[39]Senator Wayne Morse, Recorded Interview, _Lehman Papers_, 13-14.

[40]_New York Times_, 25 January 1955, 3.

[41]S.R. 55, complete text, _Executive Sessions_, 770-71.

[42]S.J.R. 28, Formosa Resolution, complete text, Ibid., 756-57. See full text of Resolution in Appendix D.

[43]Author interview with Adams.

[44]Recorded Interview, _Lehman Papers_, 9.

[45]Ibid., 10.

[46]_Cong. Rec._, 101, pt 1: 738-47.

[47]_New York Times_, 27 January 1955, 1, 2.

[48]Ibid.

[49]Ibid., 28 January 1955, 2. However, with respect to Radford, Sherman Adams later claimed that he was not "trigger-happy" and that any such concern would have originated from "a lack of communication between Eisenhower and his admirals which is not a reasonable assumption to make." Author interview.

[50]_Cong. Rec._, 101 pt 1: 820-1.

[51]_New York Herald Tribune_, 20 January 1955, 1.

[52]Ibid.

[53]Complete text of speech in reprint from _Cong. Rec._, 28 January 1955, _Lehman Papers_.

[54]Eisenhower, _Mandate For Change_, 559-60.

[55]Ibid., 560-61.

[56]_United Nations Document_, S/3354, 28 January 1955.

[57]Ibid., S/3355, 30 January 1955.

[58] Ibid., S/3356, 31 January 1955.

[59] Ibid., S/3358, 3 February 1955.

[60] New York Times, 8 February 1955, 1, 5.

[61] U.S. Congress, Senate, Committee on Foreign Relations, Mutual Defense Treaty With The Republic of China, S. Exec. Rept. 2, 84th Cong., 1st sess., 1955, 1-7.

[62] For remarks by Senators George and Morse see New York Times, 9 February 1955, 1, 14. For Senator Lehman's description of the treaty see letters to constituents, 22 & 26 March 1955, Lehman Papers.

[63] Cong. Rec., 101, pt 1: 1398.

[64] New York Times, 10 February 1955, 14. Democratic standard bearer Adlai Stevenson strongly supported Lehman's efforts. He sent the Senator a "Bravo!" for his opposition speech on the treaty and also remarked, "I pray that our misgivings will not be realized and this document won't embarrass us for years to come." See postcard, 26 February 1955, Lehman Papers.

[65] The Nixon Administration disclaimed the Formosa Resolution on 12 March 1970, and it was terminated by Act of Congress on 26 October 1974. The Carter Administration terminated the Mutual Defense Treaty on 31 December 1979, over unsuccessful congressional opposition to his unilateral termination of a treaty.

[66] Eisenhower, Mandate For Change, 563.

VI

CONGRESS AND THE MIDDLE EAST:

THE EISENHOWER DOCTRINE, 1957*

United States rivalry with the Soviet Union in the Middle East provided one of the earliest incidences of Cold War conflict between the two superpowers following World War II. The first complaint the Security Council of the United Nations received (January 19, 1946), was British supported and lodged by the Iranian Government against the Soviet Union. Soon thereafter the Iranians charged the U.S.S.R. with keeping their troops in Iranian Azerbaijan past the agreed upon date for their withdrawal. The Soviet Union retaliated by claiming that British troops in Greece and Indonesia were a threat to peace. However, the Security Council, by a vote of 8 to 3 overruled a Russian request that the Iranian dispute not be placed on the agenda. All Soviet troops were evacuated from Iran on May 6, 1946 after President Harry S. Truman sent Premier Joseph Stalin an ultimatum stating that he "would send troops if he (Stalin) did not get out."[1]

---

*Author's "Congress and the Middle East: The Eisenhower Doctrine, 1957" was originally published as Chapter 21 in DWIGHT D. EISENHOWER: Soldier, President, Statesman, Joanne P. Krieg, Ed. (Contributions in Political Science, No. 183, Greenwood Press, Inc., Westport, CT, 1987).

During that same year the Soviet Union also sought an agreement whereby British influence would be eliminated in Turkey and strategic bases commanding the Dardanelles Straits would be obtained. Strongly backed by the United States which quickly dispatched a naval task force to the Mediterranean, the Turks rejected these proposals.

The following year the United States adopted the Truman Doctrine which was aimed at stopping Communist supported partisans in Greece through the unilateral intervention of American economic and military aid. Via the implementation of this policy, governments friendly to the United States were maintained in both Greece and Turkey. The Truman Doctrine was also a general statement of American foreign policy which substantially differed from the nation's pre-World War II isolationism which had only given way to collective security as the new foreign policy four years before (1943), with congressional approval of the Fulbright and Connally Resolutions.[2]

As Britain formally terminated her Palestine mandate Jewish leaders proclaimed the state of Israel on May 14, 1948. The Truman Administration demonstrated its sympathy for a Jewish homeland in the Middle East by immediately recognizing the new state--despite State Department opposition. Arab League armies immediately attacked Israel and were decisively defeated in a short but bloody war. By 1949 Egypt signed an armistice with Israel and other Arab states quickly followed suit. The armistice was shaky at best: border raids continued with the Arabs refusing to recognize the existence of Israel and vowing to eventually destroy the new Jewish state in a war of annihilation.

American political commitments in the Middle East rose sharply during May, 1950 when through American initiative a Tripartite Declaration with Britain and France was announced guaranteeing the shaky Israeli-Arab armistice. Arab resentment of the new Jewish state continued to manifest itself, however, and on June 17th five Arab states signed a collective security pact followed by a prohibition against Israeli shipping through the Suez Canal imposed by Egypt on July 19th.

By 1951 the forces of nationalism were clearly sweeping across the Middle East. On March 15th Iran nationalized the British held Anglo-Iranian Oil Company. In Egypt, potentially the most powerful Arab state, Parliament abrogated the treaty that had assigned the defense of the Suez Canal to the British. London answered by reinforcing its Suez garrison with Washington backing the British position. In October, Egypt turned down an opportunity to participate in an Anglo-American-French-Turkish Middle East Command which was to defend the whole area against communism. During 1952 the decadent Egyptian King Farouk was ousted in an army coup which vowed a campaign against corruption and colonialist forces in Egypt. By April 1954 Col. Gamal Abdel Nasser had risen to lead the military clique that ruled Egypt; his policies were anti-Israeli and anti-colonial with an ultimate goal of pan-Arab unity.

The year 1954 also saw the development of an American protectorate over oil-rich Iran on the Soviet Union's borders. Iran had been gripped by an economic paralysis and faced bankruptcy after it seized the Anglo-Iranian oil fields and British technicians had left the country. Via a Central Intelligence Agency organized coup, Premier Mossadegh was overthrown during August 1953 and an oil accord was promulgated during 1954 between Washington, London and Teheran. Through this agreement the Anglo-Iranian Oil Company formally lost its monopoly, but the United States gained substantial concessions for its own oil concerns. It had been, according to one high American oil corporation official involved, "most profitable patriotism."[3]

Dulles and the Middle East

John Foster Dulles dominated the formulation of American foreign policy during his tenure as Secretary of State in the Eisenhower Administration with the strong backing of the President. Innovations in policy such as the Formosa Resolution 1955 were clearly Dulles in conception and motivated by a fervent anti-communism.[4]

Dulles also jealously guarded who could speak for the administration on American foreign policy and to this end President Eisenhower admonished cabinet members during the 1956 Middle East war that "it is the Department of State which is to be the public spokesman for the Executive Branch on foreign affairs, especially during the present delicate international situation."

At the same time Dulles guarded the flow of foreign policy information to other administration members. During March 1957 he met cabinet members' requests for more information with an agenda memorandum which stated that while he would be "happy to make some remarks" on the general international situation, he would "not go into detail about the Middle East."[5]

It was Dulles' judgment that any possible Communist penetration of the area could best be prevented by the establishment of yet another regional security organization such as the recently completed Southeast Asia Treaty Organization (SEATO) in 1954. Also, the Secretary was concerned with the effect of rising Arab nationalism on American access to Middle East oil. Consequently on November 22, 1955, Britain, Turkey, Iran, Iraq and Pakistan announced the establishment of the Baghdad Pact. Although the United States initiated this arrangement and participated in some of its key committees, it did not sign the pact for fear that a formal American alliance with Iraq would antagonize Egypt and Israel.[6]

However, the existence of the pact inadvertently triggered an eventuality Dulles wished to avoid: a retaliation by both Egypt and Syria in the form of their cultivation and acceptance of Soviet economic and military aid. Nasser was embittered over the growing role of the United States in the Middle East as it threatened his goal of Arab leadership. Thus, the bond between certain Arab states and the Soviet Union grew stronger.

During September 1955 a Czech arms deal with Egypt was announced and Israeli Prime Minister Moshe Sharett reacted by instructing his Embassy in Washington to shift their emphasis from gaining a U.S. security guarantee to the supply of arms for Israel. What followed was a "hint from a CIA source which reached Jerusalem through a highly secret channel, intimating that if Israel hit Egypt upon the arrival of the Soviet weapons, America would not protest."[7]

In November 1955 Ben-Gurion formed a new government serving as both Prime Minister and Defense Minister of Israel. Addressing the Knesset on November 2, 1955 Ben-Gurion reminded his nation's adversaries, especially Egypt which blocked Israeli shipping through the Suez Canal and was in the process of seeking the same effect through the Red Sea Gulf that: "Our aim is peace - but not suicide."[8]

Dulles now sought to counteract the increasing alienation of Nasser by making a joint offer with the British Government of $70 million to Egypt during December 1955 for the building of the Aswan High Dam and, on the other hand, by denying the sale of arms to Israel the following month. Israel sought these arms to counterbalance the military shipments Egypt was receiving from Soviet sources. Washington also continued to pressure London to complete the withdrawal of her large garrison from Suez as agreed to with Egypt the previous year.

Dulles also dispatched the Texas oil magnate and later Secretary of the Treasurer, Robert Anderson, to negotiate between Israel and Egypt for the purpose of reaching a compromise political and territorial settlement. The Secretary tried to link these negotiations to support for the High Dam--which only made Nasser furious and the mission failed.[9]

During February, Cairo came tentatively to terms with the International Bank for Reconstruction and Development for an additional loan with which to build the Aswan Dam. However, Middle East tensions continued to rise as young King Hussein of Jordan dismissed Gen. John Bagot Glubb as Commander of the Arab Legion on March 2, 1956 and insisted that all British advisers and troops leave Jordan. During the spring of 1956 Nasser was active seeking more aid for his High Dam project and he continued to cultivate his position in the Arab world as champion of Arab nationalism and major proponent of anti-imperialist and anti-Israeli policies.

Bloody raids continued to be mounted from the Sinai Peninsula and the Gaza Strip into Israel. On April 19th the UN Secretary General Dag Hammarskjold was able to announce a cease-fire on the Egyptian-Israeli frontier. However, King Hussein of Jordan signed a military accord with Syria on May 31st and appointed a pro-Nasser premier, completing an increasingly hostile encirclement of Israel.

Nasser continued a buildup of arms from the Soviet

Union with the avowed intention of annihilating Israel. He also recognized The Peoples Republic of China, hinted that the Russians would, under favorable terms, underwrite the costs of the Dam, sent aid to anti-British guerillas on Cyprus and their counterparts in French Algeria, and celebrated the final British withdrawal from Suez on June 13th as a triumph for Arab nationalism.

The following month the State Department stunned Nasser with an announcement that it would not finance the Aswan Dam. Both London and the International Bank quickly concurred in this decision. The U.S.S.R. announced they never had offered aid to build the Dam. Nasser struck back swiftly on July 27th by nationalizing the Suez Canal and announcing that compensation to the stockholders would be made and revenues from the canal would be used to build the Dam. Dulles' decision led directly to war. It was made without specific directives from Eisenhower or consultation with other members of the cabinet. There was, however, significant opposition in the Congress to funding the Dam.

Congress and the High Dam

By 1956 the Republicans had long been castigating the Democrats for over-spending, thus making it doubly difficult for them to argue that the Congress, with its Democratic majorities since the 1954 midterm elections, should support such a huge and controversial undertaking as the High Dam. It was also an election year and the enormous amount of ongoing funding required for the Dam was clearly unpopular with the Congress. Senators and representatives prefer annual appropriations which are based upon yearly justifications; not the kind of long-term commitment of funds required for the Dam.[10]

However, Democratic Senator J. William Fulbright of Arkansas was incorrect when he later claimed that opposition to the project "was confined to the Committee on Appropriations." A most important link existed between United States China policy and funding for the High Dam. Nasser's recognition of the Peoples Republic of China during May 1956 triggered a strong response from the China Lobby (advocates of the Republic of China on Taiwan). Republican Senate Minority Leader William Knowland of California was the outspoken head of the powerful China Lobby who quickly narrowed

Dulles' options via some friendly advice. The Minority Leader told the Secretary that the foreign aid bill was soon to be voted upon in Congress and it contained two controversial country programs--assistance to Nasser who was drawing closer to communism and assistance to Tito of Yugoslavia who had broken away from Moscow. Both men were strongly disliked by Knowland who suggested that the entire foreign aid bill would be jeopardized if the administration insisted upon aid for both. Under the circumstances Dulles chose aid for Yugoslavia.[11]

Knowland was not a Progressive Republican in the Eisenhower mold and his strong views on China were well-known. Only the year before in Senate debate he had used the extremist tactic of accusing Oregon Senator Wayne Morse of having endangered the security of the United States, because Morse had previously claimed that passage of the Formosa Resolution "would legalize the position of the proponents of a preventive war." Subsequent passage of a Mutual Defense Treaty with the Republic of China was nevertheless characterized by Morse as a "treaty with Knowland." However, the outspoken Morse also opposed funds for the Dam. He disliked the financing of a giant dam in Egypt instead of one or several dams in the Northwest United States.[12]

Additional congressional opposition existed on behalf of Israel. Abba Eban, Israeli Ambassador to the United States at that time has since recorded that American funding of the Dam was "more than Israel could afford. Here was Nasser getting arms from Moscow. He would now get the Dam from America." As a result, according to Eban, Nasser "would become insufferable through the sheer extremity of arrogance." Thus, he added in the same interview, "Israeli influence, I will say quite frankly, was exercised against American support of the Dam." Although Eban described his country's influence as "not a very ponderable thing," the Ambassador added that "it counts and certainly in that context there were many in the Senate and the House who opposed the Aswan Dam proposal in Israel's interest."[13]

There was also important opposition from the Cotton Lobby in the Congress whose influence has probably been underestimated in relation to the Aswan High Dam proposal. Cotton-growing states are almost exclusively found in the south including Texas, but the southwest and southern California also contain areas of high yields. During the 1950's the United States remained the number one producer of ginned cotton in the world. However, American cotton exports were temporarily hurting in 1955 with exports down about two million bales from what they had been in 1950. American cotton producers quite naturally opposed funding the High Dam for fear that it would lead to significantly greater cotton exports and therefore competition from Egypt. Moreover, their southern representatives in the 84th Congress (1955-57) were heavily represented in positions of power to defend their interests. Under the circumstances the opposition of King Cotton could not be overlooked.[14]

Dulles and the Doctrine

By the end of August 1956, British, French and Israeli representatives were meeting in secret to coordinate their plans for an attack upon Egypt. The Suez Canal was viewed as vital to British economic interests with twenty-five percent of the island nation's total imports traversing the canal. It was also "an oil pipeline, an economic lifeline," according to a London *Star* editorial on July 27th. Finally, canal revenues were a significant source of funds for the British treasury. French motivations were more political and military--to strike back at a government that was supporting the Algerian rebels in their bitter struggle against France.[15]

However, a severe miscalculation was in the making. The United States was not informed as to the secret arrangements for war being made by the three states. Shimon Peres, the Israeli Director General of the Ministry of Defense, returned from France on September 25th where the meetings were taking place. He reported that the French "do not think the United States will interfere; as for the Soviet Union, they just cannot guess what the reaction will be."[16]

The administration did have at least some inkling of the impending attack when an overflight of the eastern Mediterranean by Francis Gary Powers (of later U-2 fame) discovered a large military build-up on the island of Malta. Also, American Ambassador to Israel Edward B. Lawson cabled Washington that "an enormous mobilization in Israel" with "tanks on all the roads" was occurring. On October 27th Ambassador Eban was called to the State Department. With Dulles and his advisers grouped around a great map of the Israeli-Jordan frontier, the Ambassador was confronted with Lawson's observations and the question--was not Israel preparing for war? However, Eban had not yet been notified as to his government's final war decision and the administration remained in the dark.[17]

Events in the Soviet bloc countries of Eastern Europe became closely related with the imminent Middle East War. In an effort to increase his personal power, and allow the Soviet economy to expand by removing Stalinist restrictions, Krushchev had detailed Stalin's crimes against the Communist Party at the 20th Party Congress in February, 1956. As a result of this de-Stalinization process, liberal forces in Poland and Hungary were seeking greater independence from Moscow. On October 29, 1956, the Israeli army attacked and almost completely destroyed the Egyptian army. On October 30th England and France delivered ultimatums to Egypt and Israel to keep their armies away from the canal. When Nasser rejected their ultimatum the previously planned British-French intervention began. The resulting war gave the Kremlin an ideal time period for counteraction in Eastern Europe. As Anglo-French columns advanced into the Suez Canal area during the first week in November, the Hungarian rebellion was suppressed by Soviet tanks.

The initial reaction of Eisenhower to the Middle East War may be summarized in one word--furious. Ike called Downing Street directly and issued forth a tirade against one of the Prime Minister's aides whom he mistook for Anthony Eden. By the time the Prime Minister got on the phone the President had hung up. Ambassador Eban has also recalled that in the absence of Dulles, who entered the hospital on November 3rd, "we had to deal with Eisenhower in his full righteous fury."[18]

The Soviet Union suggested a Moscow-Washington joint effort to settle the crisis on November 5th which the United States rejected. However, under enormous pressure from the United Nations, the Soviet Union and most significantly the United States, the ailing Eden announced a British-French cease-fire would take place at midnight, November 6th. That same day Eisenhower easily defeated his Democratic opponent Adlai E. Stevenson in the presidential election with a popular vote lead of over nine million and more than six times as many electoral votes (457 to 73). Despite the President's popularity both houses of Congress remained firmly in control of the Democratic opposition.

After having played an important role in destroying the Middle Eastern colonial power of England and France, the administration became convinced a power vacuum was developing in the Middle East which the Soviet Union would attempt to fill. As Vice President Richard Nixon would later note: "For better or worse, the colonial empires were disintegrating. The great question in the 1950s was who would fill the vacuum." Also, even though the administration did not wish to identify its role in the area with former colonial traditions, Nasser's pan-Arab ambitions were feared as much as the presumed Russian threat. Therefore it was certainly not the purpose of U.S. foreign policy "or of the involved oil companies to push too far a unified Arab world, to abdicate the hold over the oil concessions, or to allow any further British-French vacuums to remain unfilled."[19]

The administration was also faced with the problem of whether or not to stand with the majority at the UN and vote for withdrawal of all belligerent forces, or abstain from voting so as not to further exacerbate relations with its North Atlantic Treaty allies. At the November 16th cabinet meeting the State Department's legal adviser Herman Phleger, speaking for Dulles, reported that "Nasser had assured the United States that he had no intent at present of permitting the entry of volunteers and thus flaunt the UN position, but he reserved judgment as to the future should the French and British not withdraw promptly." Under the circumstances, Dulles was convinced that the UN position was the legal position and the United States voted on November 24th for a resolution ordering a "forthwith" withdrawal of all invaders.[20]

Also, the oil interests had warned the State Department that rushing oil to Western Europe to replace her cut-off supplies might endanger American oil holdings in the Middle East whose leaders sided with Nasser. Therefore, "the diplomatic strategy was to promise oil but to go slow in delivery, first ensuring the end of the conflict and the withdrawal from Egypt of the invading armies." Under these American pressures England and France completely backed down and by December 22nd all of their troops had evacuated Suez. However, their withdrawal only heightened Washington's conviction that a dangerous power vacuum was developing in the Middle East.[21]

Dulles now decided upon a plan in the tradition of the Formosa Resolution of 1955. Still recuperating in his room at Walter Reed Hospital, he formulated a resolution in which the Congress would be asked to share responsibility in promulgating a new defense doctrine aimed at stopping any overt Communist aggression in the Middle East. Prior congressional approval was to be obtained via a joint resolution to assist area nations in defending against aggression "from any country controlled by international communism." The President would be authorized to use force in meeting any attack if assistance was requested under Article 51 of the UN Charter. Broad economic and military aid amounting to $200 million in total would also be made available to any such state upon request. Thus, the Eisenhower Doctrine was born.[22]

A Bipartisan Strategy

Administration efforts were aimed at gaining bipartisan support quickly from the Congress for the joint resolution. Eisenhower presented it first to Republican congressional leaders on the last day of 1956. The following day leaders of both parties in the Senate and the House were brought in for consultation in an effort to gain their approval and insure prompt attention for the resolution when the Congress convened its first session of the new year. The President assured Republican leaders that the resolution implied no intention to enter local conflicts in the Middle East in which the question of Communist aggression was not clearly involved. He assured the Democratic leaders that if Congress would grant him the authority to use military force if necessary in the Middle East, he believed he would never have to use it. Eisenhower then stated the power vacuum thesis that motivated his administration: "I just do not believe that we can leave a vacuum in the Middle East and prayerfully hope that Russia will stay out."[23]

However, the administration was soon confronted with strong criticism of the proposed resolution from within Democratic Party ranks. Adlai E. Stevenson was applauded by both Republicans and Democrats as he sat in the diplomatic gallery at the opening session of the Senate on January 3rd. He issued a statement criticizing the administration's Middle East proposal in which he claimed the President "is evidently trying frantically to fill the vacuum his own policies helped create before Russia does." Stevenson also warned that Eisenhower "was going to ask for another military blank check, this time the right to send our forces to fight in the Middle East."[24]

Two days later on January 5, 1957, Eisenhower countered with a special message to Congress on the proposal emphasizing his personal responsibility over its military provision. He claimed that "Russia's rulers have long sought to dominate the Middle East," but they would have nothing to fear from the United States in the Middle East or elsewhere so long as they "do not themselves first resort to aggression. That statement I make solemnly and emphatically."[25]

Overseas the British Foreign Office welcomed the resolution in brief general terms, but a London Times editorial on January 7th observed that "it comes very late, that it is fearfully vague in parts, and that it is largely irrelevant to the main causes of the Middle East upheavals, tensions and dangers." Yet, the editorial continued, "when everything has been said against it, it can be welcomed as a step forward."[26]

Another prominent Democrat attacked the proposal on January 10th. Former Secretary of State Dean Acheson, while testifying before the House Foreign Affairs Committee, referred to it as being "not only unnecessary but undesirable." He claimed the President already possessed the power to use the military and to dispense aid. What was needed, according to Acheson, was a Vandenberg type resolution which would simply express the "sense of the Senate" and in that way strengthen the hand of the executive. The joint resolution, he concluded, was an "undesirable exercise of the legislative power of Congress." Furthermore, it was "vague" and did not direct itself at the greater threat in the area which was subversion.[27]

Alternative resolutions were quickly introduced in both the House and Senate. House Speaker Sam Rayburn circulated a substitute among his colleagues that was aimed at specifying more exactly those Middle Eastern countries the United States would be pledged to defend. Eisenhower balked at this suggestion claiming that as in the Formosa Resolution, exact boundaries of the American commitment could not be specified lest the enemy feel free to attack elsewhere. Also, Dulles did not approve of the Rayburn proposal, claiming it would look like an effort to establish an "American protectorate" over the Middle East countries.[28]

In the Senate, Foreign Relations Committee member Fulbright also offered an alternative. The Fulbright approach was related to Acheson's suggestion to formulate a Vandenberg type resolution which would simply be an expression of the "sense of the Senate" and would not result in a law as would passage of a joint resolution signed by the President. The Fulbright approach would also have eliminated any specific authorization of aid. His alternative expressed the concern of Senators who were against granting the President the right to use force in advance as he saw fit, plus the allocation of 200 million dollars in aid for unspecified purposes.[29]

Dulles, who returned to his State Department office during December, testified before the combined Senate Foreign Relations and Armed Services Committee on January 14th. The Secretary was "strongly and skeptically examined" by this key Senate group--mainly on his contention that some Arab states needed economic assistance. Democratic Senator Richard B. Russell of Georgia, Chairman of the Armed Services Committee, commented that the Middle East had in fact very considerable "liquid assets," referring to the enormous oil resources of the region. Nevertheless, Dulles applied pressure for approval. He urged action claiming that "every day's delay means that the Soviet is getting that much deeper into the area." More ominously, he claimed that if they either gutted or rejected the administration's resolution, "the responsibility for peace or war would lie with them."[30]

However, Congress was also concerned that two of America's closest allies in NATO (Great Britain and France) deeply resented the administration's Middle

East policies with the result that unity in the Atlantic Alliance had almost been destroyed. Also, friends of Israel in Congress were closely watching as pressure from the UN and Washington mounted on Israel to pull its armies back to their pre-war frontiers. These developments, plus the State Department's efforts to effect a more friendly posture toward certain Arab states during this period, would play a significant role in contributing to senatorial reluctance to pass the resolution. United Nations pressure on Israel mounted further on January 17th when the General Assembly recalled several previous resolutions (Nov. 2, 4, 7, 24, 1956), and once again noted that Israeli forces had not withdrawn from Egypt.

On January 23rd Israel announced that it would not withdraw its forces from the Gaza Strip or from the Gulf of Aqaba strongpoint unless the UN dispatched forces to these areas to insure they would not be used as a basis for future Arab attacks upon Israel. That same day Eisenhower held a news conference during which he attempted to defend the economic portions of the resolution which were now heavily under fire in the Senate. He claimed that if the economic aid section of the proposal was not approved it "would destroy what we are really trying to do." In answer to the recurring criticism that the President already possessed constitutional authority to employ the armed forces, he commented that a strong expression from Congress was needed to make it plain that the nation is "largely one in our readiness to assume burdens, and where necessary, to assume risks to preserve the peace."[31]

In fact, the Dulles-authored Middle East Resolution dovetailed well with the second basic rule Eisenhower used as a guide to his decision-making. According to Presidential Assistant Sherman Adams, those two rules were: "Don't make mistakes in a hurry and secondly, if you do, share them." Thus, upon approval of the Eisenhower Doctrine the Congress would share with the President the responsibility of American foreign policy in the Middle East--especially in the advent of war.[32]

Despite congressional criticism the House Democratic leadership moved to bring the resolution, unchanged, to a vote the following week. However, the real battle was to take place in the Senate where deliberations would be slower and more critical and where

Secretary Dulles' policies and performance in particular were to be severely criticized.

Dulles Under Fire

Secretary Dulles testified before a Foreign Relations Committee different from that over which Democratic Senator Walter George of Georgia had presided during the 84th Congress. George had retired and the administration could no longer count on his prestigious leadership to dominate the committee and successfully guide key administration proposals such as the Formosa Resolution of 1955 through the Senate. The Chairman of the Foreign Relations Committee was now the elderly Theodore Francis Green, a Rhode Island Democrat whom Carl Marcy (the Committee's Chief of Staff) described as possessing "quite a different kind of mind from his predecessors. He was quite interested in details and not that interested in policy."[33]

As a result, younger more liberal members of the committee, especially Senator Fulbright, were making themselves heard. Fulbright's strong criticism of Dulles' policies in the Middle East were based upon two primary reasons. The first reason is an observation by Carl Marcy that Fulbright believed Dulles "tended not to appreciate the depth of Arab nationalism and confused Arab nationalism with communism." Secondly, he shared Adlai E. Stevenson's stated view in correspondence that "the world has lost confidence in Dulles."[34]

Dulles was also faced with the implication that his Middle East policies may have been tinged with an anti-Israeli bias. Republican Senator Jacob K. Javits of New York noted that these charges began in 1953 when the administration cut off aid to Israel because of a retaliatory raid it conducted against Egypt. By 1956, according to Javits, "Dulles was at a really very, very low ebb with the Jewish people and with many, many other people in the country at that time." In his sharp disagreement with the Secretary over the Middle East policy, Javits recalled leading large delegations of congressmen, "I mean large - 50 or 60," to confront Dulles. Senator Javits felt he played a key role in the transformation of Dulles' attitude. Javits believed Dulles' policies began to sound less suspect when he offered economic aid to both the Arab states and Israel, held Nasser to his commitments, cancelled Nasser's Aswan Dam funds, and developed a growing understanding of the "vital character" of Israel. This last point was driven home to Dulles later during the Lebanon crisis (1958), according to Javits, when "Israel turned out to be the most reliable country, by far, and not only reliable but effective." Thus, by the late fifties Javits described Dulles as becoming "a hero in the relations between Israel and the United States."[35]

During the early hearings on the resolution Senator Fulbright led the attack on Dulles by reading a lengthy indictment of his policies while the Secretary sat on the witness stand before the combined Senate Foreign Relations and Armed Services Committees. Fulbright criticized the Secretary's "reluctance to be specific" as to what would be done with the requested funds. He also noted that Britain and France were "grievously wounded by our policies." Fulbright then characterized the resolution as a "blank check for the administration to do as it pleased with our soldiers and with our money." He described Dulles' performance as being "harmful to our interests" and "calculated to weaken the influence of the free world in the Middle East," as well as disastrous to NATO. The Senator stated that no "vote of confidence in the stewardship of Secretary Dulles" should be given before more information was available. More specifically, he proposed on January 24th that Dulles furnish the joint committee with an official White Paper on American policy in the Middle East before a committee vote on the resolution was taken.[36]

The resolution's implications for Congress' power to declare war was of special concern to a number of senators including Democratic Senator Estes Kefauver of Tennessee, a member of the Armed Services Committee. He stated that the congressional right and duty to declare when the United States should be at war was, under the resolution, being delegated "to people who are going to decide it on facts which may or may not be convincing enough to the Senate." When Kefauver asked for assurances that the President would ask for a declaration that a state of war existed before American armed forces were committed, Dulles stated flatly: "Not prior to their use; no, sir." This could not be done according to Dulles, because the purpose of the resolution was to "make clear that the armed forces will be available to resist open, armed aggression by a country controlled by international communism." Senator Morse also pressed Dulles on this issue. Morse asked if the Secretary of State thought "the power vested in the Congress to declare war carries with it the power to rescind any act of the President that may lead to war." Dulles answered by stating he knew of "no way in the world" to rescind acts of the President once they had been taken.[37]

Dulles attempted to strike back at his critics during his testimony on January 25th. He objected to the Fulbright White Paper proposal claiming that "any investigation of his policies and this country's relationship with Britain and France in the Suez crisis of last autumn" would cause an "infinite delay" of the administration's plan and do "irreparable damage" to the country's association with France and Great Britain. He then resorted to the familiar time is running out argument to demonstrate his concern regarding a Russian attack and thus spur the Senate to action. He cited "desperate appeals from Iran, Iraq, Turkey and Pakistan seeking assurances that the United States would come to their aid in case of Russian attack." However, Dulles also undiplomatically indicated that he preferred that British and French troops be deployed in Europe rather than in the Middle East if a real emergency with the Soviet Union arose, claiming he would "rather not have a French and a British soldier beside me." By this blunder he further exacerbated strains in the Atlantic Alliance that a number of Senators were accusing him of provoking in the first place.[38]

The attack upon Dulles and his policies continued to mount. Democratic Senator Sam J. Ervin, Jr. of North Carolina suggested during the January 25th hearings that if the United States had become a member of the Baghdad Pact it would have insured this country of "at least five" committed allies, Dulles retorted that the United States did not join the Baghdad Pact because it didn't wish to become "embroiled in Arab politics." Ervin then noted that the administration's resolution might very well "embroil" the United States in Arab politics anyway.[39]

On January 28th the New York Times reported that criticism against the Secretary of State "was apparently beginning to create a serious question as to Mr. Dulles' future prestige and influence with Congress and in the eyes of other nations." The same article also reported that during a televised interview Senator Fulbright stated he would vote against the resolution "unless Mr. Dulles' conduct of foreign policy were investigated first." However, it was also reported that Senator Humphrey felt Congress had "no choice" other than to give the administration some military and economic aid for the Middle East, but he contended the resolution "is not directed at the real danger of Communist infiltration of the Middle East." He then added: "We are being prescribed the wrong medicine and I'm afraid we need to change doctors."[40]

Eisenhower came to the defense of his Secretary of State on January 29th. To a meeting of legislative leaders at the White House he noted that Dulles felt very much "down" because of his slip of the tongue regarding fighting next to British and French soldiers. He then told how he had begun to press critics of Dulles to be more specific about these "supposed blunders of Foster's." At the same time a potential deadlock between the Senate and the Secretary over the requested White Paper information was averted when Senator Green, Chairman of the Joint Committee hearings informed Dulles that: "The committees desire such information, but they will not delay action on Senate Joint Resolution 19 pending receipt of such information."[41]

The following day at a press conference the popular President strongly reiterated his support for Dulles, claiming that the Secretary had personal approval from him for all of his Middle East negotiations "from top to bottom." That same day (January 30, 1957), Speaker Sam Rayburn, in cooperation with the Republican floor leader Joseph W. Martin, Jr. of Massachusetts, successfully steered the resolution to a vote in the House. It passed decisively, 355 to 61. A bipartisan mixture of 188 Democrats and 167 Republicans had backed the administration's resolution; 35 Democrats and 26 Republicans had opposed its passage. The opposition was primarily a mixture of isolationist Republicans and liberal Democrats.[42]

The Senate Balks

Throughout December and January the administration applied pressure upon England, France and Israel to withdraw their troops from the occupied territories. The State Department's efforts to meet the now crucial oil needs of Western Europe were deliberately slow so as not to offend anti-colonial Arab leaders who might jeopardize American oil industry holdings in the Middle East. Under these pressures England and France evacuated their forces, but Israel did not. Instead, Israel sought guarantees that it would not be subject to renewed terrorist raids plus assurance that free transit in the Gulf of Aqaba would be maintained. Israeli Prime Minister Ben-Gurion made it clear that Israel's armies would not withdrew without such guarantees. However, King Saud of Saudi Arabia had obtained a pledge from the administration that Israel would leave the occupied territories "unconditionally."[43]

On February 1st the United States proposed a UN resolution stipulating that Israel withdraw from both the Gaza Strip and Gulf of Aqaba "without further delay." A second American resolution proposed that following such withdrawal, a UN force be stationed on the armistice line. On February 3rd the Israeli Cabinet reiterated their position: they would not withdraw without guarantees against Arab terrorist raids and a guarantee that the right of free transit in the Gulf of Aqaba would be protected.[44]

The Israeli Embassy and its press officials soon began a strong campaign of presenting their side of the question to the American people. These spokesmen contended that as far as their nation was concerned, only Aqaba and Gaza remained real trouble areas; their arguments were aided by the high esteem in which the American public held the recently victorious Israeli armies. Also, Democratic party leaders Lyndon B. Johnson, Hubert H. Humphrey and J. W. Fulbright sympathized with the Israeli position.[45]

It was now becoming increasingly clear to the administration that the Senate did not agree with its determination to have Israel withdraw without guarantees and under a growing implied threat of sanctions. Under these conditions the Senate might choose to deliberate a very long time on the resolution whose quick passage Dulles continued to insist was vital in his effort to fill the Middle East "power vacuum."

An important defection in Republican party ranks

over this issue occurred on February 6th when Senate Minority Leader Knowland voiced his criticism of the administration's "double standard" policy, referring to the recent Soviet intervention in Hungary. Knowland declared that punishing Israel while ignoring the Soviet Union's aggression would be both "immoral and unsupportable."[46]

Behind the scenes Herman Phleger, State Department Deputy Secretary Robert Murphy and Dulles worked with Israeli Ambassador Eban on a proposal. The result of their collaboration was the Department aide-memoire of February 11th which Eban believed was the "turning point in the whole affair because we could get out of Aqaba and Gaza and yet get our main interests." Its stipulations were as follows:

> (1) The Israeli Government should withdraw from both Sharm el Sheikh guarding the Gulf of Aqaba, and the Gaza Strip in accordance with U.N. recommendations.
>
> (2) The Egyptian Government should respect the right of passage of all ships through the Gulf of Aqaba.
>
> (3) The United States would support the principle of free passage through Aqaba.[47]

In the meantime, the Foreign Relations and Armed Services Committees continued to scrutinize the administration's resolution. They finally agreed upon a substitute proposal which would back the administration's use of force if it was in accordance with previous treaties including the UN Charter. The original resolution included an authorization to commit troops against any overt aggressor. Thus, many Democrats felt they had eliminated an authorization for "blank-check" military authority via the substitute proposal. The committee vote on the authorization issue was made along party lines with 15 Democrats lining up behind it and 13 Republicans voting against the modification.[48]

On February 14th the administration announced it would accept the substitute resolution. Eisenhower made this decision on the advice of Senate Republicans who warned him that to insist upon the administration version might only provoke a losing fight on the floor of the Senate. Lyndon Johnson let it be known that he "strongly" hoped the President would accept the substitute as the Democrats also wished to avoid a head-on confrontation. Johnson stressed that the substitute resolution could be used abroad with all the force the President could have used for the administration version. Also, according to the future Commander in Chief, the granting of authority to commit troops by Congress contained in the original resolution would have "created a precedent for a weaker Presidency."[49]

This was a significant breakthrough in the deadlock between the executive and congressional branches over the resolution. Via their substitute proposal, the majority Democrats had divested themselves of some anxiety over the authorization issue raised in the original resolution. Nevertheless, passage of the resolution would still give credence to the prior consent argument for military action many senators feared. Although the Senate was moving closer to voting on the resolution, the administration's position on the question of Israeli withdrawal and the possible use of sanctions would block final approval until it was resolved.

On February 15th the Israeli Government rejected the aide memoire because it lacked sufficient guarantees, especially that Egypt be forbidden to return to Gaza. On February 17th a White House statement was issued justifying the contents of the aide memoire and the administration's growing pressure on Israel to withdraw. Soon thereafter Democratic leader Johnson sent a letter to Dulles vigorously protesting the possible use of sanctions against Israel by the United Nations. He especially attacked the double standard being used on the Soviet Union and Israel, claiming that "Israel has in large part complied with the directives of the U.N.; Russia has not even pretended to be polite." On February 19th the Senate Democratic Policy Committee endorsed Johnson's statement and called on the President to "resist any United Nations attempts to impose sanctions on Israel."[50]

In the meantime Dulles saw Eban on the rejected aide memoire. The Israeli Ambassador has recalled that Dulles said "he thought we would take this thing like a shot, instead of which we were bargaining and haggling, and meantime the situation was getting worse." Dulles also stated: "If you and I can't work this out, then we are no use at all. Can't you get your people to see that this is the turning point?" Eban explained that he "couldn't possibly succeed by cable;" instead he would return to Israel if the United States could hold up any action at the UN for three or four days. Eban had himself recalled on the 18th and American UN Ambassador Henry Cabot Lodge approached the President of the General Assembly, saying that the situation should be kept in abeyance.[51]

Although there was now common agreement on the wording of the resolution, a major schism had developed between the administration and the Democratic controlled Senate over the question of sanctions. The Democrats and a number of leading Republicans had no intention of endorsing a resolution that would be interpreted as supporting administration policies which might include sanctions against Israel.

Eisenhower and Dulles attempted to meet this critical concern on February 20th by calling together in the cabinet room at the White House a bipartisan group of congressional leaders. In a meeting described as "tense and strained," Eisenhower first explained why his administration was in favor of pressuring Israel to comply with the UN demand for unconditional withdrawal. He reiterated his belief that Russian influence would increase among the Arabs if Israel did not pull back its forces. "And then the whole thing might end up in a general war," the President added. He concluded by stating that nobody wants to impose sanctions, "but how else can we induce Israel to withdraw to the line agreed on in the 1949 armistice? The Arabs refuse to discuss a permanent settlement until that move is made." Senate Majority Leader Johnson quickly reminded Eisenhower and Dulles that both he and Minority Leader Knowland were not in favor of sanctions against Israel. "After all," Johnson added, "there are times when Congress has to express its own views." Eisenhower responded that he "certainly had no objection to that." Staring at the President with a wry smile, Johnson said, "Thank you."[52]

Eisenhower then turned the meeting over to Dulles. The Secretary added that on crucial questions such as the use of sanctions the world believed Israel could control American policy because of the strong support it had in the United States. He claimed that the Arabs were therefore watching the United States closely and "if we confirmed this belief, they would feel compelled to turn to Russia." However, in spite of all the administration's protestations and admonitions that a vote on sanctions at the UN was unavoidable and the United States would have to take a stand, senatorial support for sanctions was not obtained. According to Sherman Adams, "They were anxious to let Eisenhower have all of the credit for this declaration." That night the President took his case to the people via national television; he referred to his earlier meeting with congressional leaders, but not to the disagreement over sanctions. Although he spoke in general terms, he left no doubt as to what his final decision would be if left "no choice but to exert pressure on Israel to comply with the withdrawal resolution."[53]

The Senate Consents

On February 21st the deadlock began to break when Israeli Prime Minister Ben-Gurion stated his government would make further efforts to come to an understanding with the United States. In fact, Ambassador Eban obtained from Ben-Gurion new directives for reaching an understanding regarding the doctrine of free maritime passage and the maintenance of a force in Gaza to prevent the Egyptian Army from returning. Eban explained these conditions to Dulles upon his return on February 24th, recalling that they "were really in the spirit of the February 11th memorandum." Dulles responded: "I think we have settled this." A memorandum was drawn up by Eban and Dulles in which Israel received American assurances that the Gulf of Aqaba would remain open, plus promises that the United States would exert all effort to make Gaza a United Nations administered area. On March 1st the Israeli Foreign Minister Golda Meir announced to the General Assembly that Israel was "now in a position to announce its plans for a full and complete withdrawal." On March 4th Ben-Gurion ordered Israeli forces to pull back from Gaza and Sharm el-Sheikh.[54]

In the meantime an additional modification was made in the resolution with reference to the commitment of armed forces by the President. An amendment to the previously approved amendment which had eliminated the word "authorized," substituted "Constitution of the

United States" for "Charter of the United Nations." The change was proposed by Senator Joseph O'Mahoney, Democrat of Wyoming, and received Senate approval on February 28th by an 82 to 0 vote. The final wording of this section of the Eisenhower Doctrine now read with reference to the employment of armed forces: "Provided: That such employment shall be consonant with the treaty obligations of the United States and with the Constitution of the United States."[55]

On March 5, 1957, two months from the day Eisenhower had originally asked Congress for passage of the joint resolution, it received Senate approval, 72 to 19. The opposition on the final roll call was made up of a small number of liberal Democrats, a larger group of southern Democrats, plus three conservative Republicans. The opposition's main effort centered around an amendment sponsored by Senator Morse. It stipulated that if the President intended to use the armed forces he must first give the Congress a justification for their use or in case of an emergency and the Congress is not so notified he must immediately request approval or disapproval from the Congress after the troops have been committed. The Morse proposal was defeated by a 64 to 28 vote with both future Presidents, Lyndon B. Johnson and John F. Kennedy, voting with the majority.[56]

On March 7th the House brought their version of the resolution into line with that of the Senate's by a vote of 350 to 60. Debate among the representatives was concerned "almost as much with ill-concealed resentment at the Senate, for having rewritten the House version, as with the basic issue of the policy itself." Two days later, the President signed the joint resolution into law.[57]

Summing Up

John Foster Dulles dominated American foreign policy formulation during the Eisenhower Administration with the strong backing of the President. The Secretary's refusal to fund the High Dam was a turning point in Middle East history and his decision was undoubtedly motivated in part by Nasser's growing relationship with the Soviet Union. However, congressional opposition to funding the Dam was substantial and has been underestimated as a contributory factor in Dulles' final decision.

Congressional opposition was strong and broadly based. Its most significant element was probably the China Lobby whose spokesman was the Senate Republican Minority Leader. It may still have been possible for the administration to overcome opposition to funding the Dam, but much goodwill with the Congress would have been expended in any such effort over an issue that had strong opponents in both political parties.

The President's reaction to the Suez War had been underestimated. Ike was in a wrath about the whole matter with the result that American opposition was a key factor in the eventual British-French withdrawal and Anthony Eden's subsequent resignation. However, the demise of European power in the Middle East left what the administration believed was a power vacuum that must be filled immediately. The resulting Middle East Resolution was a Dulles contrivance in the mold of the Formosa Resolution and in line with Eisenhower's penchant for sharing responsibility for major decisions.

However, congressional approval of the resolution proved to be a most difficult task with significant resistance occurring at several junctures. The first hurdle was Senator Fulbright's demand for a White Paper before any "vote of confidence" could be given on Dulles' policies. Senator Green's letter to Dulles accepting the White Paper information after action on the resolution overcame this obstacle. Secondly, the presidential employment of armed forces which was authorized in the original text was changed by two amendments which provided that any such employment be "consonant with the treaty obligations of the United States and with the Constitution of the United States." Finally, the <u>aide memoire</u> formulated by Ambassador Eban and members of the State Department including Dulles, broke the final deadlock over Israeli withdrawal and the possible use of sanctions.

The Congress therefore played a substantial role in American Middle East policy during this period. First, it heavily influenced the decision to reject funding the High Dam in 1956--a decision that led directly to war. Secondly, although the Eisenhower Doctrine was clearly an administration formulation, the Senate modified its wording and would not give it final approval until certain guarantees had been given to Israel by the administration.

In addition to Dulles, several key actors emerged in the development of the doctrine. Senator Fulbright is easily identifiable as Dulles' chief critic in the Senate, although he did not see the depths of his colleagues' opposition to funding the Dam. Israeli Ambassador Eban, whose joint authorship of the aide memoire and skillful diplomacy broke the final impasse between his government and the administration, played an important role. Senator Knowland, whose opposition to both the Dam and any possible sanctions against Israel, played a pivotal role. Majority Leader Johnson's similar opposition to sanctions brought highly important additional pressure on the administration. Senator Morse's last ditch effort to eliminate any prior consent loopholes in the resolution are notable considering the later and continuing conflicts in executive-congressional relations over the war powers.

The position of Israel was quite different than either of its two European allies in the Suez War. Israel had acted under mounting threats and attacks against its vital national interests and not the essentially colonial interests that motivated Britain and France. It was therefore logical that Israel would resist withdrawal without guarantees and that its friends in the Senate would support its position under the circumstances.

Finally, the President's backing of Dulles in this policy area "from top to bottom" gave the forceful Secretary of State greatly enhanced strength in dealing with the Congress. Yet, congressional influence was surely demonstrated in the development of the Eisenhower Doctrine.

Notes

[1]John C. Campbell, Defense Of The Middle East: Problems of American Policy, rev. ed. (New York: Harper & Brothers, 1960), 33.

[2]The Fulbright and Connally Resolutions are examined in chapter II.

[3]Robert Engler, The Politics of Oil: A Study of Private Power and Democratic Directions (New York: The MacMillan Co., 1961), 209.

[4]Dulles' central role in the formation of American foreign policy and the Formosa Resolution are examined in chapter V.

[5]Washington, D.C., The White House, Minutes and Agenda of The Cabinet, 16 November 1956 and 29 March 1957.

[6]Congressional Quarterly, Inc., The Middle East: U.S. Policy, Israel, Oil and The Arabs, A Contemporary Affairs Report, 4th ed. (Washington, D.C.: Congressional Quarterly, Inc., 1979), 37.

[7]Moshe Sharett, Yeoman Ishi (Personal Diary) (Tel Aviv: Sifriyat Maariv, 1980), 4: 1180-88, as cited in Avi Shlaim, "Conflicting Approaches To Israel's Relations With The Arabs: Ben Gurion And Sharett, 1953-1956," The Middle East Journal 37 (Spring 1983): 193.

[8]David Ben-Gurion, Israeli: A Personal History (Tel Aviv: American Israel Publishing Co., 1971), 449.

[9]Chester L. Cooper, The Lion's Last Roar: Suez, 1956 (New York: Harper & Row, 1978), 95. Cooper was an assistant to Central Intelligence Agency Director Allen Dulles. Beginning in 1955 he acted as a liaison between the American and British analytical intelligence services.

[10]Cooper, The Lion's Last Roar, 94.

[11]Congressional Record, 85th Cong., 1st sess., 1957, 103, pt 11: 14706; Cooper, The Lion's Roar, 96.

[12]See references in previous chapter and Cooper, The Lion's Roar, 95.

[13]Ambassador Abba Eban, recorded interview, Rehovot, Israel, 28 May 1964, The John Foster Dulles Oral History Project, Princeton University Library, 30-31.

[14]Townsend Hoopes, for instance, describes cotton proponents as "most curious" in The Devil and John Foster Dulles: The Diplomacy of the Eisenhower Era (Boston: Little, Brown & Company, 1973), 331; cotton export figures in the National Advisory Commission on Food and Fiber, Cotton and other Fiber problems and Policies in the United States (Washington, D.C.: U.S. Government Printing Office, 1967), 113. On southern representation see Donald R. Matthews, U.S. Senators And Their World (New York: W.W. Norton & Company, Inc., 1973), 165.

[15]London Star quote and reference to British economic interests in Cooper, The Lion's Roar, 107.

[16]Peres' assessment in Major-General Moshe Dayan, Diary Of The Sinai Campaign (New York: Harper & Row, 1966), 25.

[17]Robert H. Ferrell, ed., The Eisenhower Diaries (New York: W. W. Norton, 1981), 330-31; Eban, recorded interview, 33-34, Lawson's cable as referred to by Eban.

[18]Cooper, The Lion's Roar, 167; Eban, recorded interview, 36.

[19]The Memoirs of Richard Nixon, 2 vols. (New York: Warner Books, 1978), 1: 166; Engler, The Politics of Oil, 260.

[20]Minutes of the Cabinet, 16 November 1956. On 10 November the Soviet Union warned that it would allow Russian volunteers to join Egyptian forces if a withdrawal did not take place.

[21]Engler, The Politics of Oil, 261.

[22]Text of resolution as passed by Congress in U.S. Congress, House, Collective Defense Treaties, H. Doc., 90th Cong., 1st sess., 1967, 199. Genesis of Article 51 explained in author's "Senator Vandenberg, Bipartisanship and the Origin of United Nations Article 51," Mid-America: An Historical Review 60 (October 1978): 163-69.

[23]As quoted in Sherman Adams, Firsthand Report: The Story of the Eisenhower Administration (New York: Harper & Brothers, 1961), 271-72.

[24]Walter Johnson, ed., The Papers of Adlai E. Stevenson: Toward a New America, 1955-1957, 8 vols. (Boston: Little, Brown & Company, 1976), 6: 402-3. Democratic-Liberal Senator Herbert H. Lehman of New York had referred to the Formosa Resolution as a "blank check" in a Senate speech two years earlier.

[25]Adams, Firsthand Report, 272. For full text of Eisenhower Doctrine see Appendix E. Text quoted from, Public Papers Of The President Of The United States: Dwight D. Eisenhower, 1957 (Washington, D.C.: Federal Register Division, National Archives and Records Service, General Services Administration, 1958), 6-16.

[26]The Times (London), 7 January 1957, 9.

[27]New York Times, 11 January 1957, 1, 4.

[28]Dwight D. Eisenhower, The White House Years: Waging Peace, 1956-1961, 2 vols. (New York: Doubleday & Company, Inc., 1965), 2: 180-81.

[29]New York Times, 12 January 1957, 1, 6.

[30]Ibid., 15 January 1957, 1, 11.

[31]Ibid., 24 January 1957, 1, 13.

[32]Author interview with Sherman Adams in Hanover, New Hampshire, 14 November 1967.

[33]Author interview with Carl Marcy, Washington, D.C., 12 December 1967.

[34] Ibid.; see Stevenson letter dated 24 January 1957, to Fulbright and reference to Senator's response in The Papers of Adlai E. Stevenson, 6: 434-35.

[35] Senator Jacob K. Javits, recorded interview, Washington, D.C., 2 March 1966, The John Foster Dulles Oral History Project, Princeton University Library, 12-15.

[36] Hearings before the Senate Committees on Foreign Relations and Armed Services on S. J. Res. 19 & H. J. Res. 117, The President's Proposal On The Middle East, 85th Cong. 1st sess., 1957, 216-19.

[37] Ibid., 268-69.

[38] New York Times, 26 January 1957, 1, 8; Adams, Firsthand Report, 274.

[39] New York Times, 26 January 1957, 8.

[40] Ibid., 28 January 1957, 1, 3.

[41] Adams, Firsthand Report, 274; full text of Senator Green's letter dated 29 January 1957, reprinted in Cong. Rec.., 103, pt 11: 14702.

[42] Adams, Firsthand Report, 275; New York Times, 31 January 1957, 8.

[43] Herman Finer, Dulles Over Suez: The Theory and Practice Of His Diplomacy (Chicago: Quadrangle Books, 1964), 478.

[44] New York Times, 2 February 1957, 1; Finer, Dulles Over Suez, 469.

[45] Ibid., 470.

[46] Ibid., 475.

[47] Eban, recorded interview, 41; New York Times, 12 February 1957, 1.

[48] Ibid., 14 February 1957, 1, 6.

[49] Ibid., 15 February 1957, 6.

[50]Finer, *Dulles Over Suez*, 476-77.

[51]Eban, recorded interview, 43-44.

[52]Adams, *Firsthand Report*, 280-82.

[53]Ibid., 283-86.

[54]Ibid., 286-87; Eban, recorded interview, 44-45; Finer, *Dulles Over Suez*, 486-87.

[55]*Cong. Rec.*, 103, pt 2: 2800-02.

[56]Ibid., 3121-29.

[57]*New York Times*, 8 March 1957, 2. For full text of resolution see Appendix F. Text quoted from, U.S. Congress House, *Collective Defense Treaties*, H. Doc., 90th Cong., 1st sess., 1967, 199.

VII

KENNEDY AND THE CONGRESS:

THE NUCLEAR TEST BAN TREATY, 1963*

The continuing quest for nuclear disarmament remains of central importance to national state survival in general and Soviet-American relations in particular. The administration of John F. Kennedy produced a milestone in that quest--the Limited Nuclear Test Ban Treaty of 1963. Yet, its successful conclusion was constitutionally dependent upon senatorial consent. How that consent was achieved and the particular role of bipartisanship is the subject of the following case study.

Early Attempts

Congressional suspicion and conflict with executive efforts to negotiate limitations on nuclear arms has been a recurring pattern since the inception of atomic weaponry. As early as December 27, 1945, when American Secretary of State James Byrnes, British Foreign Secretary Ernest Bevin and Soviet Foreign Minister Vyacheslav Molotov issued a communique from Moscow with

---

*Author's "Kennedy and the Congress: The Nuclear Test Ban Treaty, 1963" was originally published as Chapter 2 in JOHN F. KENNEDY: The Promise Revisited, Paul Harper and Joann P. Krieg, Eds. (Contributions in Political Science, No. 219, Greenwood Press, Inc., Westport, CT, 1988). Copyright (c) 1988 by Hofstra University. Subtitles have been added for this volume.

several proposals including the exchange of basic atomic energy information for peaceful purposes, Republican foreign policy spokesman Senator Arthur H. Vandenberg of Michigan "nearly resigned" as a United States delegate to the United Nations General Assembly.[1] Vandenberg's near revolt was due to his disagreement with Secretary Byrnes about when the sharing of atomic energy secrets should take place and his understanding of what bipartisan consultation means--consultation prior to the implementation of policy, not simply to be informed about impending developments. Vandenberg did not resign because President Harry S. Truman subsequently agreed with the Republican Senator's position that adequate arrangements for security must accompany each stage of disclosure regarding atomic information.[2]

The Baruch Plan of 1946 did in fact include such assurances on disclosure. This plan, which was put forward by Bernard Baruch, U.S. Representative on the U.N. Atomic Energy Commission, called for the placing of all atomic resources under an international authority. However, all countries were required to submit to inspection by the authority--a provision insisted upon by Vandenberg in a public exchange of telegrams with Baruch before he was confirmed by the Senate as U.S. Representative on the Atomic Energy Commission. The Soviet Union offered a counter-proposal with more restricted verification provisions and the Baruch Plan was not implemented.[3]

During the fall of 1949 President Truman announced that the Soviet Union had detonated a nuclear bomb and by 1952 the United States had successfully tested a hydrogen bomb. The following year the Soviet Union announced that they too had detonated a hydrogen bomb. The nuclear arms race between the super powers was spiraling in the absence of agreement and the United States clearly no longer possessed a nuclear monopoly.

As public concern mounted over increasing radioactive fallout from testing in the atmosphere, the Soviet Union initiated an effort in May, 1955, to bring about an agreement ending nuclear tests. The Soviet proposal was at first linked to an overall disarmament agreement to reduce conventional forces, but by late 1955 their proposal had dropped its linkage aspects and sought a separate test ban. For the next three years, however, the administration of Dwight D. Eisenhower and the governments of Britain and France insisted upon linking a test ban with other disarmament proposals such as safeguards against surprise attack.[4]

During the presidential election year of 1956 the test ban became an issue. The Democratic party's nominee for President, Adlai E. Stevenson, proposed that all further testing of hydrogen bombs by the powers that possessed them should cease. According to Stevenson in a nationwide television address on October 15, 1956, his reasons included the fact that "testing of an H-bomb anywhere can be quickly detected." He also added: "with every explosion of a superbomb huge quantities of radioactive material are pumped into the air currents of the world at all altitudes - later to fall to earth as dust or in rain."[5]

Shortly thereafter Soviet Premier Nikolai A. Bulganin in a letter to President Eisenhower dated October 17, 1956, argued in favor of an immediate agreement because, ". . . any explosion of an atomic or hydrogen bomb cannot in the present state of scientific knowledge, be produced without being recorded in other countries." However, Eisenhower continued to insist upon additional verification--even for possible hydrogen bomb tests.[6]

The Democratic Party platform for 1956 did not specifically state its support for a test ban proposal, but it did pledge the party to "pursue vigorously this great goal of enforced disarmament." The Republican platform simply approved President Eisenhower's "determined resistance to disarmament without effective inspection." The President's easy defeat of Stevenson in the November election temporarily ended the quest for a limited test ban agreement. Yet, Stevenson's endorsement of a limited nuclear test ban had broken new ground on the American side.[7]

By the next presidential election year growing fear of nuclear war and radioactive fallout brought both party platforms in line with one another on the test ban issue. The Democratic platform called for proposals to end "nuclear tests under workable safeguards, cutting back nuclear weapons, reducing conventional forces, preserving outer space for peaceful purposes," and the establishment of a "national peace agency" to develop data for disarmament negotiations.

The Republicans declared their readiness "to negotiate and to institute realistic methods and safeguards for disarmament, and for the suspension of nuclear tests."[8]

However, the Eisenhower Administration was not without an important first, post-World War II arms limitation agreement to its credit. On December 1, 1959, the representatives of twelve countries signed the Antarctic Treaty in Washington, D.C., which would internationalize and demilitarize the seventh continent. It accomplished the latter by specifically forbidding military bases, maneuvers and fortifications, "as well as the testing of any type of weapons" on the frozen continent.[9]

Senate approval was not, however, easily obtained even though disarming Antarctica did not mean dismantling installations, but rather prohibiting their introduction. Senate debate on the Antarctic Treaty culminated on August 10, 1960, when 66 yeas versus 21 nays (13 members not voting) were recorded and the resolution of ratification was approved. The sizable number of nays came from a combination of conservative Republicans and southern Democrats who were concerned with the question of national claims on the continent coupled with a basic mistrust in the international administration of the treaty. Prophetically, conservative Republican Senator and future presidential nominee Barry Goldwater of Arizona voted against approval; Democratic Senator and future President John F. Kennedy of Massachusetts voted for its ratification.[10]

Kennedy's Efforts

John F. Kennedy's efforts to obtain a nuclear disarmament treaty with the Soviet Union began almost immediately upon his becoming the 35th President of the United States. Of specific significance was that the process which achieved this goal for the administration was bipartisanship.

According to presidential aide Theodore Sorensen, Kennedy "sincerely believed in a test ban treaty." To that effect he asked the distinguished Republican statesman John J. McCloy to head up a new negotiating effort at Geneva to see if a treaty could be put forward that both the United States and Great Britain could sign and had a real opportunity to be approved by the Soviet Union. A renewed effort was put forward, but failed over Soviet insistence that a "Troika" be the form of any inspection team which would require unanimous agreement - a position unacceptable to the United States.[11]

Nuclear testing, which neither the Soviet Union nor the United States had carried out for three years, was resumed by the U.S.S.R. in the atmosphere during September, 1961, and underground by the U.S. shortly thereafter. Kennedy's response to the resumption of Soviet nuclear testing had been carefully measured despite conflicting advice which ranged from a "wait and see attitude" from the State Department to a suggestion that the U.S. "wipe out the Soviet test site, presumably through a nuclear air attack." Politically, however, he felt he must respond for reasons of world public opinion and "for reasons of the American Congress. . . ."[12]

Yet, the year 1961 did not end without the fulfillment of at least one of the Democratic Party's stated disarmament objectives in its 1960 platform--the establishment of the U.S. Arms Control and Disarmament Agency. Remarking upon its formation, Kennedy noted the two-party support it had received in the Congress: "I am pleased and heartened by the bipartisan support this bill enjoyed in the Congress. The leaders of both political parties gave encouragement and assistance." He also announced that the first Director would be William Foster, who Kennedy added, "is a Republican, and I think his appointment indicates the bipartisan, national concern of both parties - and really, in a sense, all Americans - for this effort to disarm mankind with adequate safeguards."[13]

The Cuban Missile Crisis of October, 1962, dramatically demonstrated to the entire world the distinct possibility of a nuclear holocaust. Soon thereafter on November 4th, the President announced the conclusion of present U.S. atmospheric tests in the Pacific (the U.S. announced its resumption of atmospheric tests in March, 1962). Although Kennedy added that underground tests were continuing in Nevada, he expressed the hope that in the near future "we can conclude an effective test ban treaty, so that the world can be free from all testing." In addition, the President's correspondence with Soviet Premier Nikita S. Khrushchev, which began during late 1961, also gave further impetus toward a test ban treaty. In a December 19, 1962, letter to Kennedy the Soviet Premier told the President that the moment head arrived "to put an end once and for all to nuclear tests, to draw a line through such tests."[14]

Clearly, a convergence of interests was developing between the Soviet Union and the United States on the nuclear disarmament issue which was spurred on by the near nuclear holocaust of October, 1962. Kennedy further demonstrated this convergence by making it clear to his Arms Control and Disarmament Agency Director that he sought a test ban treaty for two reasons: its meaning to the arms race and the role of the Peoples Republic of China. While not directly quoting from his correspondence with Khrushchev, he made it clear to National Security Council members that the Soviet Union was thinking along the same lines regarding China, i.e., a test ban treaty would reduce the possibility that the Peoples Republic would become a nuclear power.[15]

Congressional Doubts

Congressional acceptance of a test ban treaty was, however, lagging behind on the question of verification. Conversations between influential Democratic Senator Henry Jackson of Washington and the President had been discouraging. Democratic Senator Richard Russell of Georgia doubted the Soviet Union would ever agree to an acceptable system of inspection and the hardline antiCommunist Democratic Senator from Connecticut, Thomas Dodd, complained that the current administration draft of a test ban treaty lacked sufficient safeguards.[16]

However, Kennedy's efforts toward a test ban treaty continued and the verification problem was partially solved by a Khrushchev statement in an interview with Norman Cousins, the Editor of Saturday Review, on April 12, 1963. Khrushchev told Cousins that he knew an agreement with the United States could be obtained if the Soviet Union accepted three on-site inspections which in his view were not necessary as adequate policing could be achieved from outside Soviet borders. However, he added, "the American Congress has convinced itself that on-site inspection is necessary and the President cannot get a treaty through the Senate without it. Very well, then let us accommodate the President."[17]

Khrushchev's accommodation did not produce immediate results because haggling continued between the two superpowers over the inspection issue. Yet, Kennedy knew a test ban treaty was not obtainable and the Senate gave his effort a boost on May 27, 1963, when Senator Dodd reversed his earlier position and introduced a sense of the Senate resolution "banning all tests that contaminate the atmosphere or the oceans."[18]

The resolution received bipartisan support with a total of thirty-four senators (mostly Democrats) acting as co-sponsors. It neatly skirted the verification issue by noting: "Whereas all tests that contaminate the atmosphere or the oceans can be effectively monitored and requires no on-site inspection apparatus. . . ." Thus, the probable parameters of an acceptable treaty in the Senate were defined. Yet, at the next day's session Democratic Senator John Stennis of Mississippi urged a cautious approach upon his colleagues from his position as Chairman of the Preparedness Investigating Subcommittee which was conducting closed hearings on nuclear test ban proposals. Stennis believed the Senate should first "have available to it essentially the same body of detailed evidence which is available to the Executive branch" in determining its own position.[19]

Within two weeks President Kennedy was finalizing his plans to make a major foreign policy speech. In this effort he consulted with Senate Majority Leader Mike Mansfield of Montana. In fact, Kennedy invited Mansfield to join him on a short trip to Hawaii just before he was to give the speech and the Majority Leader recalled talking "this matter over with me on the plane coming back from Honolulu." Mansfield agreed with Kennedy's idea for the speech which was "more exploratory," according to the Senator.[20]

The address Kennedy delivered at American University on June 10, 1963, is generally considered his most important public statement on foreign policy and the search for peace. He called for a "fresh start" in the negotiations to end nuclear testing, announced that high level discussions would begin shortly in Moscow on a comprehensive test ban treaty and pledged that the

U.S. would not be the first to resume atmospheric tests. The President also emphasized the common interests of both countries in ending the arms race by observing that "in the final analysis, our most basic common link is that we all inhabit this small planet. We all breath the same air. We all cherish our children's future. And we are all mortal."[21]

Khrushchev's reaction to the President's speech was positive. On June 20, 1963, the United States and the Soviet Union agreed to establish a Direct Communications Link or "Hot Line" between Washington and Moscow. On July 2, 1963, Khrushchev called for an agreement that did not include underground tests, but was limited to environments that both sides could effectively check with existing verifications systems. These environments were underwater, the atmosphere and in outer space. Khrushchev's new proposal was similar to the sense of the Senate resolution introduced on May 27th and presumably acceptable to the administration since an Anglo-American proposal of one year earlier (rejected by the Soviet Union) also did not include underground tests.

In an undated letter to Attorney General Robert F. Kennedy, Khrushchev would later remark that the President's speech at American University "can be called courageous and more realistic than what the Soviet Union and other countries of the socialist world often heard from American shores." He also added: "Regretfully, only a few months had passed since President John F. Kennedy made this important statement, and he was no more."[22]

Congressional reaction was not, however, totally supportive of Kennedy's speech. Of particular importance was the immediate reaction of Senate Republican Minority Leader Everett McKinley Dirksen of Illinois. Dirksen questioned Kennedy's wisdom in dealing with the Russians whom he believed you could not trust. In addition, he and House Republican Minority Leader Charles Halleck issued a joint statement that the treaty proposed by the administration might mean "virtual surrender" by the United States.[23]

Dirksen's power in the Senate was recently secured by his own re-election. In addition, the less assertive role Majority Leader Mansfield played as compared with his predecessor, Lyndon B. Johnson, who was now Vice President, heightened Dirksen's influence. It was also believed that the power vacuum left in the Senate by Johnson's election to the Vice Presidency would be filled by the aggressive Democratic Senator and oil millionaire from Oklahoma, Robert Kerr, who has been characterized as "one of the most ruthless politicians ever to enter the Senate." However, Kerr suffered a heart attack during mid-December, 1962, and died shortly thereafter with the result that Dirksen emerged as the dominant leader, albeit on the minority side.[24]

A Bipartisan Strategy

Kennedy nevertheless moved quickly to involve Senate Republicans in the upcoming three-power meeting in Moscow. He was determined to have a bipartisan representation for the Test Ban Treaty signing and he was successful in this endeavor. Republican Senator Leverett Saltonstall of Kennedy's home state was one of two Republican members of the Senate to accept the administration's offer to go to Moscow. Secretary of State Dean Rusk asked Saltonstall, the ranking Republican member of the Armed Services Committee, to go and he in turn discussed it with Minority Leader Dirksen and the ranking Republican member of the Senate Foreign Relations Committee, Bourke B. Hickenlooper of Iowa. Actually, both Dirksen and Hickenlooper had already been invited to Moscow, but they declined wishing to preserve their independence.[25]

According to the Bay State Senator, ". . . I think they personally questioned the wisdom of Republicans going," but expressed no objections. Saltonstall went and later described it as ". . . one of the most important meetings that I have had in my lifetime. I assume that that came about with President Kennedy's assent, although I did not talk personally with him about it."[26]

The administration's bipartisan strategy emerged more clearly when the senior Republican Senator from Vermont and second-ranking Republican on the Foreign Relations Committee, George D. Aiken, was also invited. The administration clearly wanted the highest ranking Republican members available from the most important Senate committees concerned with approval of the Test

Ban Treaty to be included in the American delegation to Moscow.

The concern with which the administration approached Aiken is evident based upon his own recollection. The Vermont Senator recalled receiving "a call from the White House asking if I would be willing to go to Moscow with a delegation, and intimating that--very strongly--that no effort would be made to send a delegation unless I went." Also, according to Aiken, "The President didn't want a delegation unless it was bipartisan."[27]

Senate Majority Leader Mansfield had been delegated to call Aiken immediately following a leadership meeting and he wanted to be sure that Aiken would accept the offer to go to Moscow. Mansfield started the conversation by saying: "Don't say 'no,' don't say 'no,' don't say 'no,'" until he could explain the situation to Aiken. Then, according to the Vermont Senator, ". . . he finally convinced me that it was important that I should go, and although I would have given most anything not to have gone, I did agree to go. And we did have a bipartisan committee of Senators go over there."[28]

The final U.S. delegation attending the signing ceremony in Moscow included six senators; two Republicans and four Democrats. All six senators were in foreign policy leadership positions. In addition to Saltonstall and Aiken on the Republican side, Democratic Senator John O. Pastore from Rhode Island, Chairman of the Joint Committee on Atomic Energy, plus J. William Fulbright of Arkansas, Hubert H. Humphrey of Minnesota and John Sparkman of Alabama--the three ranking Democrats on the Foreign Relations Committee--were included. Also joining the delegation was U.N. Ambassador Adlai E. Stevenson who had made the test ban a national issue in 1956. Stevenson's inclusion was a further indication of the administration's desire for unity on the treaty.

Conspicuous by their absence in the delegation were members of the important Senate Armed Services Committee. According to Kennedy's Chairman of the Atomic Energy Commission, Glenn T. Seaborg, who was also included in the U.S. delegation to Moscow, "none of its Democratic members were willing to attend," thus, according to Seaborg, "presaging the hostility of the Armed Services Committee toward the treaty."[29]

Nine days after the American delegation left for Moscow aboard Air Force One at 11:00 p.m. on August 2, 1963, a State Department memorandum was sent from Abram Chayes, the Department's legal adviser, to Under Secretary of State George W. Ball expressing concern over the words "or any other nuclear explosion," in Article I of the already initialed, but not yet formally signed Test Ban Treaty. Chayes' concern was that the wording "could be construed as prohibiting any use of nuclear weapons in self-defense against armed attack." This interpretation, according to Chayes, would be "an obvious target for attack in the Senate during the ratification process." He suggested several recommendations including a protocol that would state: "Nothing in this treaty shall impair the right recognized in Article 51 of the Charter of the United Nations."[30]

Ball immediately accepted Chayes' recommendation for a protocol which he restated as "Nothing in this treaty shall impair the right of individual or collective self-defense against armed attack recognized in Article 51 of the Charter of the United Nations." He informed McGeorge Bundy, White House special assistant for national security affairs, of these developments and that Chayes had been asked to draft a telegram to the head of the U.S. delegation, W. Averell Harriman, "instructing him to try to negotiate such a protocol." Harriman raised the issue with Andrei Gromyko, the Soviet Foreign Minister, who objected to any word changes observing that the treaty's terms related only to nuclear tests. Harriman tended to agreed with Gromyko and the matter was dropped. However, former Presidont Eisenhower's later call for a reservation on this very point gave the administration considerable concern. The Limited Nuclear Test Ban Treaty was signed on August 5, 1963, in Moscow.[31]

President Kennedy's attention to Senate prerogatives remained constant throughout the effort to secure the treaty. According to Seaborg: "At each turn in the road he and leading members of the administration had been scrupulous about informing and consulting with Senate leaders." Secretary of State Rusk briefed the Armed Services and Senate Foreign Relations Committees as well as the Joint Committee on Atomic Energy while negotiations were progressing in Moscow. Rusk, Harriman and Adrian Fisher, of the Arms Control and Disarmament Agency, conducted a further series of briefings after the treaty was signed. The President "also played the leading role in orchestrating the presentations of administration witnesses before the Foreign Relations Committee," including his own, according to Seaborg. In sum, the Chairman of the Atomic Energy Commission has stated: "Kennedy threw himself into the ratification process with every resource available to him."[32]

On August 8, 1963, President Kennedy transmitted in a Special Message the treaty banning nuclear weapons tests in the atmosphere,in outer space and underwater "with a view to receiving the advice and consent of the Senate to ratification." In his message Kennedy listed ten considerations for his former colleagues to carefully consider. They included an assurance that there were no secret agreements made at Moscow: "This Treaty is the whole agreement. United States negotiators in Moscow ere instructed not to make this agreement conditional upon any other understanding, and they made none." The President also noted that the treaty "cannot be amended without the consent of the United States, including the consent of the Senate."[33]

Of special interest was the tenth and last consideration which was totally devoted to the executive-congressional relationship and the role of bipartisanship. It began by noting that the treaty "is the product of the steady effort of the United States Government in two Administrations, and its principles have had the explicit support of both great political parties." Kennedy also reminded his former colleagues that the platforms of both political parties in 1960 contained pledges that the treaty carried out and that a nuclear test ban was consistent "with the Resolution introduced in the Senate, with wide bipartisan support in May of 1963."[34]

Despite the President's persuasive arguments in favor of Senate approval, Stennis' Preparedness Subcommittee submitted a negative report to the Senate on the treaty the same day debate was scheduled to begin. The subcommittee report was signed by Democratic Senators Stennis, Henry M. Jackson of Washington, Strom Thurmond of South Carolina and Stuart Symington of Missouri. Republican signers were Senators Barry Goldwater of

Arizona and Margaret Chase Smith of Maine. Although Symington had signed the report he added a statement indicating that he would vote for the treaty. Republican Senator Saltonstall, who was also a member of the subcommittee, did not sign the report.[35]

Kennedy's bipartisan strategy was already reaping important dividends. Senator Saltonstall's defection from the subcommittee report may reasonably be linked with his invited participation in the Moscow delegation which returned from the Soviet Union during the first week in August.

The actual hearings on the Test Ban Treaty began on August 12th and were conducted before the members of the Foreign Relations, Atomic Energy and Armed Services Committees, plus other senators who chose to sit in. The hearings took eleven days; it included the testimony of forty-four witnesses with 1,010 pages, including appendices, officially recorded. Of the witnesses, eleven were from the administration, seventeen represented organized interest groups and the rest were private individuals who wished to testify before the combined committees. The first two witnesses were Secretary of State Rusk and Secretary of Defense Robert McNamara. Their testimony made up one-fifth of the record of the hearings and on-the-scene observers believed that McNamara's testimony was the most significant part of the hearings in general.[36]

Probably the most important part of McNamara's testimony dealt with his ability to blunt, if not refute outright, the anti-treaty argument of Dr. Edward Teller--the scientist known as the Father of the Hydrogen Bomb. Teller's position was that the treaty would weaken U.S. defenses by eliminating its right to test an antiballistic missile system (ABM) in the atmosphere under the circumstances it would, if necessary, be used. Senator Goldwater queried McNamara on this point during the second day of the hearings. Goldwater's central question and McNamara's answer were recorded as follows:

> If you were asked to develop an ABM system for this country, and you turned your scientists loose on it, and you went to the manufacturers with their recommendations, and you

> finally had the completed weapon all ready to go, could you say to the President of the United States that we have an ABM that will work without having tested it in the atmosphere?
>
> Secretary McNamara. Yes, sir--with the knowledge that I now have, based on prior tests, I could.[37]

Senator Barry Goldwater had become a national political figure by 1963. With the defeat of former Vice President Richard Nixon in this bid for the California Governor's office in 1962, Goldwater emerged as a probable candidate for his party's 1964 presidential nomination. In fact, during the summer and early fall of 1963, work continued at the precinct, county and state convention levels by the Draft Goldwater Committee, although it did so without any help from either the Arizona Republican or his campaign manager.[38]

Goldwater's view of McNamara's defense policies was very negative. While President Kennedy believed, according to the Senator, that the Secretary was providing a strong capability for national defense, he thought instead that "McNamara was deliberately and systematically reducing our defense posture in pursuit of parity with the Russians."[39]

Yet Goldwater's opposition to the Test Ban Treaty was not an easy decision for him to make according to then Majority Leader Mansfield who recalled the Arizona Senator "really being torn--and I mean that sincerely--as to what he should do." Although Goldwater told Mansfield that he wanted to vote for the test ban, he was also concerned about some advice he had received from Stanford University raising questions about the treaty. In the end, according to Mansfield, Goldwater "made up his mind to vote against it, but I think he went through a real struggle and the advice of some of those friends of his may have been the decisive factor."[40]

Of particular significance was the testimony of General Maxwell Taylor, Chairman of the Joint Chiefs of Staff on August 15th. Taylor's well prepared testimony stated the criteria upon which the Joint Chiefs had reviewed the treaty and noted the consultation that followed with government officials and technicians to determine whether or not the treaty met the criteria. He then recommended four safeguards which the Joint Chiefs thought necessary:

> (a) The conduct of comprehensive, aggressive, and continuing underground nuclear test programs designed to add to our knowledge and improve our weapons in all areas of significance to our military posture for the future.
>
> (b) The maintenance of modern nuclear laboratory facilities and programs in theoretical and exploratory nuclear technology which will attract, retain, and insure the continued application of our human scientific resources to these programs on which continued progress in nuclear technology depends.
>
> (c) The maintenance of the facilities and resources necessary to institute promptly nuclear tests in the atmosphere should they be deemed essential to our national security or should the treaty or any of its terms be abrogated by the Soviet Union.
>
> (d) The improvement of our capability, within feasible and practical limits, to monitor the terms of the treaty, to detect violations, and to maintain our knowledge of Sino-Soviet nuclear activities, capabilities and achievements.

Taylor then stated that if the safeguards were established any risks inherent in the treaty were acceptable.[41]

At his August 20th news conference President Kennedy expressed his support for the safeguards. Actually, Kennedy had met both individually and collectively with the Chiefs during July before the Foreign Relations Committee hearings began and according to Seaborg: "The president's support of the four safeguards probably also had its genesis at this time."[42]

However, former President Eisenhower submitted a requested written statement to Senator Fulbright, Chairman of the Foreign Relations Committee, dated August 23, 1963, in which he suggested a reservation. Eisenhower's concern was evidently that the language in the first article of the treaty was ambiguous and could be interpreted as meaning that the United States was prohibited from using nuclear weapons in war--the kind of concern predicted by Abram Chayes, legal adviser to the State Department, at the time the treaty was signed in Moscow. The former Commander in Chief therefore proposed a reservation stating, "that in the event of any armed aggression endangering a vital interest of the United States, this Nation would be the sole judge of the kind and type of weaponry and equipment it would employ as well as the timing of their use."[43]

Nevertheless, on September 3rd the Foreign Relations Committee issued its report on the treaty. The committee recommended that the Senate give its consent to ratification by a 16 to 1 vote with the lone dissenter being Democratic Senator Russell B. Long of Louisiana. Thus, the Foreign Relations Committee recommendation stood in contrast with the previously reported Preparedness Subcommittee findings.[44]

Dirksen's Role

The role of Senator Everett McKinley Dirksen, Republican Minority Leader, now moved to center stage in the treaty approval process. Clearly Dirksen's role was of special significance. He had begun by opposing its ratification, but he was destined to drop his opposition and publicly endorse the Test Ban Treaty in a memorable Senate speech during the floor debate.

Dirksen had discovered belatedly that the Republican platform of 1960 did in fact advocate the suspension of nuclear testing in the atmosphere. In addition, he could clearly see majority public opinion favoring ratification and he was influenced further by Fulbright's August 26th announcement that Eisenhower supported the treaty with one reservation. Dirksen therefore proposed a meeting with the President regarding the treaty and an appointment was arranged by Majority Leader Mansfield and presidential Special Assistant

Lawrence O'Brien. Kennedy was at first "furious" upon learning of the appointment because Dirksen had long opposed the administration's program and also because the Senator had opposed the treaty when Kennedy thought he needed him.[45]

However, the next day (Friday), Democratic Senator Richard B. Russell of Georgia, Chairman of the Armed Services Committee, and Senator Stennis, Chairman of the Preparedness Subcommittee, announced their formal opposition to the treaty. Thus, Kennedy once again believed he might need Dirksen's support. The following Monday, September 9th, Dirksen and Kennedy met in the President's office and the Senator began by stating his fears and doubts regarding the treaty. Finally, the President realized that the Minority Leader wanted something specific and a brief exchange began with Kennedy asking:

> "You got your notes?"
> "Yes," Dirksen said.
> "Can I have them?"
> "Yes, Mr. President."

Dirksen then handed Kennedy the draft of a letter he had written which he wanted the President to send to him and Mansfield giving assurances that the nuclear weapons program would not be relaxed if the Senate approved the treaty. "The President laughed. 'It will be done' he said."[46]

The following day the Republican Minority Leader received a letter from the President in which Kennedy pledged all of the assurances Dirksen had asked. On September 11, 1963, Dirksen read the letter to the Senate in the same dramatic speech in which he completely endorsed the treaty "with no reservations whatsoever."[47] It was an important, if not critical turning point in the treaty's approval.

On September 23rd a number of amendments to the treaty were introduced in the Senate. These amendments would have had the effect of destroying the treaty by either requiring its renegotiation or because of their unacceptableness to the Soviet Union. Senator Goldwater introduced an amendment requiring that the Soviet Union first remove its military forces from Cuba before the implementation of the treaty. Another amendment introduced by Republican Senator John Tower of Texas would have delayed the treaty's implementation until the Soviet Union brought its dues bill at the United Nations up to date. Senator Tower also proposed an amendment to the treaty adding an on-site inspection provision. All of these amendments were rejected.[48]

However, one amendment was added. It was introduced by Senator Russell of Georgia, but it did not change the language of the treaty because it was an amendment to the resolution of ratification, thus avoiding any question of renegotiation. It had to do rather with the prerogatives of the Senate in the area of treaty-making, most especially the concern of many senators that the treaty might be amended by executive agreement. Russell's amendment therefore asserted the Senate's right to pass on all future amendments to the treaty. The Russell amendment was approved by a vote of 79 to 9, with 12 senators not voting.[49]

The final vote on the treaty occurred on September 24, 1963, with every able-bodied senator present. The approving vote was 80 to 19, which was thirteen votes more than the required two-thirds majority necessary for treaties. Fifty-five Democrats and twenty-five Republicans made up the eighty approving votes. Eleven Democrats and eight Republicans made up the nineteen opposing votes. With the exception of Senator Frank J. Lausche, all the Democrats who opposed the treaty were southerners. All Republican nay votes were cast by senators from western states except Margaret Chase Smith from the state of Maine. The only missing vote was that of Senator Clair Engle, Democrat, of California who was ill, but it was announced that if he were present and voting he would vote "yea."[50]

On October 7, 1963, President Kennedy signed the document of ratification for the United States in the Treaty Room of the White House. Standing immediately behind him at the ceremony was a bipartisan grouping that included Democratic Senator J. W. Fulbright and Republican Senators George Aiken and Everett Dirksen. According to Senate Majority Leader Mansfield, Kennedy regarded the treaty as a "small step." However, of most importance according to the Majority Leader, Kennedy "thought it might give mankind as a whole some hope of not being subjected to nuclear destruction or radioactive fallout."[51]

Summing Up

The road to the 1963 Test Ban Treaty had been long and arduous. Three important developments occurred during the Eisenhower Administration. First, Adlai E. Stevenson raised the issue of a test ban as part of his campaign during the 1956 presidential election. Secondly, the Antarctic Treaty excluded nuclear testing from the seventh continent and thirdly, the 1960 platforms of both political parties endorsed the ending (Democrat) or suspension (Republican) of nuclear tests.

John F. Kennedy's commitment to an arms control treaty was strong from the beginning of his administration. He established the U.S. Arms Control and Disarmament Agency during 1961 with William Foster, a Republican, as its first Director. By so doing he clearly demonstrated his determination to proceed toward an arms limitation treaty in a bipartisan manner.

The Cuban Missile Crisis of October, 1962, provided a special impetus for nuclear arms control in both Moscow and Washington. The recognition that a nuclear holocaust was a distinct possibility softened attitudes toward the difficult question of verification and within seven months Democratic Senator Dodd's sense of the Senate resolution banning tests in the atmosphere and oceans received wide bipartisan support amongst his colleagues and essentially established the parameters of a treaty acceptable to the Senate.

During June, 1963, President Kennedy made his important American University speech which called for a fresh start in Soviet-American arms limitation negotiations. In his preparation for this notable effort he consulted closely with Senate Majority Leader Mansfield before the speech was given. The subsequent high-level delegation sent to Moscow included two senior Republican Senators on the Foreign Relations and Armed Services Committees--Aiken and Saltonstall.

The administration's emphasis upon consultation with congressional foreign policy leaders and the Joint Chiefs of Staff did not slacken as the treaty negotiations ended successfully in Moscow and the Test Ban Treaty was presented to the Senate for approval. Important potential objections by the Joint Chiefs of Staff were eliminated by the President's acceptance of the four safeguards prior to the congressional testimony of General Taylor. In addition, Senator Goldwater's criticisms were successfully met by the strong, reassuring testimony of Secretary McNamara.

Republican Minority Leader Dirksen's opposition to the treaty was of special concern to the administration's effort to secure Senate approval. Yet, the Senator himself provided the road map via which he and the President could achieve consensus on the issue and John F. Kennedy was quick to seize upon Dirksen's plan. Kennedy's letter to Dirksen enabled the Senator to retain his conservative credentials amongst his constituents and like-minded colleagues in the Senate, while at the same time fall into line with his own party's 1960 platform and the majority will of the public.

Executive-congressional agreement on the 1963 limited nuclear test ban has left us with a landmark nuclear arms treaty and a successful example of how such an agreement may be approved--through bipartisanship.

Notes

[1]Vandenberg letter (excerpt) to B.E. Hutchinson, dated 29 December 1945 in, Arthur H. Vandenberg, Jr., ed., The Private Papers of Senator Vandenberg (Boston: Houghton Mifflin Company, 1952), 232.

[2]Vandenberg, Private Papers, 230, 234.

[3]United States Arms Control and Disarmament Agency, Arms Control and Disarmament Agreements: Texts and Histories of Negotiations (Washington, D.C.: U.S. Government Printing Office, 1982), 5, 6; Vandenberg, Private Papers, 235.

[4]Arms Control and Disarmament Agreements, 35.

[5]Walter Johnson, ed., The Papers of Adlai E. Stevenson, vol. 6: Toward a New America, 1955-1957 (Boston: Little, Brown & Company, 1976), 283-84.

[6]Arms Control and Disarmament Agreements, 36.

[7]Donald Bruce Johnson and Kirk H. Porter, comps., National Party Platforms: 1840-1972 (Chicago: University of Illinois Press, 1975), 525, 546.

[8]Ibid., 576, 606.

[9]Treaty text in Arms Control and Disarmament Agreements, 22-27.

[10]Congressional Record, 86th Cong., 2nd sess., 1960, 106, pt 12: 16114.

[11]Presidential Assistant Theodore Sorensen, recorded interview by Carl Kaysen, 15 April 1964, 75-76, John F. Kennedy Library Oral History Program.

[12]Ibid., 77.

[13]Public Papers Of The Presidents Of The United States: John F. Kennedy, 1961 (Washington, D.C.: Office of the Federal Register, National Archives and Records Service, General Services Administration, 1962), 626-27.

[14] Idem, Public Papers: John F. Kennedy, 1962, 821; Arthur M. Schlesinger, Jr., A Thousand Days: John F. Kennedy in the White House (Boston: Houghton Mifflin Company, 1965), 895.

[15] Herbert S. Parmet, JFK: The Presidency of John F. Kennedy (New York: The Dial Press, 1983), 310.

[16] Ibid., 311.

[17] Norman Cousins, "Notes on a 1963 Visit With Khrushchev," Saturday Review 47 (NOvember 1964), 21.

[18] See full text of resolution in Cong. Rec., 88th Cong., 1st sess., 1963, pt 7: 9483.

[19] Ibid., 9483, 9772.

[20] Senator Mike Mansfield, recorded interview by Seth P. Tillman, 23 June 1964, 30, 31, John F. Kennedy Library Oral History Program.

[21] Public Papers: John F. Kennedy, 1963, 462-64.

[22] Premier Nikita S. Khrushchev, letter to Robert F. Kennedy, Attorney General of the United States, (undated), 2, 4, John F. Kennedy Library.

[23] Neil MacNeil, Dirksen: Portrait of a Public Man (New York: The World Publishing Company, 1970), 219.

[24] Ibid., 212-13.

[25] Senator Leverett Saltonstall, recorded interview by Daniel J. Lynch, 19 November 1964, 12, John F. Kennedy Library Oral History Program; Ronald J. Terchek, The Making of the Test Ban Treaty (The Hague: Martinus Nyhoff, 1970), 145.

[26] Saltonstall, recorded interview, 12, Kennedy Library.

[27] Senator George Aiken, recorded interview by Pat Holt, 25 April 1964, 12, John F. Kennedy Library Oral History Program.

[28] Ibid., 13.

[29]Glenn T. Seaborg with the assistance of Benjamin S. Loeb and a foreword by W. Averell Harriman, Kennedy, Khrushchev and the Test Ban (Berkeley: University of California Press, 1981), 259.

[30]Chayes' memorandum, 24 July 1963, National Security File, Box No. 265, 1-2, John F. Kennedy Library.

[31]Ball memorandum, 24 July 1963, National Security File, Box 265, John F. Kennedy Library; Seaborg, Kennedy, Khrushchev and the Test Ban, 274. Development of U.N. Article 51 is examined in author's "Senator Vandenberg, Bipartisanship and the Origin of United Nations Article 51," Mid-America: An Historical Review, 60 (October 1978), 163-69.

[32]Seaborg, Kennedy, Khrushchev and the Test Ban, 264-65.

[33]Public Papers: John F. Kennedy, 1963. 622-23.

[34]Ibid., 624. Kennedy was referring to Senator Dodd's sense of the Senate resolution introduced on 27 May 1963.

[35]Mary Milling Lepper, Foreign Policy Formulation: A Case Study of the Nuclear Test Ban Treaty of 1963 (Columbus: Charles E. Merrill Publishing Company, 1971), 101.

[36]Ibid., 102-104.

[37]U.S. Congress, Senate, Committee on Foreign Relations, Hearings, Nuclear Test Ban Treaty, 88th Cong., 1st sess. (Washington, D.C.: U.S. Government Printing Office, 1963), 160.

[38]Stephen Shadegg, What Happened to Goldwater? The Inside Story of the 1964 Republican Campaign (New York: Holt, Rinehart and Winston, 1965), 66.

[39]Barry M. Goldwater, With No Apologies: The Personal and Political Memoirs of United States Senator Barry M. Goldwater (New York: William Morrow and Company, Inc., 1979), 156.

[40]Mansfield, recorded interview, 30-31, Kennedy Library.

[41]Hearings, Nuclear Test Ban Treaty, 272-76.

[42]Public Papers: John F. Kennedy, 1963, 630-31; Seaborg, Kennedy, Khrushchev and the Test Ban, 271.

[43]Full text of Eisenhower's letter in Hearings, Nuclear Test Ban Treaty, 846-48.

[44]Cong. Rec., 109, pt 12: 16217, 16270.

[45]MacNeil, Dirksen, 220-21; New York Times, 27 August 1963, 1.

[46]MacNeil, Dirksen, 221-22.

[47]Cong. Rec., 109, pt 12: 16788-91. Full text of Kennedy's letter in Appendix G. Text quoted from, Public Papers: John F. Kennedy, 1963, 669-71. Another version (unverified) of why Dirksen changed his position is told by Bobby Baker in his Wheeling and Dealing: Confessions Of A Capitol Hill Operator (New York: W. W. Norton & Company, 1978), 97-99. According to Baker a federal grand jury was about to indict Eisenhower's former aide a "Mr. Jones" for income tax evasion and the former President asked Dirksen to intercede with Kennedy to halt the indictment. Kennedy agreed, but later insisted that both Eisenhower and Dirksen endorse the treaty. "Mr. Jones" is identified as Sherman Adams by Arthur M. Schlesinger, Jr. in his Robert Kennedy And His Times (Boston: Houghton Mifflin Company, 1978), 385-87. Schlesinger has also noted that "gaps remained in the evidence" against Adams and the head of the Tax Division recommended that he not be prosecuted. However, Schlesinger adds, ". . . Eisenhower presumably did not know this, and the apparent favor may well have, for a period, restrained his criticism of his successor." Ibid., 386-87.

[48]Cong. Rec., 109, pt 13: 17113-34.

[49]Ibid., 17745-55.

[50]Ibid., 17832. Full text of treaty in Appendix H. Text quoted from, Arms Control and Disarmament Agreements, 41-43.

[51]Mansfield, recorded interview, 31-32, Kennedy Library.

VIII

NIXON VERSUS THE CONGRESS;

THE WAR POWERS RESOLUTION, 1973*

"The congressional bombing cutoff, coupled with the limitation placed on the President by the War Powers Resolution in November 1973, set off a string of events that led to the Communist takeover in Cambodia and, on April 30, 1975, the North Vietnamese conquest of South Vietnam."[1] So stated Richard M. Nixon, 37th President of the United States, in what is arguably one of the strongest indictments ever leveled by a President against the Congress in the formulation of foreign policy.

The following case study will examine the context, issues and political positions taken by leading members of the congressional and executive branches of government in the development and enactment of the War Powers Resolution, which placed restrictions upon the President's ability to "make war." A final section will summarize and evaluate why passage of this act occurred despite the President's veto.

---

*Author's, "Nixon versus the Congress: The War Powers Resolution, 1973" will be published in <u>RICHARD NIXON: A Retrospective on His Presidency</u>, Leon Friedman and William F. Levantrosser, Eds. (Contributions in Political Science, Greenwood Press, Inc., Westport, CT, 1991).

Constitutional Setting

Beginning with the Constitutional Convention of 1787 in Philadelphia where the war power was briefly discussed on August 17th, a determination was made empowering the Congress to "declare" war with the President retaining the power to "make" war as recorded:

> "To make war"
>
> Mr. Pinkney opposed the vesting this power in the Legislature. Its proceedings were too slow. It wd. meet but once a year. The Hs. of Reps. would be too numerous for such deliberations. The Senate would be the best depositary, being more acquainted with foreign affairs, and most capable of proper resolutions. If the States are equally represented in Senate, so as to give no advantage to large States, the power will notwithstanding be safe, as the small have their all at stake in such cases as well as the large States. It would be singular for one-authority to make war, and another peace.
>
> Mr. Butler. The Objections agst the Legislature lie in a great degree agst the Senate. He was for vesting the power in the President, who will have all the requisite qualities, and will not make war but when the Nation will support it.
>
> Mr. M(adison) and Mr. Gerry moved to insert "declare," striking out "make" war; leaving to the Executive the power to repel sudden attacks.[2]

The completed Constitution, therefore provided in Article I, Section 8, that the Congress "shall have the power . . . to declare War, grant Letters of Marque and Reprisal, and make rules concerning Captures on Land and Water." Letters of marque and reprisal authorized private individuals to prey upon the property and shipping of enemy nations without being considered pirates.

This practice was banned by the Pact of Paris in 1865.

In Article II, Section 2, of the Constitution, it is stated that, "The President shall be Commander in Chief of the Army and Navy of the United States. . . ." The Congress shares with the President authority over the armed forces by supplying the necessary appropriations and regulations for its governance. Nevertheless, the President's authority to "conduct" war was not in question at the Constitutional Convention as evidenced by Connecticut's change of vote on the substitution of "declare" war for "make"war as a congressional power. The Connecticut delegate had first cast one of the two votes against the substitution, but, "on the remark by Mr. King that 'make' war might be understood to 'conduct' it which was an Executive function, Mr. Elseworth gave up his objection (and the vote of Cont was changed to--ay)."[3]

The treaty power and the power to appoint ambassadors are given as shared powers to the President and the Senate and it is the sharing of these foreign policy powers, including the war power, that the eminent constitutional authority Edward S. Corwin described as "an invitation to struggle for the privilege of directing American foreign policy."[4] And struggle they have since the first administration of George Washington to the present day.

However, an historical pattern clearly emerged with reference to the war power: Declarations of war by the Congress would be infrequent--there having been only five such declarations since the inception of the Republic to the present day. Involvement of the armed forces in hostilities abroad as directed by the President and without a declaration of war would be frequent--with 199 such cases being documented for the time period 1798 to 1972, one year prior to passage of the War Powers Resolution.[5]

In addition, successive Presidents have interpreted the Commander in Chief power as one of their most important in the formulation of foreign policy and the Supreme Court has upheld their position as sole judge and responsible actor in several landmark cases. In <u>Martin v. Mott</u> (1827) the Court held that the President, when acting under the authority of a 1795 congressional act, is the only judge as to when an exigency has occurred that necessitates action by the militia.[6]

On the eve of the Civil War in Durand v. Hollins (1860), Supreme Court Justice Samuel Nelson held that naval Captain Hollins had acted correctly in 1854 when his ship bombarded a Central American port in the execution of his orders from the Commander in Chief, President Franklin Pierce, although no congressional sanction for the bombardment had been obtained. In the **Prize Cases** (1863), during the Civil War, the Court upheld President Abraham Lincoln's action in seizing blockade runners in violation of a presidential proclamation, but once again without any special legislative approval by declaring: "He (the President) does not initiate the war, but is bound to accept the challenge without waiting for any special legislative authority."[7]

In the Senate debate over the War Powers Resolution during July, 1973, both its opponents and proponents included in their arguments the positions of certain Founders during the ratification period following the Constitutional Convention of 1787. Republican Senator Barry M. Goldwater of Arizona, a former presidential candidate for his party, was the chamber's leading opponent of the resolution. Goldwater referred to Federalist No. 38 in which James Madison, the principal architect of the Constitution itself, revealed that the Framers had intentionally removed the direction of war from Congress, where it had been placed under the Articles of Confederation, because, in his words, it is -

> Particularly dangerous to give the keys of the Treasury and the command of the army into the same hands.[8]

Senator Jacob K. Javits, Republican of New York and architect of the War Powers Resolution, countered Goldwater's reference with the following excerpt from a letter of Thomas Jefferson to James Madison in 1789:

> We have already given in example one effectual check to the Dog of war by transferring the power of letting him loose from the Executive to the Legislative body, from those who are

to spend to those who are to pay.[9]

Political Context

The immediate political context in which to view the passage of the War Powers Resolution is the legislative-executive conflict over the power to conduct the Vietnam War. Yet, earlier events in the long history of conflict and cooperation between the two branches are also highly relevant and include certainly President Franklin D. Roosevelt's relations with the Congress during the World War II period. Roosevelt recognized the necessity of maintaining supply convoys to England during the summer and autumn of 1941 and he issued his famous "shoot-at-sight" order to the Navy for their protection in the North Atlantic. The President's order was issued without congressional consent, but according to Arthur M. Schlesinger, Jr. in _The Imperial Presidency_, "His choice was to go to Congress and risk the fall of Britain to Hitler or to proceed on his own. . . ."[10]

President Roosevelt was also a committed internationalist who wished to avoid the bruising and fruitless conflict that ensnared Woodrow Wilson in his epic struggle with the Senate over consent for the League of Nations following World War I. It was FDR's tactic to commit the Untied States to an international peacekeeping organization before victory was achieved. Initially, the President proceeded toward his goal without congressional involvement, but Republican Senator Arthur H. Vandenberg of Michigan "won for the Republicans the right to be consulted, and thus made bipartisanship possible."[11] The result was full congressional support for internationalism via passage of the Fulbright and Connally resolutions in 1943. Importantly, the methodology for his historic turn away from isolationism was bipartisanship.

An era of bipartisanship had begun in the formulation of U.S. foreign policy which would produce during a "brief but generative" period from the middle to the late 1940's, the hallmarks of American post-World War II foreign policy.[12] This period would end with the so-called "loss of China" issue beginning in 1949, followed by the Korean War and the onset of McCarthyism. While the bipartisan era had passed, its practice by President John F. Kennedy in 1963, played a critical role in obtaining Senate approval for the limited nuclear test ban treaty, thus demonstrating its utility for various kinds of foreign policies on the eve of the Vietnam debacle.

During early 1964, Walt W. Rostow, a presidential adviser to Lyndon B. Johnson, suggested that it would be useful to have a bipartisan congressional resolution which would give the President "discretionary authority to conduct war in Asia," similar to the Formosa Resolution obtained by President Dwight D. Eisenhower in 1955, in the eventuality that the Peoples Republic of China might attack Formosa, the Pescadores and related positions. William P. Bundy, Assistant Secretary of State for Asian and Pacific affairs, supported the congressional resolution plan and drafted one for a floor debate in June. By mid-June the President decided to postpone the congressional request until after the November presidential election because he did not wish to appear eager to expand America's military role in Vietnam before the election.[13]

While the presidential campaign between President Johnson and Republican Senator Goldwater was underway in the summer of 1964, two American destroyers reported attacks upon them by North Vietnamese PT boats in the Gulf of Tonkin. Although subsequent congressional hearings would cast a degree of doubt upon the authenticity of the attacks, the President seized the moment to gain congressional support for future military actions via the previously prepared congressional resolution.

The Tonkin Gulf Resolution that resulted was steered through the Congress, at the President's request, by Democratic Senator J. William Fulbright, Chairman of the Foreign Relations Committee. Later, Fulbright would become a severe critic of the resolution and the Vietnam War, but under his guidance it received almost complete support by the Congress with a Senate vote of 82 to 2 and a House vote of 416 to 0. The sweeping language of the joint resolution itself read in part that, "the United States is, therefore, prepared, as the President determines, to take all necessary steps, including the use of armed force, to assist any member or protocol state of the Southeast Asia Collective Defense Treaty requesting assistance in defense of its freedom."[14]

The year 1965 saw a fateful turning of the American role in the Vietnam War from that of limited involvement to major participation in numerous combat operations, accompanied by a large-scale buildup of U.S. forces on the ground, at sea and in the air. The Americanization of the war occurred despite the fact that during the previous year's election, Johnson had appeared less willing to commit American forces to the Southeast Asia imbroglio than his opponent Goldwater. By the summer of 1965, a formal declaration of war was considered by the President's top advisers, but Johnson "was afraid that it would provoke retaliation by Communist China and also provoke opposition in Congress."[15]

The remaining years of the Johnson Administration saw a developing spiral of hostility between the President and the Congress, plus ever-increasing student demonstrations against the war. Escalation of the war also continued with more and more U.S. troops embarking for Vietnam and in 1965, the ordering of a substantial air war against North Vietnam code named Operation Rolling Thunder. Casualties continued to mount with 4,000 Americans losing their lives in 1966, and the draft becoming ever more unpopular at home.

By 1967, Senate Foreign Relations Committee Chairman Fulbright was claiming that the Congress had abandoned its constitutional role in foreign policy to Presidents who acted in foreign affairs without consulting Congress.[16] On the executive branch side during the same time period, The Pentagon Papers described the administration as divided into three camps: a "dove" group led by Secretary of Defense Robert S. McNamara who wished to limit and reduce the war; a military group led by the commander in Vietnam, General William C. Westmoreland and the Joint Chiefs of Staff, who wished to widen the war; and a third group led by the President and civilian officials at the White House and State Department who took a middle of the road position.[17]

All the military and political efforts of the Johnson Administration in Vietnam received a severe jolt when 70,000 Viet Cong troops broke a late January, 1968 truce proclaimed to celebrate Tet, the lunar new year holiday, and attacked 30 provincial capitals and five major cities including Saigon. Militarily the Tet offensive was a failure for the Viet Cong and North

Vietnamese who suffered 40,000 killed. Yet, its psychological impact upon the American public and the administration was devastating. In the New Hampshire Democratic Primary during February, 1968, Senator Eugene J. McCarthy of Minnesota came close to defeating Lyndon Johnson. McCarthy's unprecedented voter strength against an incumbent President soon brought a more formidable Democratic opponent into the nomination contest --Senator Robert F. Kennedy of New York. It was all over for Johnson and on March 31, 1968, he announced a cessation of the bombing campaign against most of North Vietnam, the sending of veteran diplomat W. Averell Harriman to Paris to negotiate a peace agreement with the North Vietnamese, and his own plan to withdraw from politics.

Nixon and the War

> The main subject was Vietnam. The travail of the long war was etched on the faces around me. These were all able and intelligent men. They had wanted desperately to end the war before leaving office, but they had not succeeded.[18]

So observed President-elect Richard Nixon on his visit to the cabinet room of the White House and a meeting with Johnson's top advisers. Nixon had just accomplished one of the greatest "comebacks" in American electoral history given his defeats at the pools in 1960 for President and in 1962 for Governor of California. His 1968 presidential election had nevertheless been a narrow popular vote victory which left the Democrats in full control of the Congress. In fact, he was the first President in 120 years to assume the office with both chambers of the Congress controlled by the opposition party. He had made a significant promise to the American people upon receiving the Republican nomination: "And I pledge to you tonight that the first priority foreign policy objective of our next Administration will be to bring an honorable end to the war in Vietnam."[19] The war was now his to direct and end as Commander in Chief, but the mood in Congress was increasingly restive, assertive and critical of the war.

The withdrawal of American troops from Vietnam, already begun during the waning months of the Johnson

Administration, continued during the Nixon Administration and was clearly tied to the administration's policy of "Vietnamization." According to this policy, the United States would gradually reduce its troop strength in Vietnam while training and increasing the troop strength of the Saigon forces. Concurrent with this process would be strong diplomatic efforts to bring a negotiated peace, plus direct military pressure against North Vietnam. Under these conditions, the American withdrawal could occur in an "honorable" fashion as pledged by Nixon at the Republican nominating convention.

For Richard Nixon and his chief foreign policy adviser Henry A. Kissinger, who served as National Security Adviser during the President's first administration, the strategic significance of Vietnam as a bulwark against Chinese Communist expansion had been significantly altered by the growing Sino-Soviet rift and developing rapprochement with the Peoples Republic of China. President Nixon also redefined United States foreign policy in Asia by the enunciation of the Guam Doctrine (later called the Nixon Doctrine), on July 23, 1969. Nixon declared that in the future the United States would aid only those countries with economic and military assistance that were ready with their own military forces to defend themselves. The doctrine's emphasis upon a lower profile for U.S. military forces dovetailed well with the Nixon-Kissinger policy of Vietnamization of the Southeast Asian war.

Bringing an "honorable end to the war in Vietnam," as promised by the new President would nevertheless be very costly. As Nixon took office in January, 1969, "there were 550,000 American troops in Vietnam, 30,000 men were being drafted every month, and combat casualties were as high as 300 a week."[20] The administration's policy of gradual withdrawal of U.S. groundtroops from the high watermark established by President Johnson was not matched by a de-escalation of the air war. U.S. bombing campaigns escalated, particularly in technically neutral Cambodia which the North Vietnamese had long used to send troops into South Vietnam. These "secret" bombings were soon discovered and reported in The New York Times during March, 1969. The President then established a "Plumbers" unit to stop such leaks to the press. Eventually this decision led to a series of criminal acts by the Plumbers, especially an attempted break-in at the headquarters of the Democratic party in Washington's Watergate Hotel during 1972.[21]

But the "Side-Show"[22] in Cambodia was not over. Following a successful coup against the Cambodian leadership in early 1970, South Vietnamese and U.S. forces crossed into Cambodian territory in an effort to disrupt North Vietnamese supply lines. The administration's decision to enter Cambodia with ground forces was taken without any consultation with the Congress, even though a national frontier had been crossed (however ill-defined) by U.S. armed forces. The U.S.-South Vietnamese incursion touched off a new wave of student demonstrations and tragic incidents on American campuses and an ever deepening conflict between President and Congress. At the same time, American ground forces were continuing their slow withdrawal from Vietnam.

Congressional Assertiveness

The War Powers Resolution which eventually became public law in 1973, was passed by the Congress during a period of reform and assertiveness which roughly coincided with Richard Nixon's years in office as President of the United States. The major fueling mechanism for congressional assertiveness and reform during this period was clearly the Vietnam War. Yet, earlier incidences such as the previously noted "shoot-at-sight" orders by FDR in 1941, and the use of joint resolutions such as the Formosa Resolution, 1955, and the Tonkin Gulf Resolution, 1964, upon which to justify future war actions also played an important role.

During Nixon's first year in the White House the Senate fired an opening salvo against the presidential commitment of troops to battle without an explicit authorization from Congress. The Senate brought forward a resolution claiming that a "national commitment" could only come about through a concurrent action by the President and the Congress. The Senate resolution failed in the House, but the long march culminating in the War Powers Resolution had begun.[23]

The Cambodian incursion had acted as a lightning rod amongst anti-war members of Congress and in 1970, it attempted to ban the use of funds for operations in Cambodia via passage of the Cooper-Church amendment and the Senate repealed the 1964 Gulf of Tonkin Resolution upon which the Johnson Administration had Americanized the war. Yet, the Nixon Administration claimed in a May 30, 1970 letter to Senator Fulbright that it "does not depend on the Tonkin Gulf Resolution, as legal or constitutional authority for its present conduct of foreign relations, or its contingency plans." Instead, the President acted upon "his constitutional authority as Commander-in-Chief." From the standpoint of international law, according to the letter, "the action in Cambodia was an exercise by the United States and the Government of Viet-Nam of their right of individual and collective self-defense under Article 51 of the UN Charter."[24]

Congressional assertiveness in the foreign policy area was also expressed by passage of the Case Act in 1972 which required that executive agreements between the President and foreign governments be reported to the Congress for its information. This form of agreement, which is similar to a treaty but does not require Senate consent, had long been controversial. President Franklin D. Roosevelt had made a number of such agreements during World War II, most notably at Yalta, and a series of such agreements had been made between Washington and Saigon during the 1950's and 1960's, "promising American support for the government of South Vietnam."[25]

In the presidential election of 1972, Richard Nixon's opponent came from the U.S. Senate. Liberal Senator George McGovern of South Dakota was a strong anti-war critic and his dovish positions aided him enormously in gaining the Democratic nomination. But in the general election his strong stance against the war, which included a quick withdrawal of American troops and the refusal of future military aid to South Vietnam, became a liability. "Thus the issue that may have been McGovern's trump card in winning the nomination could only do him harm if it remained salient in the general election."[26]

The result was a Nixon triumph at the polls as American units continued to withdraw from Vietnam. Yet, the President was in a melancholy mood on his own victorious election night. In an effort to explain why, he added: "To some extent the marring effects of Watergate may have played a part, to some extent our failure to win Congress, and to a greater extent the fact that we had not yet been able to end the war in Vietnam."[27]

Independent congressional efforts to reduce the role of U.S. military forces in the war continued in the Democratic controlled Congress despite the President's strong endorsement at the polls in November. In May, 1973, a supplemental appropriations bill for the Defense Department with an attached amendment by Senator Thomas Eagleton, a Missouri Democrat, prohibiting the use of any funds for combat activities in Cambodia or Laos was passed by the Senate. By June the House had agreed to a similar language bill which President Nixon vetoed. However, the Eagleton Amendment was soon attached to other appropriations bills he could not veto without interfering with normal government operations. By the end of June the President, increasingly besieged by the unfolding Watergate scandal, accepted the Eagleton Amendment.

The War Powers Resolution

As various war power proposals were working their long way through the legislative process the American phase of the Vietnam War was finally ending. On January 11, 1973, a cease-fire agreement was reached with North Vietnam and on January 16, 1973, Richard Nixon made a commitment to South Vietnamese President Thieu that, "We will react strongly in the event that the agreement is violated." He also added his "firm intention to continue full economic and military aid."[28] However, the Congress would later cut appropriations for South Vietnam and after Nixon's resignation in August 1974, the Saigon regime was defeated during the spring of 1975.

On March 7, 1973, a House Foreign Affairs subcommittee opened hearings with both Senate and House sponsors of different war powers proposals appearing as witnesses. These hearings in the 93rd Congress would represent the final phase of the legislative effort, begun in 1969 with the Senate introduction of the National Commitment Resolution, to reassert the congressional war power.

The clear relationship of the Vietnam War to the perceived necessity for a war powers resolution to curb the Chief Executive's ability to commit American forces into hostile actions was evident in the statements of witnesses such as Democratic Representative Spark M. Matsunaga of Hawaii. According to Matsunaga, ". . . we need definite, unmistakable procedures to prevent future undeclared wars. 'No more Vietnams' should be our objective in setting up such procedures."[29]

On July 18th the House passed H J Res 542, sponsored by Wisconsin Democrat Clement J. Zablocki, leader of the war powers movement in the House. The Zablocki bill set a 120 day limit on the commitment or enlargement of American fighting forces abroad unless the Congress specifically so authorized. In addition, it would allow the Congress to terminate military commitments at any time by passage of a concurrent resolution not requiring presidential signature and thus avoiding the veto. President Nixon's opposition to both of these provisions was spelled out in a June 26th telegram sent to House Minority Leader Gerald R. Ford, a Michigan Republican and future President. Ford read aloud from the Nixon telegram on July 18th during the debate over the Zablocki bill. The President declared that he was "unalterably opposed to and must veto any bill containing the dangerous and unconstitutional restrictions."[30]

In the same telegram, however, Nixon also noted that he would "fully support the desire of members to assure Congress its proper role in national decisions of war and peace," and that he "would welcome appropriate legislation providing for an effective contribution by the Congress."[31] But as to what that "proper role" should be the President did not elaborate and Minority Leader Ford could offer almost no specifics, except that he thought the President was in "sympathy"[32] with a substitute bill offered by Indiana Republican David W. Dennis which would require approval or disapproval by the Congress within 90 days of a presidential report of U.S. involvement. The Dennis proposal was subsequently defeated on a recorded teller vote of 166-250.

The President had failed to coordinate his resistance to the Zablocki bill with representatives who were opposed, and the House Republican Policy Committee failed to agree on a Republican amendment alternative and issued no policy statement. Therefore, House opponents of the bill, whose efforts remained scattered, went down to final defeat on July 18th--despite the fact that those opposed claimed the use of a concurrent resolution to end a U.S. troop commitment was both unconstitutional and not binding on the President.[33]

In the Senate a similar pattern of Republican members either supporting their chamber's war power measure or not coordinating their opposition was repeated despite strong opposition from the President. The Senate bill (S440) was sponsored by Senators Eagleton, Javits and John C. Stennis, a Mississippi Democrat, plus 50 other senators as cosponsors. It received near unanimous approval from the Senate Foreign Relations Committee on May 17th with Senator Fulbright voting "present" and none of the Republican members voting against it. It differed from H. J. Res 542 in that it identified the emergency circumstances under which the President could commit troops and it provided a 30 day termination period for a U.S. military commitment without specific authorization, instead of 120 days as in the House version. However, the House bill would allow congressional termination of a military commitment at any time via passage of a concurrent resolution.

During the full Senate debate on S440, liberal Democrats voiced their concern that the bill was not restrictive enough. Senator Eagleton offered an amendment that would have broadened the scope of armed forces committed to include CIA or other civilian personnel because he believed "that presidential warmaking in the future will be conducted just through this loophole."[34] However, S440's floor manager, Democratic Senator Edmund S. Muskie of Maine, spoke against the amendment and it was defeated on a 34-53 roll call vote.

Republican opponents of S440 were well aware that it had strong support in the Senate given its near unanimous endorsement by the Foreign Relations Committee. Administration supporters were equally confident that President Nixon would veto S440 should it reach the White House. This knowledge probably influenced Senate Republican Minority Whip Robert P. Griffin of Michigan to withdraw his own amendment during the debate which would have established consulting procedures between the President and the Congress on questions concerning any commitment and for Congress to either approve the commitment or vote to cut off funds.[35]

A brickbat was tossed at S440 by Republican John

G. Tower of Texas who proposed an amendment to change the bill's title to read: "A bill to make rules governing the use of the Armed Forces of the United States in the absence of a declaration of war by the Congress, and thereby reduce the United States of America to the status of a second rate power."[36] Tower's proposal was ruled out of order and withdrawn. It was similar to Senator Griffin's withdrawn amendment in that it did not represent a strong or serious effort to block or modify the bill. Therefore, the only concerted Republican challenge was left to Barry Goldwater.

On July 18th Goldwater submitted a detailed list of 25 major problems with S440. Under number 25 the Conservative Republican noted that General George Washington, "was harassed, second-guessed, and over-ruled with respect to his military plans and strategy throughout the War of Independence." Therefore, according to Goldwater, "the Founding Fathers realized the Congressional control of military functions had very nearly led to disaster during the Revolutionary War. For this reason, the use of the armed forces in the defense of American rights and freedoms was left with the President as Commander in Chief."[37]

The Senate's leading proponent and cosponsor of S440, Jacob Javits, countered Goldwater's Commander in Chief argument by noting that, "out of the crisis of World War II and the ensuing cold war, lawyers for the President had spun a spurious doctrine of 'inherent' Commander-in-Chief powers--broad enough to cover virtually every 'national security' contingency that could be thought of."[38] On July 20th Goldwater further buttressed his Commander in Chief argument by having printed in the Congressional Record 199 cases of U.S. military hostilities abroad without a declaration of war from 1798 to 1972, as opposed to the five declarations of war by the Congress during the same time period. The Arizona Republican then declared that he was "convinced" that "the President does have the warmaking power under the Constitution, that the Congress' right to declare war means nothing except to declare." Furthermore, Goldwater stated to his Senate colleagues, "We can declare war every 5 minutes, but not one man will leave the shores of America until the President says so."[39]

Despite the additional support of the Senate's

recognized authority on constitutional law, Democrat Sam J. Ervin, Jr. of North Carolina, who would not support S440 because it said "expressly that the President of the United States cannot perform his constitutional duty and cannot exercise his constitutional power to protect his country against invasion for more than 30 days without the affirmative consent of Congress,"[40] the bill was passed by the Senate.

Agreement was reached by a House-Senate conference on October 4th which set a 60 day limit on any commitment of U.S. forces without a war declaration or specific congressional authorization. Also, Senate conferees agreed upon a general policy statement instead of the specific delineation of circumstances upon which the President could act without congressional authority. On October 10th the Senate approved the conference report by a vote of 75-20 with 26 Republicans and 49 Democrats voting in the affirmative and 14 Republicans and 6 Democrats voting against the report. House action on the conference report took place on October 12th. An approving vote of 238-123 was recorded with 163 Democrats and 75 Republicans supporting the compromise and 38 Democrats and 85 Republicans opposed. Thus, Republican voting opposition was clearly more evident in the House than in the Senate.[41]

Nixon versus the Congress

In President Richard Nixon's veto message of October 24, 1973, returning House Joint Resolution 542--The War Powers Resolution--to the Congress without his approval, he declared that: "The Founding Fathers understood the impossibility of foreseeing every contingency that might arise in this complex area. They acknowledged the need for flexibility in responding to changing circumstances. They recognized that foreign policy decisions must be made through close cooperation between the two branches and not through rigidly codified procedures."[42]

The President especially objected to the 60 day limit on troop commitments abroad which were not authorized by the Congress while at the same time allowing the Congress "to eliminate certain authorities merely by the passage of a concurrent resolution. . . ." According to Nixon: "I believe that both these provisions are unconstitutional. The only way in which the constitutional powers of a branch of the Government can be altered is by amending the Constitution - and any attempt to make such alterations by legislation alone is clearly without force."[43]

Nixon was also "particularly disturbed"[44] that certain of the President's powers as Commander in Chief would be automatically terminated in 60 days unless the Congress authorized an extension. His veto defense of the Commander in Chief power was consistent with previous positions taken by Republican Senator Goldwater and Democrat Sam J. Ervin, Jr.

The President, however, did not object to all of the Joint Resolution's provisions. He referred to Section 3's call "for consultations with the Congress before and during the involvement of the United States forces in hostilities" as a "constructive measure." He further stated that he would "welcome the establishment of a non-partisan commission on the constitutional roles of the Congress and the President in the conduct of foreign affairs."[45]

It was all to no avail. On November 7, 1973, the House of Representatives and the Senate voted to override the President's veto. It was the first successful override of a presidential veto in the 93rd Congress, and in the House, which was required to vote first, it was a cliff-hanger. The 284-135 House vote was only four votes more than the two-thirds majority required to override a veto by the Constitution. The vote, according to political party, was as follows: 103 Republicans voted to sustain, 86 voted to override; 198 Democrats voted to override, 32 voted to sustain of which 23 were Southern Democrats. In the Senate, where the veto was expected to be overridden, the vote was 75-18, providing a 13 vote margin beyond the two-thirds requirement.[46]

The main immediate reason for the successful override in the House was the Watergate crisis that had enveloped the Presidency. Only hours after the successful congressional override of the War Powers Resolution on November 7th, Richard Nixon ended a televised speech on the energy crisis with a direct reference to the increasing demands that he resign over Watergate: "Tonight I would like to give my answer to those who have suggested that I resign. I have no intention whatever of walking away. . . ."[47] Representative William S. Mailliard of California, who led the Republican forces in the House seeking to sustain the President's veto, believed that several weeks prior to the override vote a veto could have been sustained, but that the Watergate crisis and other matters related to the scandal had contributed to a favorable override climate.[48]

While the White House was embattled over Watergate, lobbying efforts coordinated by Americans for Democratic Action aimed their pro-resolution efforts at fifteen House liberals, many of whom believed the joint resolution gave the President too much power. The A.D.A., plus congressional supporter's efforts, paid off--on the final House vote eight of the fifteen voted in favor of the override (7 Democrats, 1 Republican).[49]

After these immediate reasons for the override in the House, a broader analysis is necessary to assess Nixon's defeat by the Congress over passage of the War Powers Resolution. Certainly the Vietnam War itself, which so poisoned executive-congressional relations during the late 1960's and into the 1970's, must be considered a major contributory reason. But any assessment of the causes of the conflict between President and Congress during the Vietnam War period must take into account two salient factors. First, the near unanimous congressional approval of the Tonkin Gulf Resolution in 1964, with its sweeping language of commitment, represented an historic foreign policy error by the legislative branch. Secondly, President Nixon's Cambodian incursion across a national frontier in 1970, without any consultation with the Congress, obviously widened the Vietnam War and greatly exacerbated the continuing feud over the war powers between President and Congress.

The War Powers Resolution must also be viewed as partially the product of a period of congressional reassertion and reform that roughly coincided with Richard Nixon's years in the White House. Congressional assertiveness not only encompassed the War Powers Resolution in 1973 but was, for instance, preceded by the Case Act in 1972, and followed by the Budget Act of 1974. The Budget Act was a legislative effort to reassert congressional control over government spending and curb the presidential impoundment of funds. This period of congressional reassertion and reform had been brewing a long time, but its culmination during the Nixon Presidency and after was fueled especially by the notion that the Presidency had become imperial, i.e., gorged with power and indifferent toward the Congress.

The Commander in Chief power of the President remains at the center of the controversy over the war power between the executive and legislative branches. The President's power to conduct war was not in question at the Constitutional Convention of 1787, and numerous Presidents have, in fact, committed the armed forces into hostile situations without declarations of war by the Congress. Indeed, the defense of the Commander in Chief power was a primary reason for Nixon's veto as stated in his message: "House Joint Resolution 542 would attempt to take away, by a mere legislative act, authorities which the President has properly exercised under the Constitution for almost 200 years."[50]

Viewing the War Powers Resolution in an historical context, it represents (especially Section 3 regarding consultation), an effort by the Congress to mandate by legislation what had been accomplished voluntarily beginning thirty years before through bipartisanship. Because bipartisanship is a process and not a policy, its utility in the formulation of various foreign policies, including the development of an alliance or a disarmament treaty, is equally germane. Bipartisanship enhances trust between President and Congress, conversely the War Powers Resolution bespeaks of mistrust on the part of the Congress toward the President--a mistrust that was certainly understandable during the Vietnam War years, but may not serve the long-range interests of U.S. foreign policy formulation.

Richard Nixon has been at least partially vindicated in his conflict with the Congress over the War Powers Resolution. In 1983 the Supreme affirmed a lower court ruling that invalidated the legislative veto provisions in hundreds of laws.[51] Section 5(c) of the War Powers Resolution provides for a legislative veto by empowering the Congress, in the absence of a war declaration or statutory authorization, to force the removal of armed forces from hostilities abroad by concurrent resolution.

Yet, Nixon must bear at least part of the responsibility for bringing about a resolution he so strongly opposed. He did not sufficiently consult with the Congress, especially during a period when his own party was in the minority in both chambers. He did not sufficiently rally Republican Representatives in the House during the struggle over the veto override--undoubtedly due to his own preoccupation with Watergate.

Notes

[1]Richard M. Nixon, RN: The Memoirs Of Richard Nixon (New York: Grosset & Dunlap, 1978), 889 (hereinafter cited as Memoirs).

[2]Max Farrand, ed., The Records Of The Federal Convention of 1787, 4 vols. (New Haven: Yale University Press, 1937), 2: 318.

[3]Ibid., see footnote, 319.

[4]Edward S. Corwin, The President: Office and Powers, 1787-1957 (New York: New York University Press, 1957), 171.

[5]See chronological list in, Congressional Record, 93rd Cong., 1st sess., 1973, 119, pt 20: 25066-74.

[6]Edward Conrad Smith, ed., The Constitution of the United States With Case Summaries (New York: Barnes & Noble Books, 1979), 96-97.

[7]Fred W. Friendly and Martha J. H. Elliott, The Constitution: That Delicate Balance (New York: Random House, 1984), 266-81; Smith, The Constitution, 97.

[8]Cong. Rec., 119, pt 20: 25077.

[9]Ibid., 25078.

[10]Arthur M. Schlesinger, Jr., The Imperial Presidency (New York: Popular Library, 1974), 118.

[11]See chap. 11, 33.

[12]See author's, "Senator Vandenberg, Bipartisanship, and the Origin of United Nation's Article 51," Mid-America: An Historical Review 60 (October 1978): 163.

[13]James E. Dougherty and Robert L. Pfaltzgraff, Jr., American Foreign Policy: FDR to Reagan (New York: Harper & Row Publishers, Inc., 1986), 227.

[14]Neil Sheehan, Hedrick Smith, E. W. Kenworthy and Fox Butterfield, The Pentagon Papers (New York: Bantam Books, Inc., 1971), 265.

[15]Amos Yoder, The Conduct of American Foreign Policy Since World War II (New York: Pergamon Press, 1986), 95.

[16]Robert A. Diamond, ed., Origins and Development of Congress (Washington, D.C.: Congressional Quarterly, Inc., 1976), 260.

[17]Pentagon Papers, 511.

[18]Nixon, Memoirs, 336.

[19]See Nixon acceptance speech in, Arthur M. Schlesinger, Jr., ed., History of American Presidential Elections, 1789-1968, 4 vols. (New York: McGraw-Hill Book Co., 1971) 4: 3834-35.

[20]Henry T. Nash, American Foreign Policy: Changing Perspectives on National Security (Homewood, Illinois: The Dorsey Press, 1978), 247.

[21]Walter LaFeber, America, Russia, and the Cold War 1945-1984 (New York: Alfred A. Knopf, 1985), 263.

[22]Quote from title of study on Cambodian aspect of Vietnam War by William Shawcross, Side-Show: Kissinger, Nixon and the Destruction of Cambodia (New York: Pocket Books, 1974), iii.

[23]James A. Nathan and James K. Oliver, Foreign Policy Making and the American Political System (Boston: Little, Brown & Company, 1983), 102.

[24]Letter from Elliot Richardson, Acting Secretary, Department of State, in Cong. Rec. 119, pt 8: 10421. U.N. Article 51 was included in the Charter at U.S. insistence. See author's, "Senator Vandenberg, Bipartisanship, and the Origin of United Nation's Article 51," Mid-America 60 (October 1978): 163-69.

[25]Cecil V. Crabb, Jr. and Pat M. Holt, Invitation to Struggle: Congress, the President and Foreign Policy (Washington, D.C.: Congressional Quarterly Inc., 1980), 13.

[26]Nelson W. Polsby and Aaron Wildavsky, Presidential Elections: Strategies of American Electoral Politics (New York: Charles Scribner's Sons, 1984), 179.

[27]Nixon, Memoirs, 717.

[28]Quoted in Yoder, Conduct of American Foreign Policy, 112.

[29]Quoted in 1973 Congressional Quarterly Almanac (Washington, D.C.: Congressional Quarterly Inc., 1974), 908.

[30]Cong. Rec., 119, pt 19: 24664.

[31]Ibid.

[32]Ibid., 24663.

[33]See 1973 Quarterly Almanac, 910-11.

[34]Quoted in, Ibid., 914.

[35]Ibid.

[36]Ibid.

[37]Cong. Rec., 119, pt 19: 24533-36.

[38]Ibid., 24537.

[39]Ibid., pt 20: 25066-78.

[40]Quoted in 1973 Quarterly Almanac, 913-14.

[41]Voting results in 1973 Quarterly Almanac, 916-17. Full text of War Powers Resolution in Appendix I. Text quoted from United States Statutes At Large 87 (1973): 555-59.

[42]See full text of Nixon's Veto Of The War Powers Resolution in Appendix J. Text quoted from Public Papers Of The Presidents Of The United States: Richard Nixon, 1973 (Washington, D.C.: Office of the Federal Register, National Archives and Records Service, General Services Administration, 1975), 893-95.

[43]Ibid.

[44]Ibid.

[45]Ibid.

[46]Voting results in 1973 Quarterly Almanac, 905.

[47]Nixon, Memoirs, 947.

[48]1973 Quarterly Almanac, 906.

[49]Ibid.

[50]See Appendix J.

[51]Immigration and Naturalization Service v. Chadha, 103 S. Ct. 2764 (1983).

IX

CONCLUSIONS AND A LOOK AT POST-VIETNAM DEVELOPMENTS

Illuminating the complex and at times conflict-ridden President-Congress relationship in the formulation of American foreign policy has been the subject of the seven consecutive case studies examined in this volume. Taken together, these studies provide us with a liberal sample of the ways in which the two branches related to each other during a thirty year time period. In addition, the wars that occurred during the time period of the first and last study, proved to be important turning points for both United States diplomacy and the executive-congressional relationship.

In 1943 during World War II, the Congress declared its resolution to end isolationism and adopt collective security as the postwar foreign policy of the American Republic. By so doing, a conflict begun one generation earlier between President and Congress over the same general issue was finally resolved and an historic new direction in U.S. diplomacy was established.

Yet, with the end of World War II in 1945, the Grand Alliance that had defeated the Axis Powers dissolved and a Cold War between the Soviet Union and the United States was soon observable. Containment of Russia and its allies became the focus of executive branch planners, largely replacing the internationalist foreign policy so recently agreed upon with the Congress. This new direction meant congressional consent would be needed to formulate and become part of entangling peace-time alliances, a foreign policy position long avoided by the United States.

Containment eventually led the United States into foreign policy commitments and situations that strained the President-Congress relationship. A major schism between the two branches finally occurred over the war power during a period of congressional reassertion. The Vietnam War had brought these strains to a head and was a major contributory reason for the breakdown in relations between the two branches--a far cry from their status 30 years earlier during World War II.

Constitutional Issues

Constitutional issues between President and Congress may be found in the initial congressional acceptance of collective security during World War II, to passage of the War Powers Resolution in 1973. During the struggle to embrace collective security in 1943, the first impulse of the Roosevelt Administration was to bypass the Congress in the establishment of a United Nations Relief and Rehabilitation Administration (UNRRA) agreement whereby the United States would participate in UNRRA via an executive agreement instead of a treaty. A strong protest by the minority Republicans in the Congress ended this effort, but the consultation procedures that then developed between the two branches established a bipartisan foreign policy approach that led directly to congressional acceptance of collective security.

Controversy over presidential use of executive agreements instead of treaties nevertheless continued. Several such agreements were made by President Franklin D. Roosevelt during World War II, with the Yalta Agreements of 1945 being an important and contentious example. During the 1950's and 1960's successive administrations made supportive agreements with South Vietnam and during the period of congressional assertiveness that followed, the Case Act became law in 1972. By that act Congress must be informed upon completion of all such agreements.

Yet, not all executive agreements are looked upon suspiciously by the Congress. An important example is the Pact of Madrid in 1953 which established U.S. ties with Franco Spain. Its objectives were sought by members of the Congress long before the Truman Administration finally relented to the establishment of formal negotiations with the Spanish Government. Therefore, the substance rather than the method of executive agreement usage remains the greater potential cause of conflict between the two branches.

The use of congressional resolutions have long been considered a useful method of achieving an expression of legislative support for administration foreign policy. However, their actual meaning has also been a source of controversy between the two branches. Senator Arthur H. Vandenberg was, for instance, well aware of the danger that supporting resolutions might be misinterpreted as actual congressional consent for executive branch foreign policy implementation. Both he and Senator Tom Connally had reassured their Senate colleagues in 1943 that the Connally Resolution was an exercise of the advice function and not the consent function; the latter being reserved for actual treaty approval. Again in 1948, Vandenberg and Under Secretary Robert A. Lovett gave the same assurance regarding the Vandenberg Resolution to members of the Foreign Relations Committee.

Clearly, Vandenberg's well-known "passionate Constitutionalism,"[1] as described by Walter Lippman, was important in calming Senate fears over possible confusion on this issue. Alas, in 1951, during a particular low point in the long Cold War, Senator Vandenberg died in office.

The use of area resolutions during the Eisenhower Administration, as devised by Secretary of State John Foster Dulles for Formosa in 1955 and the Middle East in 1957, conformed to the President's own decision-making guideline: "Don't make mistakes in a hurry and secondly, if you do, share them."[2] Yet, like the Truman Administration in 1948 when the Vandenberg Resolution was approved, the Eisenhower Administration was faced with an opposition party majority in the Congress. Therefore, despite the fact that Dwight D. Eisenhower had "friends on both sides of the aisle"[3] in the Congress, the divided government scenario he faced led his administration to depend upon supporting resolutions to insure the successful implementation of foreign policy.

Even when the executive and legislative branches are not divided by the two political parties, with one controlling the White House and the other the Congress, supporting resolutions can be very important if future policy-making requires the Senate's consent to the ratification of a treaty. The Fulbright and Connally Resolutions embracing collective security in 1943 were, for instance, sought and deemed highly important by the Roosevelt Administration in its quest to make the United States a treaty member of the evolving United Nations. Similarly, bipartisan passage of Senator Thomas Dodd's sense of the Senate Resolution in 1963 "banning all tests that contaminate the atmosphere or the oceans,"[4] was among the important supporting factors that helped assure President John F. Kennedy a test ban treaty could be achieved.

Each of these resolutions, although separated by a twenty year time span from 1943 to 1963, was approved when the congressional majority and the President were of the same political party. Yet, given the fact that political party members in Congress may, or may not, vote as a bloc for a treaty or other important external policies, Presidents naturally seek such resolutions; even though constitutionally they are an exercise of the advice function and not the consent function.

It is in the area of the war power that the question of prior consent and congressional resolutions became most conflict-ridden as evidenced in several of the case studies. Although the Constitution eloquently assigns the power "To declare War, grant Letters of Marque and Reprisal, and make Rules concerning Capture on Land and Water,"[5] to the Congress, in practice it has been the President acting as Commander in Chief who has far more often independently ordered U.S. forces into hostilities. This historical fact was clearly detailed by Senator Barry M. Goldwater in the congressional debate over the War Powers Resolution in 1973.[6] However, it was through presidential interpretation of congressional resolutions that the issue finally came to a head during the long war in Southeast Asia.

An important precursor of the impending storm between the two branches over the war power was passage of the Formosa Resolution in 1955. President Eisenhower interpreted that resolution as being tantamount to a congressional declaration of war when he gave orders to Admiral Radford "to attack Red Chinese airfields, if self-defense so required,"[7] in order to evacuate the

Tachens.

It is not as though members of the Senate were unaware of the war implications of the Formosa Resolution. Senator Wayne Morse had delivered a long speech against its approval noting that it "would legalize the position of the proponents of a preventive war."[8] Also, Senator Herbert H. Lehman had, in his opposition speech, asked the question: "Why should we write and sign this blank check?"[9] However, any broad opposition in the Senate to the Formosa Resolution was significantly reduced by the McCarthyite atmosphere still existent during the 84th Congress.

In 1964 presidential adviser Walt W. Rostow suggested to President Lyndon B. Johnson that a congressional resolution should be sought similar to the Formosa Resolution, giving the President "discretionary authority to conduct war in Asia."[10] Known as the Tonkin Gulf Resolution, it was approved that same year by a near unanimous congressional vote. The sweeping language of the resolution was interpreted by the Johnson Administration the same way that President Eisenhower had interpreted the Formosa Resolution almost one decade earlier. The difference was that the year following passage of the Tonkin Gulf Resolution, the United States embarked upon large-scale warfare in Vietnam.

During 1967, Under Secretary of State Nicholas de B. Katzenback clearly stated the Johnson Administration's interpretation of the Southeast Asia resolution before the Senate Foreign Relations Committee. According to his testimony, "the resolution gave the President all the freedom of military decision that would be his as Commander-in-Chief, under a declaration of war."[11]

Three years later in the wake of the Cambodian incursion, which occurred without any consultation with the Congress, the Senate repealed the Tonkin Gulf Resolution. The Nixon Administration, however, quickly asserted in a May 30, 1970, letter to Senator J. William Fulbright that it did not "depend on the Tonkin Gulf Resolution, as legal or constitutional authority for its present conduct of foreign relations, or its contingency plans." Instead, according to the letter, the President was acting upon "his constitutional authority as Commander-in-Chief."[12]

The congressional answer to this assertion was, in effect, the War Powers Resolution of 1973. Meant to redress a constitutional imbalance over the war power, it became law by overriding a veto cast by a Chief Executive greatly weakened by scandal. Passage of the resolution did not clarify the war power question between President and Congress. Not one President has, as of this writing (1990), accepted its validity and most, if not all, have viewed it as an unconstitutional effort to usurp their power as Commander in Chief.

Common Themes

The case studies taken together reveal several themes about foreign policy formulation and the President-Congress relationship. These themes are not hard and fast rules since exceptions undoubtedly exist. Yet, themes or patterns did emerge from the studies which deepen our understanding of the two branch relationship in the formulation of foreign policy. They are as follows:

Individual leaders in both branches play a key role in making foreign policy. In all the cases examined at least one leader emerged who was of special importance in either bringing about agreement between the two branches or who devised the policy itself and effectively worked for its approval. Although historical events, surrounding conditions, and political party-pressure group politics all played influential roles, it was usually an individual member of the executive or legislative branch that lent the necessary energy and skill to bring about results.

Certainly Secretary of State Cordell Hull's role in greatly facilitating the enactment of the Fulbright and Connally Resolutions is an example of this theme found in the first case study. Hull's great prestige amongst his former colleagues in the House and Senate and his careful attention to gaining a clear consensus for collective security in both chambers made him a crucial player in achieving the resolutions of 1943.

On the legislative side, Senator Vandenberg's role in gaining his colleagues' approval for NATO in 1948-49 was also crucial. Actually, the Michigan Republican and former isolationist must be considered one of the most important congressional foreign policy leaders in the entire postwar era. Vandenberg was both a skilled parliamentarian and defender of the Senate's constitutional prerogatives. Given his commitment to bipartisanship as well, he became an essential figure in bridging the gap between President and Congress during the late 1940's.

Senator Patrick A. McCarren's dogged support for aid to Franco Spain, plus his effort to make it a member of the western alliance during the late 1940;s and early 1950's, was certainly one of the more important reasons why the Pact of Madrid was finally negotiated in 1953. Secretary of State Dulles, as author of both the Formosa Resolution and the Eisenhower Doctrine during the 1950's, must also be included as an obvious key player in the formulation of those Eisenhower era foreign policies.

President Kennedy played a central role in bringing about the Nuclear Test Ban Treaty of 1963. His commitment to arms control was strong from the beginning of his administration and accentuated by his important American University speech calling for a fresh start in Soviet-American arms limitation. Kennedy's bipartisan approach to the treaty with the Congress and his quick acceptance of Senator Everett M. Dirksen's suggestion on how his support could be obtained, are further examples of his importance in bringing a nuclear limitation policy to fruition.

Finally, the enactment of the War Powers Resolution in 1973 was also strongly influenced by individual effort. Senator Jacob K. Javits, the leading proponent and cosponsor of the Senate version of the resolution (S440) had, in addition, effectively countered in debate Senator Goldwater's important Commander in Chief argument against the resolution.

<u>Bipartisanship is a useful method for overcoming President-Congress conflict in foreign policy formulation.</u> The several conditions identified by the first Chief of Staff of the Senate Foreign Relations Committee, Francis O. Wilcox, and this author in the second case study, provide us with a guide as to when and how bipartisanship may be utilized successfully. Senator Vandenberg's definition of bipartisanship itself remains one of the best: a common effort to "unite our official voice at the waters edge. . . ."[13]

The usefulness of this method is amply demonstrated in the first case study on the resolutions of 1943. In that beginning example an essential condition for the existence of a bipartisan foreign policy was established: "Executive consultation with party foreign policy leaders in the Congress prior to the implementation of policy."[14] The successful usage of bipartisanship at the time was an historic achievement in the formulation of U.S. foreign policy. The great Wilsonian struggle between the two branches over collective security had finally been put to rest with the resolution's endorsement of, "the establishment and maintenance of international authority with power to prevent aggression and to preserve the peace of the world."[15]

Senate approval of the Vandenberg Resolution in 1948, which led directly to U.S. participation in the North Atlantic Treaty Organization the following year, was also a bipartisan accomplishment. Both ideal and essential conditions for successful bipartisanship were present when the resolution was passed. Yet, despite the obvious success of bipartisanship in this case, it cannot be classified as a fully bipartisan achievement. Claude Pepper's strong criticism that, "At that time Senator Vandenberg dominated the policy and the position of the Senate and our government in the field of foreign affairs,"[16] must be considered when making a final evaluation.

During the last years of the Truman Administration the bipartisan foreign policy so carefully nurtured by Vandenberg had collapsed under the blows of bitter partisan attacks over the so-called loss of China and other accusations about Communists in government. At the same time, President Harry S. Truman remained resistent until near the end of his administration to closer relations with Fascist Spain, despite the blandishments of the Spanish Lobby in the Congress.

The Eisenhower Administration found it necessary to rely upon the bipartisan method to achieve congressional approval for both the Formosa Resolution in 1955 and the Middle East Resolution in 1957. Faced with an opposition party majority in the Congress following the congressional elections of 1954, bipartisanship became a necessity despite the personal popularity of the President. A bipartisan strategy was quickly mapped out with an administration promise to senior Democrat and

Republican members of the Foreign Relations and Armed Forces Committees to "participate in evolving national policy."[17] As a result, the Eisenhower Administration could usually count upon both Republican and Democratic member support in the Congress for its foreign policies.

President Kennedy also relied upon the bipartisan method to achieve the Nuclear Test Ban Treaty in 1963. His adeptness at its usage remains a model for Presidents facing a potentially strong congressional opposition to an important foreign policy initiative. Kennedy worked closely with congressional leaders in both parties throughout the treaty formulation process. The President's Chairman of the Atomic Energy Commission, Glenn T. Seaborg, commented upon the Kennedy Administration's relations with the upper chamber as follows: "At each turn in the road he and leading members of the administration had been scrupulous about informing and consulting with Senate leaders."[18]

The highly partisan politics that characterized the early 1950's had returned by the late 1960's over the Vietnam War issue, making consensus and thus bipartisan cooperation between the two branches more difficult to achieve. In addition, a period of congressional assertiveness had begun and by 1973 the President was preoccupied with the Watergate scandal, further reducing his ability to deal effectively with the Congress. In a sense then, passage of the War Powers Resolution represents the antithesis of bipartisan foreign policy formulation: it became law by a congressional override of a presidential veto and not through cooperative action between the two branches; it attempts to enforce by legislation consultation between the two branches that bipartisanship would achieve through voluntary effort; it has not engendered a cooperative spirit between the two branches since no President has yet recognized its validity.

Yet, in five of the seven case studies, bipartisanship was clearly a useful method for overcoming differences between the President and Congress in the making of foreign policies; with those policies being as divergent as the North Atlantic Treaty Organization and the Nuclear Test Ban Treaty.

Trust is an important factor in making relations

between the two branches function. "The whole thing, our whole government works on trust. If you can't trust a fellow Senator or anybody else in our government, the whole thing breaks down."[19] So spoke Harry Truman and indeed, the case studies bear out his conclusion.

Certainly Secretary of State Hull in the Roosevelt Administration had the trust of the Congress. His long previous service in the legislative branch was just the kind of background that senators and representatives believed would insure respect for their procedures and prerogatives. FDR relied upon Hull in the important area of congressional relations and his reliance was well placed given the successful passage of the Resolutions of 1943.

Likewise, Senator Vandenberg held a similar position of trust during the struggle to make the United States a charter member of the evolving Atlantic Alliance. Again, much of that trust was built around the well-known fact that the Michigan Senator possessed a deep respect for, and knowledge of, the Constitution. His colleagues in the Congress did not believe he would allow the executive branch to chip away at their prerogatives in the making of foreign policy. Thus, the Vandenberg Resolution of 1948 was in part the result of their trust in the former isolationist senator.

The Truman Administration's relationship with the Congress over the issue of Franco Spain's participation in the Western Alliance was not characterized by trust between congressional members and the President. Instead, a rather profound difference in viewpoint, or lack of consensus, may be discerned. In this case, military advice, which also favored closer ties with Spain, was deemed less suspect or more trustworthy by the President than congressional insistence that U.S. policy toward Spain be changed. Finally, in 1951, President Truman commented that American relations with the Franco Government had shifted "on the advice of the Department of Defense."[20]

The sweeping language of the Formosa Resolution in 1955 authorizing the President "to employ the armed forces of the United States as he deems necessary for the specific purpose of securing and protecting Formosa and the Pescadores against armed attack,"[21] fueled Senate fears that a preventive war might result. In order to dispel that fear, President Eisenhower declared that any decision to use American forces for self-defense of Formosa and the Pescadores "would be a decision which he would take and the responsibility for which he has not delegated."[22] Given the trust placed in the word of the elected Commander in Chief, most Senate fears were quickly reduced and a significant hurdle overcome for passage of the resolution.

Lack of trust in Secretary of State Dulles' stewardship of the administration's Middle East policy during 1956-57 was one of the important reasons for the considerable congressional opposition to the Middle East Resolution. President Eisenhower once again attempted to allay Senate fears when on January 30, 1957, during a press conference, he claimed that the Secretary had his personal approval for all of his Middle East negotiation "from top to bottom."[23]

The breakthrough Nuclear Test Ban Treaty in 1963 could not have been achieved if President Kennedy had not carefully nurtured Senate trust in the treaty-making process. The bipartisan procedures that Kennedy used aided the development of that trust between the two branches. Important members of the opposition Republican Party were consulted and included in the American delegation to Moscow for the treaty signing. Executive consultation also extended to the Joint Chiefs of Staff headed by General Maxwell Taylor. Taylor's subsequent endorsement of the treaty, with the recommendation of four safeguards, was critical for its eventual ratification.

The passage of the War Powers Resolution in 1973 may be viewed as the result of a loss of trust in the President by the Congress. The loss of that trust had significantly deepened since the Americanization of the Vietnam War in 1965. Undoubtedly, President Richard M. Nixon's Cambodian incursion in 1970, without any consultation with the Congress, quickened the pace of legislative initiative toward the resolution. Yet, given the fact of continued presidential resistance to the resolution, one must question whether or not such legislation can ever effectively substitute for trust-building methods like bipartisanship.

<u>Executive initiative of foreign policy is the general pattern, but the congressional power to pro-</u>

pose, delay and shape such policy remains substantial. In the first case study on the Fulbright and Connally Resolutions during World War II, we viewed a wary Roosevelt Administration in their relations with the Congress over the adoption of an internationalist foreign policy. Obviously they feared that a duplication of President Woodrow Wilson's tragic conflict with the Senate over the League of Nations might occur. Within this context then, the House of Representatives stepped forward and initiated the Fulbright Resolution in 1943. The later Connally Resolution was primarily administration-inspired, although its final form was to a large extent a product of collaboration between the Senate Foreign Relations Committee and the State Department.

The Vandenberg Resolution of 1948 was first suggested by members of the executive branch, but its final wording was "largely" in Senator Vandenberg's phraseology.[24] Also, it was the Republican Senator's leadership and tactics that prevented the resolution from being blocked by remaining isolationists or liberal Senators like Claude Pepper who believed the formation of a regional alliance would weaken the United Nations. The Vandenberg Resolution led directly to Senate approval of U.S. participation in the North Atlantic Treaty Organization the following year.

The Pact of Madrid, which was finally signed by the Eisenhower Administration in 1953, was not initially a product of the executive branch. President Truman's disdain for the Franco Government was well-known to the Congress, but it did not stop a determined combination of pro-Spanish members of the legislature, plus an effective foreign lobbying organization, from prodding the President and Secretary of State toward a change in U.S.-Spanish policy. That change of policy, however, did not take place until the pro-Spanish forces in the Congress received important support from the military establishment.

The Formosa Resolution was a Secretary of State Dulles' contrivance with far-reaching consequences for the President-Congress relationship. In 1964 it was used as the prototype for the fateful Tonkin Gulf Resolution which preceded the American build-up in Vietnam. The most important criticism of the Formosa Resolution in 1955 came from those senators who believed it was a "blank check"[25] upon which the President could mount a preventive war. Yet, the McCarthyite atmosphere still evident during the 84th Congress clearly inhibited a full discussion of its necessity and implications.

The Formosa Resolution and Mutual Defense Treaty with Taiwan were both initiated by the Eisenhower-Dulles Administration. However, the treaty with Taiwan was first proposed by Generalissimo Chiang Kai-shek. Although Secretary Dulles did not immediately respond to this proposal, Senator Alexander Wiley, Chairman of the Senate Foreign Relations Committee was enthusiastic. Therefore, a certain degree of Senate pressure for the treaty may be discerned.

The Middle East Resolution in 1957 was another John Foster Dulles' contrivance that reflected President Eisenhower's continuing penchant for sharing major foreign policy responsibilities with the Congress. It was clearly an administration-initiated foreign policy, but the Congress played a highly significant role in shaping and almost blocking its enactment. Beginning in 1956, China Lobby advocates in Congress opposed U.S. funding of the Aswan Dam in Egypt. Also in opposition were Cotton Lobby advocates and congressional members concerned with the effect upon Israel of U.S. funding for the dam. These congressional pressures undoubtedly influenced the Dulles decision not to finance the Aswan Dam.

The Middle East Resolution of 1957 was supposed to fill in the power vacuum left by the 1956 war, but congressional opposition to its wording soon resulted. In fact, Senate approval did not occur until modifications were made in the resolution with reference to the commitment of armed forces by the President. Of additional significance was Senate opposition to the administration position that Israel should withdraw its armies back to their pre-war frontiers without guarantees and under a growing implied threat of sanctions by the United Nations. Only until skillful diplomacy had resulted in administration guarantees to Israel was final approval of the resolution voted upon by the Senate.

The 1963 Nuclear Test Ban Treaty was initiated by the executive branch of government within the context of previous commitments given by both political parties to either endorse the ending (Democrat) or suspend

(Republican) nuclear tests in their 1960 campaign platforms. In addition, President Kennedy anticipated potential congressional opposition throughout the entire treaty-making process, and via bipartisan consultation reached a consensus with the Congress. This consensus-building included the President's acceptance of recommendations from the Joint Chiefs of Staff and assurances in letter form to Senate Republican Minority Leader Everett McKinley Dirksen allowing him, in a dramatic speech before his colleagues, to endorse the treaty "with no reservations whatsoever."[26]

The War Powers Resolution of 1973 was initiated by the Congress and strongly resisted by the President. Yet, like President Truman in the early 1950's, Richard Nixon was unable to stop a concerted congressional drive to force a foreign policy change. Congressional assertiveness and a lack of bipartisan consultation between the two branches on the commitment of troops issue, contributed to a growing determination to bring about a change in how such policy may be formulated.

The Vietnam War itself, given its length and controversial nature, also provided a strong stimulus for change. Representative Spark M. Matsunaga of Hawaii stated the need for a resolution with the war very much in mind when he testified during 1973 that, ". . . we need definite, unmistakable procedures to prevent future undeclared wars, 'no more Vietnams' should be our objective in setting up such procedures."[27] Nevertheless, congressional determination to forge a new relationship with the President regarding the war power, was significantly aided during the House veto override vote by the weakening effect of Watergate on the Commander in Chief.

The war power is a salient issue in the President-Congress relationship. The war power issue itself dates back to the Constitutional Convention of 1787 when the legislative branch was empowered to declare war, but the Presidency was left with the power to make or conduct war. This division of the war power resulted in an historical pattern whereby the Congress would declare war infrequently, but the President, as Commander in Chief, would commit the United States to hostilities on numerous occasions.

The case studies examined reveal a pattern of

congressional concern regarding the war power that was at various times paramount in its relations with the executive branch. Beginning with the first study on the resolutions of 1943 we see the great isolationist-internationalist debate moving toward its final phase. To a large extent isolationism expressed a fear of entanglement in European wars. Those fears had been historically ameliorated by an isolationist foreign policy and further checked by the Senate's power to consent, or withhold consent, to the ratification of alliance treaties that might automatically lead to war. By 1943, however, during the midst of World War II, the President's internationalist position seemed far more cogent and Senator Connally's words to his colleagues were both simple and compelling: "Isolationism has failed. Let us try collective security."[28]

The Vandenberg Resolution in 1948 and subsequent North Atlantic Treaty were also clearly concerned with the war power issue. Isolationist sentiment in the Senate was a diminishing, but still potent factor in the effort to bring the United States into the developing Atlantic Alliance. Both the resolution and the treaty were carefully constructed to reduce Senate fears regarding the possible bypassing of the congressional power to declare war. A reference to constitutional processes is contained in the Vandenberg Resolution and Article 5 of the treaty does not technically violate the war declaration power of the Congress.

The President-Congress conflict over closer relations with Spain during the Truman Administration was not concerned with the war power. During the Formosa Strait confrontation in 1954-55, however, an important conflict between the two branches occurred that was directly related to the war power issue. The introduction of the Formosa Resolution in 1955 was seen by several senators as a presidential request for a dangerous grant of authority that, as stated by Senator Morse, "could very well mean war."[29]

Congressional opposition to the Middle East Resolution in 1957 was also, in part, concerned with the war power. The Middle East Resolution was similar to the Formosa Resolution in that it would, according to several of its Senate critics, delegate to others the congressional right and duty to declare when the United States should be at war. As a result, the final wording of the resolution was modified by Senate amendments to read that the employment of the armed forces "shall be consonant with the treaty obligations of the United States and with the Constitution of the United States."[30]

The war power issue between President and Congress was not of concern in the Senate's final consent to ratification of the Nuclear Test Ban Treaty in 1963. Yet, less than one decade later during the midst of the Vietnam War, a deep schism developed between the two branches over the commitment of U.S. forces to large-scale warfare in Southeast Asia.

The War Powers Resolution of 1973 was an important congressional effort to redress its diminished role in the decision to commit the United States to war. This perceived erosion of the congressional war power had taken place over many years, but was especially highlighted by the Vietnam War. An assertive Congress had finally faced the "Imperial Presidency"[31] and overrode President Nixon's veto of the resolution. Passage of the War Powers Resolution did not put the issue to rest, but it was a significant effort by the Congress to more directly influence the commitment of troops issue, and by so doing challenge the Commander in Chief power of the President.

Post-Vietnam Developments

"The political fault line from the old Washington power game to the new Washington power game was 1974."[32] This is the assessment correspondent Hedrick Smith has given in his best-selling book on Washington politics. Surely, dramatic political events did occur in 1974, none the least of which was President Nixon's resignation from the White House due to the Watergate scandal and the threat of almost certain impeachment by the House of Representatives.[33] The period of congressional reassertion had of course begun earlier during the Vietnam War, but by 1974 that assertiveness was affecting how the Congress worked and related to the President.

Even before 1974 a pattern of congressional assertiveness toward presidential authority in the making of foreign policy had become a fixture. In 1970 the Senate repealed the Gulf of Tonkin Resolution upon which the

Johnson Administration had placed so much of its authority to prosecute the war in Southeast Asia. In 1972 Congress passed the Case Act which required that executive agreements between the President and foreign governments be reported for its information. In 1973 the War Powers Resolution itself became law, and in 1974 the Budget Act passed, reasserting congressional control over government spending and curbing the presidential impoundment of funds. By the middle 1970's Congress was investigating the role of the Central Intelligence Agency and establishing oversight committees to monitor its covert operations.

At the same time changes were occurring within the Congress that produced a less hierarchical system of power, making the legislature harder to lead than previously. In 1974 House Democrats adopted a "subcommittee bill of rights"[34] which institutionalized subcommittees, and in both the House and Senate the number of committees dramatically increased. This dispersal of power was accompanied by an enormous increase in the size of congressional staffs from about 11,500 in 1973 to more than 24,000 by 1985.[35] Staff influence also grew, especially in the Senate, as the workload on the Congress increased. This new dependency has been cryptically characterized as: "The Unelected Leading the Overburdened."[36]

The seniority system, which had long prevailed as an organizational and reward system in the Congress, was also changing. By the middle 1970's, changes were in place that allowed new and younger members critical of the old leadership to advance more quickly. The seniority system was not destroyed, but it had been significantly weakened. An additional result was that the new and younger leaders tended "to be more partisan and ideological, eager to make their mark, and less willing than the old leaders to defer to presidential authority on foreign policy. . . ."[37]

Party discipline also declined as new members of Congress were able to win elections and advancement without conforming to previous codes of stricter party loyalty. An important reason for this change was that legislators could now gain instant public recognition via the expanding use of television. In 1979 the House began televising coverage of its floor proceedings and the Senate followed suit in 1986. The establishment of their own television studios on Capitol Hill also enhanced the ability of representatives and senators to do short takes for national news programs, in effect sharing prime time with the President and the Secretary of State.

The increasing mobility of congressional members to foreign country trouble spots by jet plane is another reason for their greater involvement and assertiveness on foreign policy issues. Junketeering has long been a fixture of congressional life, but fast fact-finding trips resulting in personal contacts between senators and representatives with national leaders is a relatively recent phenomenon associated with the jet age. As a result, congressional members are enabled "to put forth alternatives that are based on a level of expertise and firsthand knowledge that rivals the executive branch."[38]

Executive decision-making has also been influenced by change. Beginning in 1974 a long-standing claim by Presidents that their private communications with principal advisers, including foreign policy advisers, need not be divulged was successfully challenged. This presumed doctrine of executive privilege, based upon the constitutional separation of powers, had been the basis for President Nixon's refusal to allow a special prosecutor investigating the Watergate scandal to review certain tape recordings of conversations between himself and his advisers. In United States v. Nixon, however, the Supreme Court ruled that while there may be a correct claim for executive privilege, especially where sensitive diplomatic or military information is involved, the President does not possess a "privilege of immunity from judicial process under all circumstances."[39]

Although the changes that have taken place in both the Congress and in the legislative-executive relationship since 1974 are substantial, they have not eliminated the continuing importance of the themes that emerged from the case studies examined during the time period 1943-73.

Individual leadership in both branches is still necessary to bring about new foreign policies or to stay the course of continuing programs. The kind of leadership exemplified by Senator Vandenberg during the

1940's is now admittedly more difficult to achieve or identify. Congress has become less hierarchical with its increase in the number of committees, reduction in the degree of party loyalty, and changes in the seniority system. Yet, the need for congressional leaders to bring together their independent and divided colleagues remains a basic necessity for the coherent formulation of foreign policy with the President.

Bipartisanship remains a useful method for overcoming President-Congress conflict in foreign policy formulation. The bipartisan method produced notable U.S. foreign policy achievements during the time period covered by the case studies, e.g., NATO and the Nuclear Test Ban Treaty. Divided government, or a situation in which at least one branch of the Congress is in the hands of one political party and the Presidency in the hands of the other, has characterized every government since 1968 with the exception of the Carter Administration years. As a result, bipartisanship has actually become a necessity for the development of a consensual foreign policy--a necessity subject to change given the predilections of the American voter.

Trust also remains an important factor in making relations between the two branches function. Given the natural divisiveness emanating from the separation of powers, it is a factor whose importance transcends any one time period. The Vietnam War and the Watergate scandal clearly diminished the degree of trust the Congress holds for the Presidency. Yet, the need for trust between President and Congress to successfully formulate foreign policy remains a constant necessity. Also, given the divided government tendency so prevalent since the Vietnam War era, the existence of trust between the two branches is perhaps even more necessary now than it has been in the past.

Executive initiation of foreign policy remains the general pattern, but the congressional power to propose, delay and shape such policy also remains substantial. Congressional assertiveness has reinforced the legislative role in foreign policy-making; and that assertiveness has been aided by other changes mentioned above including greater television access for individual members and the mobility which jet air travel increasingly provides. Yet, the concomitant dispersal of power in the Congress since 1974 mitigates the legislature's ability to coordinate its own policy agenda, thus continuing the usual presidential initiation of foreign policy.

Finally, the war power continues to be a salient issue in the President-Congress relationship. The steep decline in Cold War tensions by the last decade of the 20th century does not diminish the importance of this issue. The War Powers Resolution may or may not be reformed, although a growing consensus in the Congress believes it to be necessary. Wars unfortunately will continue to occur; prolonged wars with U.S. involvement, as happened in Vietnam, might once again cause a major schism in President-Congress relations.

Notes

[1]Clinton Rossiter and James Lare, eds., *The Essential Lippman: A Political Philosophy for Liberal Democracy* (New York: Vintage Books, 1965), 287-89.

[2]Author interview with Presidential Assistant Sherman Adams in Hanover, New Hampshire, 14 November 1967.

[3]Ibid.

[4]*Congressional Record*, 88th Cong. 1st sess., 1963, pt 7: 9483.

[5]Johny H. Killian, ed., *The Constitution of the United States of America: Analysis and Interpretation* (Washington, D.C.: U.S. Government Printing Office, 1987), 9.

[6]*Cong. Rec.*, 93rd Cong., 1st sess., 1973, 119, pt 20: 25066-78.

[7]Dwight D. Eisenhower, *Mandate For Change, 1953-1956* (New York: Doubleday & Company, Inc., 1963), 560-61.

[8]*Cong. Rec.*, 84th Cong., 1st sess., 1955, 101, pt 1: 738-47.

[9]Text of speech from *Cong. Rec.*, 28 January 1955, in *The Herbert H. Lehman Papers*, Columbia University, School of International Affairs, New York City, N.Y.

[10]James E. Dougherty and Robert L. Pfaltzgraff, Jr., *American Foreign Policy: FDR to Reagan* (New York: Harper & Row Publishers, Inc., 1986), 227.

[11]*New York Times*, 18 August 1967, 14.

[12]Letter from Elliot Richardson, Acting Secretary, Department of State, in *Cong. Rec.*, 119, pt 8: 10421.

[13]Vandenberg to a constituent, 5 January 1950, Arthur H. Vandenberg, Jr., ed., *The Private Papers of Senator Vandenberg* (Boston: Houghton Mifflin Company, 1952), 552.

[14]See author's, "Senator Vandenberg, Bipartisanship and the Origin of United Nations Article 51, *Mid-America: An Historical Review* 60 (October 1978): 164.

[15]Quoted from the Connally Resolution in *Cong. Rec.*, 78th Cong., 1st sess., 1943, 89, pt 7: 9222. For full text see Appendix A.

[16]Letter to the author from Representative Claude Pepper, 23 June 1980.

[17]*New York Times*, 15 December 1954, 1.

[18]Glenn T. Seaborg with the assistance of Benjamin S. Loeb and a foreword by W. Averell Harriman, *Kennedy, Khrushchev and the Test Ban* (Berkeley: University of California Press, 1981), 264.

[19]Merle Miller, *Plain Speaking: an oral biography of Harry S. Truman* (New York: Berkeley Publishing Corporation, 1973), 170.

[20]*New York Times*, 20 July 1951, 4.

[21]For full text of Resolution see Appendix D.

[22]*New York Times*, 27 January 1955, 1, 2.

[23]Ibid., 31 January 1957, 8.

[24]Vandenberg, *Private Papers*, 406.

[25]See Senator Lehman speech reprint from *Cong. Rec.*, 28 January 1955, in *Lehman Papers*.

[26]*Cong. Rec.*, 109, pt 12: 16791.

[27]Quoted in 1973 *Congressional Quarterly Almanac* (Washington, D.C.: Congressional Quarterly Inc., 1974), 908.

[28]*Cong. Rec.*, 89, pt 7: 8665.

[29]*New York Times*, 25 January 1955, 3.

[30]*Cong. Rec.*, 85th Cong., 1st sess., 1957, 103, pt 2: 2800-02.

[31]Quote from title of a book by Arthur M. Schlesinger, Jr., The Imperial Presidency (New York: Popular Library, 1974).

[32]Hedrick Smith, The Power Game: How Washington Works (New York: Ballantine Books, 1989), 20.

[33]Bob Woodward and Carl Bernstein, The Final Days (New York: Simon & Schuster, 1976), 390.

[34]Smith, The Power Game, 25.

[35]Ibid., 24.

[36]Ross K. Baker, House and Senate (New York: W. W. Norton & Company, Inc., 1989), 89.

[37]Howard J. Wiarda, Foreign Policy Without Illusion: How Foreign Policy-Making Works and Fails to Work in the United States (Glenview, Illinois: Scott, Foresman & Company, 1990), 206.

[38]Ibid., 211.

[39]United States v. Nixon, 418 U.S. 683 (1974).

APPENDICES

APPENDIX A

THE FULBRIGHT RESOLUTION
(21 September 1943)

Resolved by the House of Representatives (the Senate concurring), That the Congress hereby expresses itself as favoring the creation of appropriate international machinery with power adequate to establish and to maintain a just and lasting peace, among the nations of the world, and as favoring participation by the United States therein through its constitutional processes.

THE CONNALLY RESOLUTION
(5 November 1943)

Resolved, That the war against all our enemies be waged until complete victory is achieved.

That the United States cooperate with its comrades-in-arms in securing a just and honorable peace.

That the United States, acting through its constitutional processes, join with free and sovereign nations in the establishment and maintenance of international authority with power to prevent aggression and to preserve the peace of the world.

That the Senate recognizes the necessity of there being established at the earliest practicable date a general international organization, based on the prin ciple of the sovereign equality of all peace-loving states, and open to membership by all such states, large and small, for the maintenance of international peace and security.

That, pursuant to the Constitution of the United States, any treaty made to effect the purposes of this resolution, on behalf of the Government of the United States with any other nation or any association of nations, shall be made only by and with the advice and consent of the Senate of the United States, provided two-thirds of the Senators present concur.

APPENDIX B

THE VANDENBERG RESOLUTION
(11 June 1948)

Whereas peace with justice and the defense of human rights and fundamental freedoms require international cooperation through more effective use of the United Nations: Therefore be it

Resolved, That the Senate reaffirm the policy of the United States to achieve international peace and security through the United Nations so that armed forces shall not be used except in the common interest, and that the President be advised of the sense of the Senate that this Government, by constitutional process, shall particularly pursue the following objectives within the United Nations Charter:

(1) Voluntary agreement to remove the veto from all questions involving pacific settlements of international disputes and situations, and from the admission of new members.

(2) Progressive development of regional and other collective arrangements for individual and collective self-defense in accordance with the purposes, principles, and provisions of the Charter.

(3) Association of the United States, by constitutional process, with such regional and other collective arrangements as are based on continuous and effective self-help and mutual aid, and as affect its national security.

(4) Contributing to the maintenance of peace by making clear its determination to exercise the right of individual or collective self-defense under article 51 should any armed attack occur affecting its national security.

(5) Maximum efforts to obtain agreements to provide the United Nations with armed forces as provided by the Charter, and to obtain agreement among member nations upon universal regulation and reduction of armaments under adequate and dependable guaranty against violation.

(6) If necessary, after adequate effort toward strengthening the United Nations, review of the Charter at an appropriate time by a General Conference called under article 109 or by the General Assembly.

APPENDIX C

DEFENSE AGREEMENT WITH SPAIN
(26 September 1953)

PREAMBLE

Faced with the danger that threatens the western world, the Governments of the United States and Spain, desiring to contribute to the maintenance of international peace and security through foresighted measures which will increase their capability and that of the other nations which dedicate their efforts to the same high purposes to participate effectively in agreements for self defense,

Have agreed as follows:

ARTICLE I

In consonance with the principles agreed upon in the Mutual Defense Assistance Agreement, the Governments of the United States and of Spain consider that the contingencies with which both countries may be faced indicate the advisability of developing their relations upon a basis of continued friendship, in support of the policy of strengthening the defense of the West. This policy shall include:

1. On the part of the United States, the support of Spanish defense efforts for agreed purposes by providing military end item assistance to Spain during a period of several years to contribute to the effective air defense of Spain and to improve the equipment of its military and naval forces, to the extent to be agreed upon in technical discussions in the light of the circumstances, and with the cooperation of the resources of Spanish industry to the extent possible. Such support will be conditioned as in the case of other friendly nations by the priorities and limitations due to the international commitments of the United States and the exigencies of the international situation and will be subject to Congressional appropriations.

2. In consequence of the above stated premises and for the same agreed purposes, the Government of Spain authorizes the Government of the United States, subject to terms and conditions to be agreed, to develop, maintain and utilize for military purposes, jointly with the Government of Spain, such areas and facilities in territory under Spanish jurisdiction as may be agreed upon by the competent authorities of both Governments as necessary for the purposes of this agreement.

3. In granting assistance to Spain within the policy outlined above, as the preparation of the agreed areas and facilities progresses, the Government of the United States will satisfy, subject to the provisions of paragraph one, the minimum requirements for equipment necessary for the defense of Spanish territory, to the end that should a moment requiring the wartime utilization of the areas and facilities arrive, from this moment, the requirements are covered to the extent possible as regards the air defense of the territory and the equipment of the naval units; and that the armament and equipment of the Army units be as far advanced as possible.

ARTICLE II

For the purposes of this agreement and in accordance with technical arrangements to be agreed upon between the competent authorities of both Governments, the Government of the United States is authorized to improve and fit agreed areas and facilities for military use, as well as to undertake necessary construction in this connection in cooperation with the Government of Spain, to station and house therein the necessary military and civilian personnel, and to provide for their security, discipline, and welfare; to store and maintain custody of provisions, supplies, equipment and materials; and to maintain and operate the facilities and equipment necessary in support of such areas and personnel.

ARTICLE III

The areas which, by virtue of this Agreement, are prepared for joint utilization will remain under Spanish flag and command, and Spain will assume the obligation of adopting the necessary measures for there external security. However, the United States may, in all cases, exercise the necessary supervision of United States personnel facilities, and equipment.

The time and manner of wartime utilization of said areas and facilities will be as mutually agreed upon.

ARTICLE IV

The Government of Spain will acquire, free of all charge and servitude, the land which may be necessary for all military purposes and shall retain the ownership of the ground and of the permanent structures which may be constructed thereon. The United States Government reserves the right to remove all other constructions and facilities established at its own expense when it is deemed convenient by the Government of the United States or upon the termination of this Agreement; in both cases the Spanish Government may acquire them, after previous assessment, whenever they are not installations of a classified nature.

The Spanish state will be responsible for all claims made against the United States Government by a third party, in all cases referring to the ownership and utilization of the above-mentioned land.

ARTICLE V

The present Agreement will become effective upon signature and will be in force for a period of ten years, automatically extended for two successive periods of five years each unless the termination procedure hereafter outlined is followed.

At the termination of the first ten years or of either of the two extensions of five years, either of the two Governments may inform the other of its intention to cancel the Agreement, thus initiating a consultation period of six months. In the event concurrence is not reached on extension, this Agreement will terminate one year after the conclusion of the period of consultation.

In witness whereof the respective representatives duly authorized for the purpose, have signed the present agreement.

Done at Madrid, in duplicate, in the English and Spanish languages, both texts authentic, this twenty-sixth day of September, 1953.

For the Government of the United States of America:

James Clement Dunn
Ambassador of the United States of America

For the Government of Spain:

Alberto Martin Artajo
Minister of Foreign Affairs

APPENDIX D

THE FORMOSA RESOLUTION
(28 January 1955)

Whereas the primary purpose of the United States, in its relations with all other nations, is to develop and sustain a just and enduring peace for all; and

Whereas certain territories in the west Pacific under the jurisdiction of the Republic of China are now under armed attack, and threats and declarations have been made and are being made by the Chinese Communists that such armed attack is in aid of and in preparation for armed attack on Formosa and the Pescadores; and

Whereas such armed attack if continued would gravely endanger the peace and security of the west Pacific area and particularly of Formosa and the Pescadores; and

Whereas the secure possession by friendly governments of the western Pacific island chain, of which Formosa is a part, is essential to the vital interests of the United States and all friendly nations in or bordering upon the Pacific Ocean; and

Whereas the President of the United States on Jan. 6, 1955, submitted to the Senate for its advice and consent to ratification a mutual defense treaty between the United States of America and the Republic of China, which recognized that an armed attack in the west Pacific area directed against territories therein described in the region of Formosa and the Pescadores, would be dangerous to the peace and safety of the parties to the treaty: therefore be it

Resolved, (etc.,) That the President of the United States be and he hereby is authorized to employ the armed forces of the United States as he deems necessary for the specific purpose of securing and protecting Formosa and the Pescadores against armed attack, this authority to include the securing and protection of such related positions and territories of that area now in friendly hands and the taking of such other measures as he judges to be required or appropriate in assuring the defense of Formosa and the Pescadores.

This resolution shall expire when the President shall determine that the peace and security of the area is reasonably assured by international conditions, created by action of the United Nations or otherwise, and shall so report to Congress.

APPENDIX E

THE EISENHOWER DOCTRINE

SPECIAL MESSAGE TO THE CONGRESS

BY PRESIDENT EISENHOWER ON THE MIDDLE EAST

(5 January 1957)

To the Congress of the United States:

First may I express to you my deep appreciation of your courtesy in giving me, at some inconvenience to yourselves, this early opportunity of addressing you on a matter I deem to be of grave importance to our country.

In my forthcoming State of the Union Message, I shall review the international situation generally. There are worldwide hopes which we can reasonably entertain, and there are worldwide responsibilities which we must carry to make certain that freedom - including our own - may be secure.

There is, however, a special situation in the Middle East which I feel I should, even now, lay before you.

Before doing so it is well to remind ourselves that our basic national objective in international affairs remains peace--a world peace based on justice. Such a peace must include all areas, all peoples of the world if it is to be enduring. There is no nation, great or small, with which we would refuse to negotiate, in mutual good faith, with patience and in the determination to secure a better understanding between us. Out of such understandings must, and eventually will, grow confidence and trust, indispensable ingredients to a program of peace and to plans for lifting from us all the burdens of expensive armaments. To promote these objectives, our government works tirelessly, day by day, month by month, year by year. But until a degree of success crowns our efforts that will assure to all nations peaceful existence, we must, in the interests of peace itself, remain vigilant, alert and strong.

I

The Middle East has abruptly reached a new and critical stage in its long and important history. In past decades many of the countries in that area were not fully self-governing. Other nations exercised considerable authority in the area and the security of the region was largely built around their power. But since the First World War there has been a steady evolution toward self-government and independence. This development the United States has welcomed and has encouraged. Our country supports without reservation the full sovereignty and independence of each and every nation of the Middle East.

The evolution to independence has in the main been a peaceful process. But the area has been often troubled. Persistent cross-currents of distrust and fear with raids back and forth across national boundaries have brought about a high degree of instability in much of the Mid East. Just recently there have been hostilities involving Western European nations that once exercised much influence in the area. Also the relatively large attack by Israel in October has intensified the basic differences between that nation and its Arab neighbors. All this instability has been heightened and, at times, manipulated by International Communism.

THE EISENHOWER DOCTRINE AND ITS APPLICATION

II

Russia's rulers have long sought to dominate the Middle East. That was true of the Czars and it is true of the Bolsheviks. The reasons are not hard to find. They do not affect Russia's security, for no one plans to use the Middle East as a base for aggression against Russia. Never for a moment has the United States entertained such a thought.

The Soviet Union has nothing whatsoever to fear from the United States in the Middle East, or anywhere else in the world, so long as its rulers do not themselves first resort to aggression.

That statement I make solemnly and emphatically.

Neither does Russia's desire to dominate the Middle East spring from its own economic interest in the area. Russia does not appreciable use or depend upon the Suez Canal. In 1955 Soviet traffic through the Canal represented only about three fourths of 1% of the total. The Soviets have no need for, and could provide no market for, the petroleum resources which constitute the principal natural wealth of the area. Indeed, the Soviet Union is a substantial exporter of petroleum products.

The reason for Russia's interest in the Middle East is solely that of power politics. Considering her announced purpose of Communizing the world, it is easy to understand her hope of dominating the Middle East.

This region has always been the crossroads of the continents of the Eastern Hemisphere. The Suez Canal enables the nations of Asia and Europe to carry on the commerce that is essential if these countries are to maintain well-rounded and prosperous economies. The Middle East provides a gateway between Eurasia and Africa.

It contains about two thirds of the presently known oil deposits of the world and it normally supplies the petroleum needs of many nations of Europe, Asia and Africa. The nations of Europe are peculiarly dependent upon this supply, and this dependency relates to transportation as well as to production! This has been vividly demonstrated since the closing of the Suez Canal and some of the pipelines. Alternate ways of transportation and, indeed, alternate sources of power can, if necessary, be developed. But these cannot be considered as early prospects.

These things stress the immense importance of the Middle East. If the nations of that area should lose their independence, if they were dominated by alien forces hostile to freedom, that would be both a tragedy for the area and for many other free nations whose economic life would be subject to near strangulation. Western Europe would be endangered just as though there had been no Marshall Plan, no North Atlantic Treaty Organization. The free nations of Asia and Africa, too, would be placed in serious jeopardy. And the countries of the Middle East would lose the markets upon which their economies depend. All this would have the most adverse, if not disastrous, effect upon our own nation's economic life and political prospects.

Then there are other factors which transcend the material. The Middle East is the birthplace of three great religions, Moslem, Christian and Hebrew. Mecca and Jerusalem are more than places on the map. They symbolize religions which teach that the spirit has supremacy over matter and that the individual has a dignity and rights of which no despotic government can rightfully deprive him. It would be intolerable if the holy places of the Middle East should be subjected to a rule that glorifies atheistic materialism.

International Communism, of course, seeks to mask its purposes of domination by expressions of good will and by superficially attractive offers of political, economic and military aid. But any free nation, which is the subject of Soviet enticement, ought, in elementary wisdom, to look behind the mask.

Remember Estonia, Latvia and Lithuania! In 1939 the Soviet Union entered into mutual assistance pacts with these then independent countries; and the Soviet Foreign Minister, addressing the Extraordinary Fifth Session of the Supreme Soviet in October 1939, solemnly and publicly declared that "we stand for the scrupulous and punctilious observance of the pacts on the basis of complete reciprocity, and we declare that all the nonsensical talk about the Sovietization of the Baltic countries is only to the interest of our common enemies and of all anti-Soviet provocateurs." Yet in 1940, Estonia, Latvia and Lithuania were forcibly incorporated into the Soviet Union.

Soviet control of the satellite nations of Eastern Europe has been forcible maintained in spite of solemn promises of a contrary intent, made during World War II.

Stalin's death brought hope that this pattern would change. And we read the pledge of the Warsaw Treaty of 1955 that the Soviet Union would follow in satellite countries "The principles of mutual respect for their independence and sovereignty and noninterference in domestic affairs." But we have just seen the subjugation of Hungary by naked armed force. In the aftermath of this Hungarian tragedy, world respect for and belief in Soviet promises have sunk to a new low. International Communism needs and seeks a recognizable success.

Thus, we have these simple and indisputable facts:

1. The Middle East, which has always been coveted by Russia, would today be prized more than ever by International Communism.

2. The Soviet rulers continue to show that they do not scruple to use any means to gain their ends.

3. The free nations of the Mid East need, and for the most part want, added strength to assure their continued independence.

III

Our thoughts naturally turn to the United Nations as a protector of small nations. Its charter gives it primary responsibility for the maintenance of international peace and security. Our country has given the United Nations its full support in relation to the hostilities in Hungary and in Egypt. The United Nations was able to bring about a cease-fire and withdrawal of hostile forces from Egypt because it was dealing with governments and peoples who had a decent respect for the opinions of mankind as reflected in the United Nations General Assembly. But in the case of Hungary, the situation was different. The Soviet Union vetoed action by the Security Council to require the withdrawal of Soviet armed forces from Hungary. And it has shown callous indifference to the recommendations, even the censure, of the General Assembly. The United Nations can always be helpful, but it cannot be a wholly dependable protector of freedom when the ambitions of the Soviet Union are involved.

IV

Under all the circumstances I have laid before you, a greater responsibility now devolves upon the United States. We have shown, so that none can doubt, our dedication to the principle that force shall not be used internationally for any aggressive purpose and that the integrity and independence of the nations of the Middle East should be inviolate. Seldom in history has a nation's dedication to principle been tested as severely as ours during recent weeks.

There is general recognition in the Middle East, as elsewhere, that the United States does not seek either political or economic dominance over any other people. Our desire is a world environment of freedom, not servitude. On the other hand many, if not all, of the nations of the Middle East are aware of the danger that stems from International Communism and welcome closer cooperation with the United States to realize for themselves the United Nations goals of independence, economic well-being and spiritual growth.

If the Middle East is to continue its geographic role of uniting rather than separating East and West; if its vast economic resources are to serve the well-being of the peoples there, as well as that of others; and if its cultures and religions and their shrines are to be preserved for the uplifting of the spirits of the people, then the United States must make more evident its willingness to support the independence of the freedom-loving nations of the area.

V

Under these circumstances I deem it necessary to seek the cooperation of the Congress. Only with that cooperation can we give the reassurance needed to deter aggression, to give courage and confidence to those who are dedicated to freedom and thus prevent a chain of events which would gravely endanger all of the free world.

There have been several Executive declarations made by the United States in relation to the Middle East. There is the Tripartite Declaration of May 25, 1950, followed by the Presidential assurance of October 31, 1950, to the King of Saudi Arabia. There is the Presidential declaration of April 9, 1956, that the United States will within constitutional means oppose any aggression in the area. There is our Declaration of November 29, 1956, that a threat to the territorial integrity or political independence of Iran, Iraq, Pakistan, or Turkey would be viewed by the United States with the utmost gravity.

Nevertheless, weaknesses in the present situation

and the increased danger from International Communism, convince me that basic United States policy should now find expression in joint action by the Congress and the Executive. Furthermore, our joint resolve should be so couched as to make it apparent that if need be our words will be backed by action.

VI

It is nothing new for the President and Congress to join to recognize that the national integrity of other free nations is directly related to our own security.

We have joined to create and support the security system of the United Nations. We have reinforced the collective security system of the United Nations by a series of collective defense arrangements. Today we have security treaties with 42 other nations which recognize that our peace and security are intertwined. We have joined to take decisive action in relation to Greece and Turkey and in relation to Taiwan.

Thus, the United States through the joint action of the President and the Congress, or, in the case of treaties, the Senate, has manifested in many endangered areas its purpose to support free and independent governments--and peace--against external menace, notably the menace of International Communism. Thereby we have helped to maintain peace and security during a period of great danger. It is now essential that the United States should manifest through joint action of the President and the Congress our determination to assist those nations of the Mid East area, which desire that assistance.

The action which I propose would have the following features.

It would, first of all, authorize the United States to cooperate with and assist any nation or group of nations in the general area of the Middle East in the development of economic strength dedicated to the maintenance of national independence.

It would, in the second place, authorize the Executive to undertake in the same region programs of military assistance and cooperation with any nation or group of nations which desires such aid.

It would, in the third place, authorize such assistance and cooperation to include the employment of the armed forces of the United States to secure and protect the territorial integrity and political independence of such nations, requesting such aid, against overt armed aggression from any nation controlled by International Communism.

These measures would have to be consonant with the treaty obligations of the United States, including the Charter of the United Nations and with any action or recommendation of the United Nations. They would also, if armed attack occurs, be subject to the overriding authority of the United Nations Security Council in accordance with the Charter.

The present proposal would, in the fourth place, authorize the President to employ, for economic and defensive military purposes, sums available under the Mutual Security Act of 1954, as amended, without regard to existing limitations.

The legislation now requested should not include the authorization or appropriation of funds because I believe that, under the conditions I suggest, presently appropriated funds will be adequate for the balance of the present fiscal year ending June 30. I shall, however, seek in subsequent legislation the authorization of $200,000,000 to be available during each of the fiscal years 1958 and 1959 for discretionary use in the area, in addition to the other mutual security programs for the area hereafter provided for by the Congress.

VII

This program will not solve all the problems of the Middle East. Neither does it represent the totality of our policies for the area. There are the problems of Palestine and relations between Israel and the Arab States, and the future of the Arab refugees. There is the problem of the future status of the Suez Canal. These difficulties are aggravated by International Communism, but they would exist quite apart from that threat. It is not the purpose of the legislation I propose to deal directly with these problems. The United Nations is actively concerning itself with all these matters, and we are supporting the United Nations. The United States has made clear, notably by Secretary Dulles' address of August 26, 1955, that we are willing to do much to assist the United Nations in solving the basic problems of Palestine.

The proposed legislation is primarily designed to deal with the possibility of Communist aggression, direct and indirect. There is imperative need that any lack of power in the area should be made good, not by external or alien force, but by the increased vigor and security of the independent nations of the area.

Experience shows that indirect aggression rarely if ever succeeds where there is reasonable security against direct aggression; where the government disposes of loyal security forces, and where economic conditions are such as not to make Communism seem an attractive alternative. The program I suggest deals with all three aspects of this matter and thus with the problem of indirect aggression.

It is my hope and belief that if our purpose be proclaimed, as proposed by the requested legislation, that very fact will serve to halt any contemplated aggression. We shall have heartened the patriots who are dedicated to the independence of their nations. They will not feel that they stand alone, under the menace of great power. And I should add that patriotism is, throughout this area, a powerful sentiment. It is true that fear sometimes perverts true patriotism into fanaticism and to the acceptance of dangerous enticements from without. But if that fear can be allayed, then the climate will be more favorable to the attainment of worthy national ambitions.

And as I have indicated, it will also be necessary for us to contribute economically to strengthen those countries, or groups of countries, which have governments manifestly dedicated to the preservation of independence and resistance to subversion. Such measures will provide the greatest insurance against Communist inroads. Words alone are not enough.

VIII

Let me refer again to the requested authority to employ the armed forces of the United States to assist to defend the territorial integrity and the political independence of any nation in the area against Communist armed aggression. Such authority would not be exercised except at the desire of the nation attacked. Beyond this it is my profound hope that this authority would never have to be exercised at all.

Nothing is more necessary to assure this than that our policy with respect to the defense of the area be promptly and clearly determined and declared. Thus the United Nations and all friendly governments, and indeed governments which are not friendly, will know where we stand.

If, contrary to my hope and expectation, a situation arose which called for the military application of the policy which I ask the Congress to join me in proclaiming, I would of course maintain hour-by-hour contact with the Congress if it were in session. And if the Congress were not in session, and if the situation had grave implications, I would, of course, at once call the Congress into special session.

In the situation now existing, the greatest risk, as is often the case, is that ambitious despots may miscalculate. If power-hungry Communists should either falsely or correctly estimate that the Middle East is inadequately defended, they might be tempted to use open measures of armed attack. If so, that would start a chain of circumstances which would almost surely involve the United States in military action. I am convinced that the best insurance against this dangerous contingency is to make clear now our readiness to cooperate fully and freely with our friends of the Middle East in ways consonant with the purposes and principles of the United Nations. I intend promptly to send a special mission to the Middle East to explain the cooperation we are prepared to ask.

IX

The policy which I outline involves certain burdens and indeed risks for the United States. Those who covert the area will not like what is proposed. Already, they are grossly distorting our purpose. However, before this Americans have seen our nation's vital interests and human freedom in jeopardy, and their fortitude and resolution have been equal to the crisis, regardless of hostile distortion of our words, motives and actions.

Indeed, the sacrifices of the American people in the cause of freedom have, even since the close of World War II, been measured in many billions of dollars and in thousands of the precious lives of our youth. These sacrifices, by which great areas of the world have been preserved to freedom, must not be throw away.

In those momentous periods of the past, the President and the Congress have united, without partisanship, to serve the vital interests of the United States and of the free world.

The occasion has come for us to manifest again our national unity in support of freedom and to show our deep respect for the rights and independence of every nation- however great, however small. We seek not violence, but peace. To this purpose we must now devote our energies, our determination, ourselves.

Dwight D. Eisenhower

APPENDIX F

JOINT CONGRESSIONAL RESOLUTION TO

"PROMOTE PEACE AND STABILITY IN THE MIDDLE EAST"
(9 March 1957)

Resolved by the Senate and House of Representatives of the United States of America in Congress assembled,

That the President be and hereby is authorized to cooperate with and assist any nation or group of nations in the general area of the Middle East desiring such assistance in the development of economic strength dedicated to the maintenance of national independence.

Sec. 2. The President is authorized to undertake, in the general area of the Middle East, military assistance programs with any nation or group of nations of that area desiring such assistance. Furthermore, the United States regards as vital to the national interest and world peace the preservation of the independence and integrity of the nations of the Middle East. To this end, if the President determines the necessity thereof, the United States is prepared to use armed forces to assist any such nation or group of such nations requesting assistance against armed aggression from any country controlled by international communism: Provided, That such employment shall be consonant with the treaty obligations of the United States and with the Constitution of the United States.

Sec. 3. The President is hereby authorized to use during the balance of fiscal year 1957 for economic and military assistance under this joint resolution not to exceed $200,000,000 from any appropriation now available for carrying out the provisions of the Mutual Security Act of 1954, as amended, in accord with the provisions of such Act: Provided, That, whenever the President determines it to be important to the security of the United States, such use may be under the authority of section 401 (a) of the Mutual Security Act of 1954, as amended (except that the provisions of section 105 (a) thereof shall not be waived), and without regard to the provisions of section 105 of the Mutual Security Appropriation Act, 1957: Provided, further, That obligations incurred in carrying out the purposes of the first sentence of section 2 of this joint resolution shall be paid only out of appropriations for military assistance, and obligations incurred in carrying out the purposes of the first section this joint resolution shall be paid only of appropriations other than those for military assistance. This authorization is in addition to other existing authorizations with respect to the use of such appropriations. None of the additional authorization contained in this section shall be used until fifteen days after the Committee on Foreign Relations of the Senate, the Committee on Foreign Affairs of the House of Representatives, the Committees on Appropriations of the Senate and the House of Representatives and, when military assistance is involved, the Committees on Armed Services of the Senate and the House of Representatives have been furnished a report showing the object of the proposed use, the country for the benefit of which such use is intended, and the particular appropriation or appropriations for carrying out the provisions of the Mutual Security Act of 1954, as amended, from which the funds are proposed to be derived: Provided, That funds available under this section during the balance of fiscal year 1957 shall, in the case of any such report submitted during the last fifteen days of the fiscal year, remain available for use under this section for the purposes stated in such report for a period of twenty days following the date of submission of such report. Nothing contained in this joint resolution shall be construed as itself authorizing the appropriation of additional funds for the purpose of carrying out the provisions of the first section or of the first sentence of section 2 of this joint resolution.

Sec. 4. The President shall continue to furnish facilities and military assistance, within the provisions of applicable law and established policies to the United Nations Emergency Force in the Middle East, with a view to maintaining the truce in that region.

Sec. 5. The President shall within the months of January and July of each year report to the Congress his action hereunder.

Sec. 6. This joint resolution shall expire when the President shall determine that the peace and security of the nations in the general area of the Middle East are reasonably assured by international conditions created by action of the United Nations or otherwise except that it may be terminated earlier by a concurrent resolution of the two Houses of Congress.

APPENDIX G

LETTER FROM PRESIDENT JOHN F. KENNEDY TO SENATE LEADERS RESTATING THE ADMINISTRATION'S VIEWS ON THE NUCLEAR TEST BAN TREATY

(10 September 1963)

Dear Senator Mansfield and Senator Dirksen:

I am deeply appreciative of the suggestion which you made to me on Monday morning that it would be helpful t have a further clarifying statement about the policy of this Administration toward certain aspects of our nuclear weapons defenses, under the proposed test ban treaty now before the Senate. I share your view that it is desirable to dispel any fears or concerns in the minds of Senators or of the people of our country on these matters. And while I believe that fully adequate statements have been made on these matters before the various committees of the Senate by the Secretary of State, the Secretary of Defense, the Director of Central Intelligence, the Chairman of the Atomic Energy Commission, and the Joint Chiefs of Staff, nevertheless I am happy to accept your judgment that it would be helpful if I restated what has already been said so that there may be no misapprehension.

In confidence that the Congress will share and support the policies of the Administration in this field, I am happy to give these unqualified and unequivocal assurances to the members of the Senate, to the entire Congress, and to the country:

1. Underground nuclear testing, which is permitted under the treaty, will be vigorously and diligently carried forward, and the equipment, facilities, personnel and funds necessary for that purpose will be provided. As the Senate knows, such testing is now going on. While we must all hope that at some future time a more comprehensive treaty may become possible be changes in the policies of other nations, until that time our underground testing program will continue.

2. The United States will maintain a posture of readiness to resume testing in the environments prohibited by the present treaty, and it will take all the necessary steps to safeguard our national security in the event that there should be an abrogation or violation of any treaty provision. In particular, the United States retains the right to resume atmospheric testing forthwith if the Soviet Union should conduct tests in violation of the treaty.

3. Our facilities for the detection of possible violations of this treaty will be expanded and improved as required to increase our assurance against clandestine violation by others.

4. In response to the suggestion made by President Eisenhower to the Foreign Relations Committee on August 23, 1963, and in conformity with the opinion of the Legal Advisor of the Department of State, set forth in the report of the Committee on Foreign Relations, I am glad to emphasize again that the treaty in no way limits the authority of the Commander-in-Chief to use

nuclear weapons for the defense of the United States and its allies, if a situation should develop requiring such a grave decision. Any decision to use such weapons would be made by the United States in accordance with its Constitutional processes and would in no way be affected by the terms of the nuclear test ban treaty.

5. While the abnormal and dangerous presence of Soviet military personnel in the neighboring island of Cuba is not a matter which can be dealt with through the instrumentality of this treaty, I am able to assure the Senate that if that unhappy island should be used either directly or indirectly to circumvent or nullify this treaty, the United States will take all necessary action in response.

6. The treaty in no way changes the status of the authorities in East Germany. As the Secretary of State has made clear, "We do not recognize, and we do not intend to recognize, the Soviet occupation zone of East Germany as a state or as an entity possessing national sovereignty, or to recognize the local authorities as a government. Those authorities cannot alter these facts by the act of subscribing to the test ban treaty."

7. This Government will maintain strong weapons laboratories in a vigorous program of weapons development, in order to ensure that the United States will continue to have in the future a strength fully adequate for an effective national defense. In particular, as the Secretary of Defense has made clear, we will maintain strategic forces fully ensuring that this nation will continue to be in a position to destroy any aggressor, even after absorbing a first strike by a surprise attack.

8. The United States will diligently pursue its programs for the further development of nuclear explosives for peaceful purposes by underground tests within the terms of the treaty, and as and when such developments make possible constructive uses of atmospheric nuclear explosions for peaceful purposes, the United States will seek international agreement under the treaty to permit such explosions.

I trust that these assurances may be helpful in dispelling any concern or misgivings which any member of the Senate or any citizen may have as to our determination to maintain the interests and security of the United States. It is not only safe but necessary, in the interest of this country and the interest of mankind, that this treaty should now be approved, and the hope for peace which it offers firmly sustained, by the Senate of the United States.

Once more, let me express my appreciation to you both for your visit and for your suggestions.

Sincerely,

John F. Kennedy

Note: This is the text of identical letters addressed to the Honorable Mike Mansfield, Majority Leader of the Senate, and to the Honorable Everett M. Dirksen, Minority Leader of the Senate, and sent at their suggestion.

The Report of the Senate Committee on Foreign Relations, to which the President referred, is dated September 3, 1963 (Senate Executive Rept. No. 3, 88th Cong., 1st sess.).

APPENDIX H

TREATY BANNING NUCLEAR WEAPONS TESTS IN THE ATMOSPHERE, IN OUTER SPACE AND UNDER WATER

(Signed at Moscow 5 August 1963, Ratification advised by Senate 24 September 1963)

The Governments of the United States of America, the United Kingdom of Great Britain and Northern Ireland, and the Union of Soviet Socialist Republics, hereinafter referred to as the "Original Parties."

Proclaiming as their principal aim the speediest possible achievement of an agreement on general and complete disarmament under strict international control in accordance with the objectives of the United Nations which would put an end to the armaments race and eliminate the incentive to the production and testing of all kinds of weapons, including nuclear weapons.

Seeking to achieve the discontinuance of all test explosions of nuclear weapons for all time, determined to continue negotiations to this end, and desiring to put an end to the continuation of man's environment by radioactive substances.

Have agreed as follows:

Article I

1. Each of the Parties to this Treaty undertakes to prohibit, to prevent, and not to carry out any nuclear weapon test explosion, or any other nuclear explosion, at any place under its jurisdiction or control;

(a) In the atmosphere; beyond its limits, including outer space; or under water, including territorial waters or high seas; or

(b) In any other environment if such explosion causes radioactive debris to be present outside the territorial limits of the State under whose jurisdiction or control such explosion is conducted. It is understood in this connection that the provisions of this subparagraph are without prejudice to the conclusion of a treaty resulting in the permanent banning of all nuclear test explosions, including all such explosions underground, the conclusion of which, as the Parties have stated in the Preamble to this Treaty, they seek to achieve.

2. Each of the Parties to this Treaty undertakes furthermore to refrain from causing, encouraging, or in any way participating in, the carrying out of any nuclear weapon test explosion, or any other nuclear explosion, anywhere which would take place in any of the environments described, or have the effect referred to, in paragraph 1 of this Article.

Article II

1. Any Party may propose amendments to this Treaty. The text of any proposed amendment shall be submitted to the Depositary Governments which shall circulate it to all Parties to this Treaty. Thereafter, if requested to do so by one-third or more of the Parties,

the Depositary Governments shall convene a conference, to which they shall invite all the Parties, to consider such amendment.

2. Any amendment to this Treaty must be approved by a majority of the votes of all the Parties to this Treaty, including the votes of all of the Original Parties. The amendment shall enter into force for all Parties upon the deposit of instruments of ratification by a majority of all the Parties, including the instruments of ratification of all of the Original Parties.

Article III

1. This Treaty shall be open to all States for signature. Any State which does not sign this Treaty before its entry into force in accordance with paragraph 3 of this Article may accede to it at any time.

2. This Treaty shall be subject to ratification by signatory States. Instruments of ratification and instruments of accession shall be deposited with the Governments of the Original Parties--the United States of America, the United Kingdom of Great Britain and Northern Ireland, and the Union of Soviet Socialist Republics--which are hereby designated the Depositary Governments.

3. This Treaty shall enter into force after its ratification by all the Original Parties and the deposit of their instruments of ratification.

4. For States whose instruments of ratification or accession are deposited subsequent to the entry into force of this Treaty, it shall enter into force on the date of the deposit of their instruments of ratification or accession.

5. The Depositary Governments shall promptly inform all signatory and acceding States of the date of each signature, the date of deposit of each instrument of ratification of and accession to this Treaty, the date of its entry into force, and the date of receipt of any requests for conferences or other notices.

6. This Treaty shall be registered by the Depositary Governments pursuant to Article 102 of the Charter of the United Nations.

Article IV

This Treaty shall be of unlimited duration.

Each Party shall in exercising its national sovereignty have the right to withdraw from the Treaty if it decides that extraordinary events, related to the subject matter of this Treaty, have jeopardized the supreme interests of its country. It shall give notice of such withdrawal to all other Parties to the Treaty within three months in advance.

Article V

This Treaty, of which the English and Russian texts are equally authentic, shall be deposited in the archives of the Depositary Governments. Duly certified copies of this Treaty shall be transmitted by the Depositary Governments to the Governments of the signatory and acceding States.

IN WITNESS WHEREOF the undersigned, duly authorized, have signed this Treaty.

DONE in triplicate at the city of Moscow the fifth day of August, one thousand nine hundred and sixty-three.

For the Government of the United States of America	For the Government of the United Kingdom of Great Britain and Northern Ireland	For the Government of the Union of Soviet Socialist Republics
DEAN RUSK	HOME	A. GROMYKO

APPENDIX I

WAR POWERS RESOLUTION
(12 October 1973)

JOINT RESOLUTION

Concerning the war powers of Congress and the President

Resolved by the Senate and House of Representatives of the United States of America in Congress assembled,

SHORT TITLE

SECTION 1. This joint resolution may be cited as the "War Powers Resolution."

PURPOSE AND POLICY

SECTION 2. (1) It is the purpose of this joint resolution to fulfill the intent of the framers of the Constitution of the United States and insure that the collective judgment of both the Congress and the President will apply to the introduction of United States Armed Forces into hostilities, or into situations where imminent involvement in hostilities is clearly indicated by the circumstances, and to the continued use of such forces in hostilities or in such situations.

(b) Under article I, section 8, of the Constitution, it is specifically provided that the Congress shall have the power to make all laws necessary and proper for carrying into execution, not only its own powers but also all other powers vested by the Constitution in the Government of the United States, or in any department or officer thereof.

(c) The constitutional powers of the President as Commander-in-Chief to introduce United States Armed Forces into hostilities, or into situations where imminent involvement in hostilities is clearly indicated by the circumstances, are exercised only pursuant to (1) a declaration of war, (2) specific statutory authorization, or (3) a national emergency created by attack upon the United States, its territories or possessions, or its armed forces.

CONSULTATION

SEC. 3. The President in every possible instance shall consult with Congress before introducing United States Armed Forces into hostilities or into situations where imminent involvement in hostilities is clearly indicated by the circumstances, and after every such introduction shall consult regularly with the Congress until United States Armed Forces are no longer engaged in hostilities or have been removed from such situations.

REPORTING

SEC. 4. (a) In the absence of a declaration of war, in any case in which United States Armed Forces are introduced--

(1) into hostilities or into situations where imminent involvement in hostilities is clearly indicated by the circumstances;

(2) into the territory, airspace or waters of a foreign nation, while equipped for combat, except for deployments which relate solely to supply, replacement, repair, or training of such forces; or

(3) in numbers which substantially enlarge United States Armed Forces equipped for combat already located in a foreign nation;

the President shall submit within 48 hours to the Speaker of the House of Representatives and to the President pro tempore of the Senate a report, in writing, setting forth--

(A) the circumstances necessitating the introduction of United States Armed Forces;

(B) the constitutional and legislative authority under which such introduction took place; and

(C) the estimated scope and duration of the hostilities or involvement.

(b) The President shall provide such other information as the Congress may request in the fulfillment of its constitutional responsibilities with respect to committing the Nation to war and to the use of United States Armed Forces abroad.

(c) Whenever United States Armed Forces are introduced into hostilities or into any situation described in subsection (a) of this section, the President shall, so long as such armed forces continue to be engaged in such hostilities or situation, report to the Congress periodically on the status of such hostilities or situation as well as on the scope and duration of such hostilities or situation, but in no event shall he report to the Congress less often than once every six months.

CONGRESSIONAL ACTION

SEC. 5. (a) Each report submitted pursuant to section 4(a) (1) shall be transmitted to the Speaker of the House of Representatives and to the President pro tempore of the Senate on the same calendar day. Each report so transmitted shall be referred to the Committee on Foreign Affairs of the House of Representatives and to the Committee on Foreign Relations of the Senate for appropriate action. If, when the report is transmitted, the Congress has adjourned sine die or has adjourned for any period in excess of three calendar days, the Speaker of the House of Representatives and the President pro tempore of the Senate, if they deem it advisable (or if petitioned by at least 30 percent of the membership of their respective Houses) shall jointly request the President to convene Congress in order that it may consider the report and take appropriate action pursuant to this section.

(b) Within sixty calendar days after a report is submitted or is required to be submitted pursuant to section 4(a) (1), whichever is earlier, the President shall terminate any use of United States Armed forces with respect to which such report was submitted (or required to be submitted), unless the Congress (1) has declared war or has enacted a specific authorization for such use of United States Armed Forces, (2) has extended by law such sixty-day period, or (3) is physically unable to meet as a result of an armed attack upon the United States. Such sixty-day period shall be extended for not more than an additional thirty days if the President determines and certifies to the Congress in writing that unavoidable military necessity respecting the safety of United States Armed Forces requires the continued use of such armed forces in the course of bringing about a prompt removal of such forces.

(c) Notwithstanding subsection (b), at any time that United States Armed Forces are engaged in hostilities outside the territory of the United States, its possessions and territories without a declaration of war or specific statutory authorization, such forces shall be removed by the President if the Congress so directs by concurrent resolution.

CONGRESSIONAL PRIORITY PROCEDURES
FOR JOINT RESOLUTION OR BILL

SEC. 6. (a) Any joint resolution or bill introduced pursuant to section 5(b) at least thirty calendar days before the expiration of the sixty-day period specified in such section shall be referred to the Committee on Foreign Affairs of the House of Representatives or the Committee on Foreign Relations of the Senate, as the case may be, and such committee shall report one such joint resolution or bill, together with its recommendations, not later than twenty-four calendar days before the expiration of the sixty-day period specified in such section, unless such House shall otherwise determine by the yeas and nays.

(b) Any joint resolution or bill so reported shall become the pending business of the House in question (in case of the Senate the time for debate shall be equally divided between the proponents and opponents), and shall be voted on within three calendar days thereafter, unless such House shall otherwise determine by yeas and nays.

(c) Such a joint resolution or bill passed by one House shall be referred to the committee of the other House named in subsection (a) and shall be reported out not later than fourteen calendar days before the expiration of the sixty-day period specified in section 5(b). The joint resolution or bill so reported shall become the pending business of the House in question and shall be voted on within three calendar days after it has been reported, unless such House shall otherwise determine by yeas and nays.

(d) In the case of any disagreement between the two Houses of Congress with respect to a joint resolution or bill passed by both Houses, conferees shall be promptly appointed and the committee of conference shall make and file a report with respect to such resolution or bill not later than four calendar days before the expiration of the sixty-day period specified in section 5(b). In the event the conferees are unable to agree within 48 hours, they shall report back to their respective Houses in disagreement. Notwithstanding any rule in either House concerning the printing of conference reports in the Record or concerning any delay in the consideration of such reports, such report shall be acted on by both Houses not later than the expiration of such sixty-day period.

CONGRESSIONAL PRIORITY PROCEDURES FOR CONCURRENT RESOLUTION

SEC. 7. (a) Any concurrent resolution introduced pursuant to section 5(c) shall be referred to the Committee on Foreign Affairs of the House of Representatives or the Committee on Foreign Relations of the Senate, as the case may be, and one such concurrent resolution shall be reported out by such committee together with its recommendations within fifteen calendar days, unless such House shall otherwise determine by the yeas and nays.

(b) Any concurrent resolution so reported shall become the pending business of the House in question (in the case of the Senate the time for debate shall be equally divided between the proponents and the opponents) and shall be voted on within three calendar days thereafter, unless such House shall otherwise determine by yeas and nays.

(c) Such a concurrent resolution passed by one House shall be referred to the committee of the other House named in subsection (a) and shall be reported out by such committee together with its recommendations within fifteen calendar days and shall thereupon become the pending business of such House and shall be voted upon within three calendar days, unless such House shall otherwise determine by yeas and nays.

(d) In the case of any disagreement between the two Houses of Congress with respect to a concurrent resolution passed by both Houses, conferees shall be promptly appointed and the committee of conference shall make and file a report with respect to such concurrent resolution within six calendar days after the legislation is referred to the committee of conference. Notwithstanding any rule in either House concerning the printing of conference reports in the Record or concerning any delay in the consideration of such reports, such report shall be acted on by both Houses not later than six calendar days after the conference report is filed. In the event the conferees are unable to agree within 48 hours, they shall report back to their respective Houses in disagreement.

INTERPRETATION OF JOINT RESOLUTION

SEC. 8. (a) Authority to introduce United States Armed Forces into hostilities or into situations wherein involvement in hostilities is clearly indicated by the circumstances shall not be inferred--

(1) from any provision of law (whether or not in effect before the date of the enactment of this joint resolution), including any provision contained in any appropriation Act, unless such provision specifically authorizes the introduction of United States Armed forces into hostilities or into such situations and states that it is intended to constitute specific statutory authorization within the meaning of this joint resolution; or

(2) from any treaty heretofore or heretoafter ratified unless such treaty is implemented by legislation specifically authorizing the introduction of United States Armed Forces into hostilities or into such situations and stating that it is intended to constitute specific statutory authorization within the meaning of this joint resolution.

(b) Nothing in this joint resolution shall be construed to require any further specific statutory authorization to permit members of United States Armed Forces to participate jointly with members of the armed forces of one or more foreign countries in the headquarters operations of high-level military commands which were established prior to the date of enactment of this joint resolution and pursuant to the United Nations Charter or any treaty ratified by the United States prior to such date.

(c) For purposes of this joint resolution, the term "introduction of United States Armed Forces" includes the assignment of members of such armed forces to command, coordinate, participate in the movement of, or accompany the regular or irregular military forces of any foreign country or government when such military forces are engaged, or there exists an imminent threat that such forces will become engaged, in hostilities.

(d) Nothing in this joint resolution--

(1) is intended to alter the constitutional authority of the Congress or of the President, or the provisions of existing treaties; or

(2) shall be construed as granting any authority to the President with respect to the introduction of United States Armed Forces into hostilities or into situations wherein involvement in hostilities is clearly indicated by the circumstances which authority he would not have had in the absence of this joint resolution.

SEPARABILITY CLAUSE

SEC. 9. If any provision of this joint resolution or the application thereof to any person or circumstance is held invalid, the remainder of the joint resolution and the application of such provision to any other person or circumstance shall not be affected thereby.

EFFECTIVE DATE

SEC. 10. This joint resolution shall take effect on the date of its enactment.

APPENDIX J

VETO OF THE WAR POWERS RESOLUTION
(24 October 1973)

To the House of Representatives:

I hereby return without my approval House Joint Resolution 542--the War Powers Resolution. While I am in accord with the desire of the Congress to assert its proper role in the conduct of our foreign affairs, the restrictions which this resolution would impose upon the authority of the President are both unconstitutional and dangerous to the best interests of our Nation.

The proper roles of the Congress and the Executive in the conduct of foreign affairs have been debated since the founding of our country. Only recently, however, has there been a serious challenge to the wisdom of the Founding Fathers in choosing not to draw a precise and detailed line of demarcation between the foreign policy powers of the two branches.

The Founding Fathers understood the impossibility of foreseeing every contingency that might arise in this complex area. They acknowledged the need for flexibility in responding to changing circumstances. They recognized that foreign policy decisions must be made through close cooperation between the two branches and not through rigidly codified procedures.

These principles remain as valid today as they were when our Constitution was written. Yet House Joint Resolution 542 would violate those principles by defining the President's powers in ways which would strictly limit his constitutional authority.

Clearly Unconstitutional

House Joint Resolution 542 would attempt to take away, by a mere legislative act, authorities which the President has properly exercised under the Constitution for almost 200 years. One of its provision would automatically cut off certain authorities after sixty days unless the Congress extended them. Another would allow the Congress to eliminate certain authorities merely by the passage of a concurrent resolution--an action which does not normally have the force of law, since it denies the President his constitutional role in approving legislation.

I believe that both these provisions are unconstitutional. The only way in which the constitutional powers of a branch of the Government can be altered is by amending the Constitution--and any attempt to make such alterations by legislation alone is clearly without force.

Undermining Our Foreign Policy

While I firmly believe that a veto of House Joint Resolution 542 is warranted solely on constitutional grounds, I am also deeply disturbed by the practical consequences of this resolution. For it would seriously undermine this Nation's ability to act decisively and convincingly in times of international crisis. As a result, the confidence of our allies is our ability to assist them could be diminished and the respect of our adversaries for our deterrent posture could decline. A permanent and substantial element of unpredictability would be injected into the world's assessment of American behavior, further increasing the likelihood of miscalculation and war.

If this resolution had been in operation, America's effective response to a variety of challenges in recent years would have been vastly complicated or even made impossible. We may well have been unable to respond in the way we did during the Berlin crisis of 1961, the Cuban missile crisis of 1962, the Congo rescue operation in 1964, and the Jordanian crisis of 1970--to mention just a few examples. In addition, our recent actions to bring about a peaceful settlement of the hostilities in the Middle East would have been seriously impaired if this resolution had been in force.

While all the specific consequences of House Joint Resolution 542 cannot yet be predicted, it is clear that it would undercut the ability of the United States to act as an effective influence for peace. For example, the provision automatically cutting off certain authorities after 60 days unless they are extended by the Congress could work to prolong or intensify a crisis. Until the Congress suspended the deadline, there would be at least a chance of United States withdrawal and an adversary would be tempted therefore to postpone serious negotiations until the 60 days were up. Only after the Congress acted would there be a strong incentive for an adversary to negotiate. In addition, the very existence of a deadline could lead to an escalation of hostilities in order to achieve certain objectives before the 60 days expired.

The measure would jeopardize our role as a force for peace in other ways as well. It would, for example, strike from the President's hand a wide range of important peace-keeping tools by eliminating his ability to exercise quiet diplomacy backed by subtle shifts in our military deployments. It would also cast into doubt authorities which Presidents have used to undertake certain humanitarian relief missions in conflict areas, to protect fishing boats from seizure, to deal wit ship or aircraft hijackings, and to respond to threats of attack. Not the least of the adverse consequences of this resolution would be the prohibition contained in section 8 against fulfilling our obligations under the NATO treaty as ratified by the Senate. Finally, since the bill is somewhat vague as to when the 60 day rule would apply, it could lead to extreme confusion and dangerous disagreements concerning the prerogatives of the two branches, seriously damaging our ability to respond to international crises.

Failure To Require Positive Congressional Action

I am particularly disturbed by the fact that certain of the President's constitutional powers as Commander in Chief of the Armed Forces would terminate automatically under this resolution 60 days after they were invoked. No overt Congressional action would be required to cut off these powers--they would disappear automatically unless the Congress extended them. In effect, the Congress is here attempting to increase its policy-making role through a provision which requires it to take absolutely no action at all.

In my view, the proper way for the Congress to make known its will on such foreign policy questions is through a positive action, with full debate on the merits of the issue and with each member taking the responsibility of casting a yes or no vote after considering those merits. The authorization and appropriations process represents one of the ways in which such influence can be exercised. I do not, however, believe that the Congress can responsibly contribute its considered, collective judgment on such grave questions without full debate and without a yes or no vote. Yet this is precisely what the joint resolution would allow. It would give every future Congress the ability to handcuff every future President merely by doing nothing and sitting still. In my view, one cannot become a responsible partner unless one is prepared to take responsible action.

Strengthening Cooperation Between the Congress and the Executive Branches

The responsible and effective exercise of the war

powers requires the fullest cooperation between the Congress and the Executive and the prudent fulfillment by each branch of its constitutional responsibilities. House Joint Resolution 542 includes certain constructive measures which would foster this process by enhancing the flow of information from the executive branch to the Congress. Section 3, for example, calls for consultations with the Congress before and during the involvement of the United States forces in hostilities abroad. This provision is consistent with the desire of this Administration for regularized consultations with the Congress in an even wider range of circumstances.

I believe that full and cooperative participation in foreign policy matters by both the executive and the legislative branches could be enhanced by a careful and dispassionate study of their constitutional roles. Helpful proposals for such a study have already been made in the Congress. I would welcome the establishment of a non-partisan commission on the constitutional roles of the Congress and the President in the conduct of foreign affairs. This commission could make a thorough review of the principal constitutional issues in Executive-Congressional relations, including the war powers, the international agreement powers, and the question of Executive privilege, and then submit its recommendations to the President and the Congress. The members of such a commission could be drawn from both parties--and could represent many perspectives including those of the Congress, the executive branch, the legal profession, and the academic community.

This Administration is dedicated to strengthening cooperation between the Congress and the President in the conduct of foreign affairs and to preserving the constitutional prerogatives of both branches of our Government. I know that the Congress shares that goal. A commission on the constitutional roles of the Congress and the President would provide a useful opportunity for both branches to work together toward that common objective.

Richard Nixon

BIBLIOGRAPHY

Archives

Columbia University Library, School of International Affairs, New York City, New York
Herbert H. Lehman Papers

Dwight D. Eisenhower Library, Abilene, Kansas
Dwight D. Eisenhower Papers

John F. Kennedy Library, Boston, Massachusetts
John F. Kennedy Papers

Princeton University Library, Princeton, New Jersey
John Foster Dulles Papers

Correspondence

Dean Acheson
J. William Fulbright
Claude D. Pepper
Francis O. Wilcox

Interviews

Sherman Adams
Carl Marcy

Recorded Interviews

Columbia University Library:
Wayne L. Morse
Hubert H. Humphrey

John F. Kennedy Library:
George D. Aiken
Mike J. Mansfield
Leverett Saltonstall
Theodore C. Sorenson

Princeton University Library:
Abba Eban
Charles H. Hallack
Jacob K. Javits
John J. Sparkman

Documents

A Decade of American Foreign Policy Basic Documents, 1941-1949, Washington, D.C.: Department of State, 1985.

American Historical Documents, Edited by Harold C. Syrett, New York: Barnes & Noble, Inc., 1960.

Cotton and other Fiber Problems and Policies in the United States, Washington, D.C.: U.S. Government Printing Office, 1967.

Documents of American History, Edited by Henry Steele Commager, New York: Appleton-Century-Crofts 1968.

Dwight D. Eisenhower: Public Papers, volumes, 1954-1957, Washington, D.C.: U.S. Government Printing Office, 1986.

Foreign Relations of the United States, volumes, 1943-1960, Washington, D.C.: U.S. Government Printing Office, 1986.

__________, Memoranda of Conversation of the Secretary of State, 1947-1952, Microfiche Publication, Washington, D.C.: Department of State, 1988.

Francis O. Wilcox, Chief of Staff, Senate Foreign Relations Committee, 1947-1955, Oral History Interviews, Feb. 1 - June 13, 1984, Conducted by Donald A. Ritchie, Senate Historical Office, Washington, D.C., 1985.

Harry S. Truman: Public Papers, 1949, Washington, D.C.: United States Government Printing Office, 1964.

Immigration and Naturalization Service v. Chadha, 103 S. Ct. 2764 (1983.

John F. Kennedy: Public Papers, volumes, 1961-1963, Washington, D.C.: U.S. Government Printing Office, 1964.

Minutes and Documents of the Cabinet Meetings of President Eisenhower (1953-1961), Washington, D.C.: University Publications of America, 1980.

National Party Platforms: 1840-1972, Compiled by Donald Bruce Johnson and Kirk H. Porter, Chicago: University of Illinois Press, 1975.

Richard Nixon: Public Papers, volumes, 1972-1973, Washington, D.C.: U.S. Government Printing Office, 1975.

The Constitution of the United States of America: Analysis and Interpretation, Edited by Johny H. Killian, Washington, D.C.: U.S. Government Printing Office, 1987.

The Constitution of the United States With Case Summaries, Edited by Edward Conrad Smith, New York: Barnes & Noble Books, 1970.

The Federalist Papers: Alexander Hamilton, James Madison, John Jay, Introduction by Clinton Rossiter, New York: The American Library, 1967.

The Papers of Adlai E. Stevenson: Toward a New America, 1955-1957, Edited by Walter Johnson, Boston: Little, Brown & Company, 1976.

The Papers of General Lucius D. Clay: Germany 19451949, Edited by Jean Edward Smith, Bloomington: Indiana University Press, 1974.

The Pentagon Papers, Neil Sheehan, Hedrick Smith, E. W. Kenworthy and Fox Butterfield, New York: Bantam Books, Inc., 1971.

The Prize Cases, 2Bl. (67 U.S.) 635 (1863).

The Public Papers and Addresses of Franklin D. Roosevelt, volumes, 11-13, Compiled by Samuel I. Rosenman, New York: Russell & Russell, 1969.

The Records of the Federal Convention of 1787, Edited by Max Farrand, New Haven: Yale University Press, 1937.

United Nations Document, Security Council, S/3354, January 28, 1955.

__________, S/3355, January 30, 1955.

__________, S/3356, January 31, 1955.

__________, S/3358, February 3, 1955.

United States Arms Control and Disarmament Agency, Arms Control and Disarmament Agreement: Texts and Histories of Negotiations, Washington, D.C.: U.S. Government Printing Office, 1982.

U.S. Congress, House, Congressional Record, vol. 89, 1943.

__________, Senate, Ibid.

__________, Ibid., vol. 94, 1948.

__________, Ibid., vol. 96, 1950.

__________, Ibid., vol. 97, 1951.

__________, Ibid., vol. 101, 1955.

__________, Ibid., vol. 103, 1957.

__________, Ibid., vol. 106, 1960.

__________, Ibid., vol. 109, 1963.

__________, Ibid., vol. 119, 1973.

__________, Ibid., vol. 132, 1986.

__________, House, Collective Defense Treaties, H. Doc., 90th Cong., 1st sess., 1967.

__________, Senate, Assignment Of Ground Forces Of The United States To Duty In The European Area, S. Rept. 175, 82nd Cong., 1st sess., 1951.

__________, Authorizing the President to Employ the Armed Forces of the United States for Protecting the Security of Formosa, the Pescadores, and Related Positions and Territories of that Area, S. Rept. 13, 84th Cong., 1st sess., 1953.

__________, Declaration of War and Peace Aims of the United States, S. Rept. 478, 78th Cong., 1st sess., 1943.

__________, Executive Sessions of the Senate Foreign Relations Committee, Historical Series, vol. 3, 84th Cong., 1st sess., 1955.

__________, Hearings before the Senate Committee on Foreign Relations and Armed Services on S. J. Res. 19 & H. J. Res. 117, The President's Proposal On The Middle East, 85th Cong., 1st sess., 1957.

__________, Hearings before the Senate Committee on Foreign Relations, Nuclear Test Ban Treaty, 88th Cong., 1st sess., Washington, D.C.: U.S. Government Printing Office, 1963.

__________, Hearings before the Senate Subcommittee on Appropriations, State, Commerce, Justice, Judiciary Appropriations, 81st Cong., 1st sess., 1949.

__________, Hearings in Executive Session, 1948-1949, The Vandenberg Resolution and The North Atlantic Treaty, 80th Cong., 2nd sess. and 81st Cong., 1st sess., Washington, D.C.: U.S. Government Printing Office, 1973.

__________, Message From the President Of The United States Transmitting A Mutual Defense Treaty Between The United States of America and The Republic Of China, S. Doc. Executive A, 84th Cong., 1st sess., 1954.

U.S. Department of State, Restoring Bipartisanship in Foreign Affairs, Secretary of State George P. Shultz, Current Policy, No. 709, Washington, D.C.: Bureau of Public Affairs, 1985.

United States v. Curtiss-Wright Export Corp., 299 U.S. 304 (1936).

United States v. Nixon, 418 U.S. 683 (1974).

Books

Acheson, Dean. A Citizen Looks At Congress. New York: Harper & Brothers, 1956.

__________, Present at the Creation: My Years in the State Department. New York: W. W. Norton & Company, 1969.

Adams, Sherman. Firsthand Report: The Story of the Eisenhower Administration. New York: Harper & Brothers, 1961.

Adler, Selig. The Isolationist Impulse: Its Twentieth Century Reaction. New York: The Free Press, 1957.

Baker, Bobby. Wheeling and Dealing: Confessions Of A Capitol Hill Operator. New York: W. W. Norton & Company, 1978.

Baker, Ross K. House and Senate. New York: W. W. Norton & Company, Inc., 1989.

Ben-Gurion, David. Israel: A Personal History. Tel Aviv: American Israel Publishing Co., 1971.

Bemis, Samuel Flagg. A Diplomatic History Of The United States. New York: Henry Holt & Company, 1947.

Bloom, Sol. The Autobiography of Sol Bloom. New York: G. P. Putnam's Sons, 1948.

Brown, Anthony Cave. The Last Hero: Wild Bill Donovan. New York: Vintage Books, 1984.

Burns, James MacGregor. Roosevelt: The Lion and the Fox. New York: Harcourt, Brace & World, Inc., 1956.

Campbell, John C. Defense Of The Middle East: Problems of American Policy. New York: Harper & Brothers, 1960.

Cheever, Daniel S. and Haviland, Jr., H. Field. American Foreign Policy and the Separation of Powers. Cambridge, Mass.: Harvard University Press, 1952.

Clotfeter, James. The Military in American Politics. New York: Harper & Row, 1973.

Clubb, O. Edmund. Twentieth Century China. New York: Columbia University Press, 1964.

Compton, James V., ed. American and the Origins of the Cold War. Boston: Houghton Mifflin Company, 1972.

Connally, Senator Tom as told to Steinberg, Alfred. My Name is Tom Connally. New York: Thomas Y. Crowell Company, 1954.

Cook, Don. Forging The Alliance: NATO, 1945-1950. New York: Arbor House/William Morrow & Company, 1989.

Cooper, Chester L. The Lion's Last Roar: Suez, 1956. New York: Harper & Row, 1978.

Corwin, Edward B. The President: Office and Powers, 1787-1957. New York: New York University Press, 1957.

Crabb, Jr., Cecil V. Bipartisan Foreign Policy: Myth or Reality? Evanston, Ill.: Row, Peterson, 1957.

__________ and Holt, Pat M. Invitation to Struggle: Congress, the President and Foreign Policy. Washington, D.C.: Congressional Quarterly, Inc., 1980.

Dayan, Moshe. Diary Of The Sinai Campaign. New York: Harper & Row, 1966.

Diamond, Robert A., ed. Origins and Development of Congress. Washington, D.C.: Congressional Quarterly, Inc., 1976.

Donovan, Robert J. Eisenhower: The Inside Story. New York: Harper & Brothers, 1956.

Dougherty, James E. and Pfaltzgraff, Jr., Robert L. American Foreign Policy: FDR to Reagan. New York: Harper & Row Publishers, Inc., 1986.

Dulles, John Foster. War or Peace. New York: Macmillan Company, 1950.

Eden, Anthony. The Memoirs of Anthony Eden: Full Circle. Boston: Houghton Mifflin Company, 1960.

Eisenhower, Dwight D. Mandate For Change, 1953-1956. New York: Doubleday & Company, Inc., 1963.

__________. The White House Years: Waging Peace, 1956-1961. New York: Doubleday & Company, Inc., 1965.

Ebenstein, William and Pritchett, C. Herman and Turner, Henry A. and Mann, Dean, eds. American Democracy In World Perspective. New York: Harper & Row, 1973.

Englebrecht, Helmuth C. and Hanighen, F. C. Merchants of Death. New York: Dodd, Mead & Company, 1934.

Engler, Robert. The Politics of Oil: A Study of Private Power and Democratic Directions. New York: The Macmillan Co., 1961.

Ferrell, Robert H., ed. The Eisenhower Diaries. New York: W. W. Norton, 1981.

Finer, Herman. Dulles Over Suez: The Theory and Practice Of His Diplomacy. Chicago: Quadrangle Books, 1964.

Fisher, Louis. President and Congress. New York: Free Press, 1972.

Friedman, Leon and Levantrosser, William F. RICHARD NIXON: A Retrospective on His Presidency. Westport, CT: Greenwood Press, Inc., 1991.

Friendly, Fred W. and Elliott, Martha J. H. The Constitution: That Delicate Balance. New York: Random House, Inc., 1984.

Gaddis, John Lewis. The Long Peace: Inquires into the History of the Cold War. New York: Oxford University Press, 1987.

__________. The United States and the Origins of the Cold War, 1941-1947. New York: Columbia University Press, 1972.

Gamson, William A. and Modigliani, Andre. Untangling the Cold War: A Strategy For Testing Rival Theories. Boston: Little, Brown & Company, 1971.

Gladwyn, Lord. The Memoirs of Lord Gladwyn. New York: Weybright & Talley, 1972.

Goldwater, Barry M. With No Apologies: The Personal and Political Memoirs of United States Senator Barry M. Goldwater. New York: William Morrow & Company, Inc., 1979.

Graebner, Norman A., ed. An Uncertain Tradition: American Secretaries of State in the Twentieth Century. New York: McGraw-Hill Book Company, Inc., 1961.

Griffis, Stanton. Lying in State. Garden City: Doubleday & Company, Inc., 1952.

Griffith, Robert. The Politics of Fear: Joseph McCarthy and the Senate. Lexington: University Press of Kentucky, 1970.

Harper, Paul and Krieg, Joann P., eds. JOHN F. KENNEDY: The Promise Revisited. Westport, CT: Greenwood Press, Inc., 1988.

Hartmann, Susan M. Truman and the 80th Congress. Columbia: University of Missouri Press, 1971.

Henderson, Sir Nicholas. The Birth of NATO. Boulder, CO: Westview Press, 1983.

Hoopes, Townsend. The Devil and John Foster Dulles: The Diplomacy of the Eisenhower Era. Boston: Little, Brown & Company, 1973.

Hull, Cordell. The Memoirs of Cordell Hull. New York: The Macmillan Company, 1948.

Isaacson, Walter and Thomas, Evan. The Wise Men: Six Friends And The World They Made. New York: Simon & Schuster, Inc., 1986.

Israel, Fred L., ed. The War Diary of Breckenridge Long: Selections From the Years 1939-1944. Lincoln: University of Nebraska Press, 1966.

Johnson, Paul. Modern Times: The World from the Twenties to the Eighties. New York: Harper & Row, Publishers, Inc., 1983.

Kahn, Jr., E. J. The China Hands: America's Foreign Service Officers and What Befell Them. New York: The Viking Press, 1975.

Kegley, Jr., Charles W. and Wittkopf, Eugene R. American Foreign Policy: Pattern and Process. New York: St. Martin's Press, 1982.

Kennedy, Paul. The Rise and Fall of the Great Powers: Economic Change and Military Conflict from 1500 to 2000. New York: Vintage Books, 1989.

Krieg, Joann P., ed. DWIGHT D. EISENHOWER: Solider, President, Statesman. Westport, CT: Greenwood Press, Inc., 1987.

LaFeber, Walter. America, Russia, and the Cold War, 1945-1984. New York: Alfred A. Knopf, 1985.

LaRue, L. H. Political Discourse: A Case Study of the Watergate Affair. Athens: The University of Georgia Press, 1988.

Lepper, Mary Milling. Foreign Policy Formulation: A Case Study of the Nuclear Test Ban Treaty of 1963. Columbus: Charles E. Merrill Publishing Company, 1971.

Levering, Ralph B. The Cold War, 1945-1987. Arlington Heights, Il.: Harlan Davidson, Inc., 1988.

__________, with a foreword by Gallop, George. The Public and American Foreign Policy, 1918-1978. New York: William Morrow & Company, 1978.

Lowi, Theodore J. Bases In Spain. Indianapolis and New York: The Bobbs-Merrill Company, Inc., 1963.

MacNeil, Neil. Dirksen: Portrait of a Public Man. New York: The World Publishing Company, 1970.

Madariaga, Salvador de. Spain: A Modern History. New York: Frederick A. Praeger, 1958.

Matthews, Donald R. U. S. Senators And Their World. New York: W. W. Norton & Company, Inc., 1973.

Miller, Merle. Plain Speaking: an oral biography of Harry S. Truman. New York: Berkeley Publishing Corporation, 1973.

Millis, Walter, ed. with the collaboration of Duffield, E.S. The Forrestal Diaries. New York: The Viking Press, 1951.

Nash, Henry T. American Foreign Policy: Changing Perspectives on National Security. Homewood, IL: The Dorsey Press, 1978.

Nathan, James A. and Oliver, James K. Foreign Policy-Making and the American Political System. Boston: Little, Brown & Company, 1983.

Nixon, Richard M. RN: The Memoirs Of Richard Nixon. New York: Grosset & Dunlap, 1978.

O'Donnell, Kenneth P. and Powers, David F. with McCarthy, Joe. "Johnny, We Hardly Knew Ye." Boston: Little, Brown & Company, 1972.

O'Neill, Tip with Novak, William. Man Of The House: The Life and Political Memoirs of Speaker Tip O'Neill. New York: St. Martin's Press, 1987.

Oshinsky, David M. A Conspiracy So Immense: The World of Joe McCarthy. New York: The Free Press, 1983.

Parmet, Herbert S. JFK: The Presidency of John F. Kennedy. New York: The Dial Press, 1983.

Patterson, James T. Mr. Republican: A Biography of Robert A. Taft. Boston: Houghton Mifflin Company, 1972.

Pearson, Drew and Anderson, Jack. The Case Against Congress: A Compelling Indictment of Corruption on Capitol Hill. New York: Simon & Schuster, 1968.

Polsby, Nelson W. and Wildavsky, Aaron. Presidential Elections: Strategies of American Electoral Politics. New York: Charles Scribner's Sons, 1984.

Reedy, George E. The U.S. Senate: Paralysis or a Search for Consensus. New York: Crown Publishers, Inc., 1986.

Robinson, James A. Congress and Foreign Policy-Making: A Study in Legislative Influence and Initiative. Homewood, Illinois: The Dorsey Press, 1967.

Rossiter, Clinton and Lare, James, eds. The Essential Lippmann: A Political Philosophy for Liberal Democracy. New York: Vintage Books, 1965.

Schlesinger, Jr., Arthur M. A Thousand Days: John F. Kennedy in the White House. Boston: Houghton Mifflin Company, 1965.

__________, ed. History of American Presidential Elections, 1789-1968. New York: McGraw-Hill Book Co., 1971.

__________. Robert Kennedy And His Times. Boston: Houghton Mifflin Company, 1978.

__________. The Imperial Presidency. New York: Popular Library, 1974.

Seaborg, Glenn T. with the assistance of Loeb, Benjamin S. and a foreword by Harriman, W. Averell. Kennedy, Khrushchev and the Test Ban. Berkeley: University of California Press, 1981.

Shadegg, Stephen. What Happened to Goldwater? The Inside Story of the 1964 Republican Campaign. New York: Holt, Rinehart & Winston, 1965.

Sharett, Moshe. Yeoman Ishi. Tel Aviv: Sifriyat Maariv, 1980.

Shawcross, William. Side-Show: Kissinger, Nixon and the Destruction of Cambodia. New York: Pocket Books, 1974.

Sherwood, Robert E. Roosevelt and Hopkins: An Intimate History. New York: Harper & Brothers, 1950.

Smith, Hedrick. The Power Game: How Washington Works. New York: Ballantine Books, 1989.

Sorensen, Theodore C. Kennedy. New York: Harper & Row, 1965.

Terchek, Ronald J. The Making of the Test Ban Treaty. The Hague: Martinus Nyhoff, 1970.

Truman, Harry S. Memoirs: Years of Trial and Hope, 1946-1952. New York: Doubleday & Company, Inc., 1956.

Vandenberg, Jr., Arthur H., ed. with the collaboration of Morris, Joe Alex. The Private Papers of Senator Vandenberg. Boston: Houghton Mifflin Company, 1952.

Waltz, Kenneth N. Foreign Policy and Democratic Politics: The American and British Experience. Boston: Little, Brown & Company, 1967.

Westerfield, Bradford H. Foreign Policy and Party Politics: Pearl Harbor to Korea. New Haven: Yale University Press, 1955.

Whitaker, Arthur P. Spain and Defense of the West: Ally and Liability. New York: Harper & Brothers, 1961.

Wiarda, Howard J. Foreign Policy Without Illusion: How Foreign Policy-Making Works and Fails to Work in the United States. Glenview, Illinois: Scott, Foresman & Company, 1990.

Woodward, Bob and Bernstein, Carl. The Final Days. New York: Simon & Schuster, 1976.

Wormuth, Francis D. and Firmage, Edwin B. and Butler, Francis P., contributing author. To Chain the Dog of War: The War Powers of Congress in History & Law. Dallas: Southern Methodist University Press, 1986.

Yergin, Daniel. Shattered Peace: The Origins of the Cold War and the National Security State. Boston: Houghton Mifflin Company, 1977.

Yoder, Amos. The Conduct of American Foreign Policy Since World War II. New York: Pergamon Press, 1986.

Periodicals

American Political Science Review

Atlantic Monthly

China Quarterly

Congressional Digest

Congressional Quarterly Almanac

Department of State Bulletin

Foreign Affairs

Foreign Policy

Middle East Journal

Mid-America: An Historical Review
New Republic

New York Herald Tribune

New York Times

Pennsylvania Political Science Association Newsletter

Political Science Quarterly

Presidential Studies Quarterly

Review of Politics

Saturday Evening Post

Saturday Review

Vital Speeches Of The Day

World Affairs

World Politics

World Today

INDEX

About the Author

Philip J. Briggs is Professor and Chairperson of the Department of Political Science at East Stroudsburg University in Pennsylvania. He received both his M.A. and Ph.D. degrees from The Maxwell School of Citizenship and Public Affairs at Syracuse University. The author of numerous journal articles, chapters in edited volumes, and reviews on U.S. foreign policy, Dr. Briggs has lectured widely as a Commonwealth Speaker for the Pennsylvania Humanities Council, and is currently Executive Director of the Research Committee on Armed Forces and Society of the International Political Science Association.